PRAISE FOR *REVIVAL PREACHING*

"I am very grateful to Klassen and his work on revival preaching. It is a call to bold faith and bold proclamation. Using the backdrop of Jonathan Edwards's powerful preaching ministry, we are invited into a rich theological journey flavored with real-life experiences.... This is a must-read for preachers at any stage. This book will inspire you to be fearless in your preaching and passionate in your longing for revival."

—**David Hearn**, President of the Christian and Missionary Alliance in Canada

"Looking at the intersection of revival, preaching, and Edwards, Klassen provides 'lessons' that religious leaders can take from Edwards's experiences and writings as a soul counselor and a 'scientist' of conversion.... There is much wisdom to be had from his reflections on the nature of conversion, revival, and spirituality, gained from practical experience as a local pastor."

—**Kenneth P. Minkema**, Jonathan Edwards Center, Yale University

"I am so pleased to commend this book to my brothers and sisters in the English-speaking world. Those of us who live in the West stand in great need of God.... We need revival and what Jonathan Edwards called 'regeneration.' The book you hold in your hands is full of advice from Edwards himself on earnest preaching for revival.... May God stir your hearts and elevate your minds as you read, redirecting your desires and filling your life with divine things—the only things that really satisfy."

—**Doug Sweeney**, Second Dean of Beeson Divinity School and world-renowned scholar of Jonathan Edwards

"God knows this Western world needs revival.... We need a deep and broad awakening that reorients in fundamental ways both the lives of individuals and the direction of a society. There is no better Christian thinker on how to prepare for and preach toward such a revival than Jonathan Edwards. More than anyone else in the history of the church, Edwards was a theologian of revival. If we want to understand revival and how to seek it, we must turn to Edwards. This book by Dr. Klassen should help every reader do those things."

—**Gerald R. McDermott**, Anglican Chair of Divinity, retired, Beeson Divinity School

"Today, Christian churches . . . need to recapture the centrality of true biblical preaching. This timely book on revival preaching encourages us to move in this direction. It does so by emphasizing in a unique way the relationship between preaching and revival, as illustrated in the remarkable preaching and revival ministry of Jonathan Edwards.... Reading this book challenges us not only to recapture biblical preaching but to pray for revival, and to pray for and strive for Spirit-filled preaching that produces revival. I highly commend this book."

—**Raymond E. Ebbett**, former Director of the Christian and Missionary Alliance in Spain

"By highlighting the principles of revival preaching as emulated by Jonathan Edwards, Klassen challenges the next generation of preachers to a higher spiritual plane. He opens our eyes to a kind of preaching that has been almost forgotten but needed today more than ever. This book invites preachers to rediscover preaching as a powerful agent of life transformation. The principles outlined here will not only deepen your preaching ministry but will also reignite your passion for revival! When preachers catch this vision, so will the congregation, resulting in an awakening. Ernie's heart deeply longs for revival. This book is an overflow of his heart!"

—**Ashwin Ramani**, Associate Teaching Pastor, Centre Street Church, Calgary, Alberta

Revival Preaching

Revival Preaching

Twelve Lessons from Jonathan Edwards

ERNEST EUGENE KLASSEN

RESOURCE *Publications* • Eugene, Oregon

REVIVAL PREACHING
Twelve Lessons from Jonathan Edwards

Copyright © 2021 Ernest Eugene Klassen. All rights reserved. Except for brief quotations in critical publications or reviews, no part of this book may be reproduced in any manner without prior written permission from the publisher. Write: Permissions, Wipf and Stock Publishers, 199 W. 8th Ave., Suite 3, Eugene, OR 97401.

Resource Publications
An Imprint of Wipf and Stock Publishers
199 W. 8th Ave., Suite 3
Eugene, OR 97401

www.wipfandstock.com

PAPERBACK ISBN: 978-1-6667-1147-9
HARDCOVER ISBN: 978-1-6667-1148-6
EBOOK ISBN: 978-1-6667-1149-3

08/26/21

Revival Preaching: Twelve Lessons from Jonathan Edwards is dedicated to my preaching colleagues in the English-speaking world. May these reflections from Scripture and the sermons of Jonathan Edwards enable us all to more faithfully and effectively fulfill Paul's mandate to Timothy and to us:

I solemnly charge *you* in the presence of God and of Christ Jesus, who is to judge the living and the dead, and by His appearing and His kingdom: preach the word; be ready in season *and* out of season; reprove, rebuke, exhort, with great patience and instruction. For the time will come when they will not endure sound doctrine; but *wanting* to have their ears tickled, they will accumulate for themselves teachers in accordance to their own desires, and will turn away their ears from the truth and will turn aside to myths. But you, be sober in all things, endure hardship, do the work of an evangelist, fulfill your ministry (II Tim 4:1–5) (NASB).

I want to publicly thank The Christian and Missionary Alliance for their support of this project. May I encourage you to support this missions-minded and missions-hearted denomination? See www.cmacan.org (Canada).

Thanks Kenneth Minkema for coaching and guiding me along the way, and being so amazingly accessible to a novice like myself. That month spend in the Jonathan Edwards Study Center, just outside your office was so enriching.

Thanks to all who read parts of the document and provided valuable feedback. A special thanks to Steve Irvin for making numerous valuable suggestions. Any mistakes are mine!

Thanks, Marilyn, for more than 45 years (June 26, 1976) of life together!

May our Triune God be glorified by the faithful preaching of His Gospel and His Word. May He be pleased to use these thoughts to stimulate a God-honoring, Christ-centered Spirit empowered revival that leads to the revitalization of the church and the awakening and subsequent salvation of many souls.

I welcome your correspondence revernieklassen@gmail.com

J. I. PACKER'S TRIBUTE TO JONATHAN EDWARDS AS A PREACHER

"In fact, Edwards' own preaching was powerful in a high degree. Humanly speaking, he had a unique gift for making ideas live by the luminous precision with which he expounded them. He uncoils at length of reasoning with a slow, smooth exactness that is almost hypnotic in its power to rivet attention on the successive folds of truth sliding out into view. Had Edwards been no more than a pagan don teaching economics, he would without doubt have been a performer of 'Ancient Mariner' quality in the lecture-room. To this compelling expository power was added in the pulpit a terrible solemnity, expressive of the awe of God that was constantly on his spirit; and the result was preaching that congregations could neither resist nor forget. Edwards could make two hours seem like twenty minutes as he bore down on his listeners' conscience with the plain old truths of sin and salvation, and the calm majesty of his inexorable analysis was no less used of God to make men feel the force of truth than was the rhapsodic vehemence of George Whitefield."

"'His words', wrote his first biographer, Hopkins, 'often discovered a great deal of inward fervour, without much noise or external emotion, and fell with great weight on the minds of his hearers; and he spake so as to reveal the strong emotions of his own heart, which tended, in the most natural and effectual manner, to move and affect others'. Such a feeling communication of felt truth was, in fact, precisely what the Puritans had in mind when they spoke of 'powerful' preaching."

"As a Bible-lover, a Calvinist, a teacher of heart-religion, a gospel preacher of unction and power, and above all, a man who loved Christ, hated sin, and feared God, Edwards was a pure Puritan; indeed, one of the purest and greatest of all Puritans. American historians of culture have recently rediscovered Edwards as a major contributor to the American philosophical and literary heritage. It is to be wished that evangelical Christians today might themselves rediscover the important contribution that this latter-day Puritan made to the elucidation of the biblical faith."

"A Quest for Godliness—The Puritan Vision of the Christian Life"

J. I. Packer: 314, 315

All emphases are the author's

He also included this:
"If you mean by eloquence, what is usually intended by it in our cities; he had no pretensions to it. He had no studied variance of voice, and no strong emphasis. He scarcely gestured or even moved; and he made no attempt, by the eloquence of his style, or the beauty of his pictures, to gratify the taste, and fascinate the imagination. But, if you mean by eloquence the power of presenting an important truth before an audience, with overwhelming weight of argument, and with such intenseness of feeling that the whole soul of the speaker is thrown into every part of the conception and delivery, so that the solemn attention of the whole audience is riveted, from the beginning to the close, and impressions are left that cannot be effaced, Mr. Edwards was the most eloquent man I ever heard speak."

—ANONYMOUS FIRSTHAND WITNESS OF EDWARDS'S PREACHING
(quoted in J. I. Packer, A Quest for Godliness: The Puritan Vision of the Christian Life, 314)

Contents

Permissions	xiii
Biographical Sketch of The Author	xv
Introduction A: Introducing the Theme	1
Introduction B: Introducing the Thesis of this Book	8
Introduction C: Defining our Terms	18
Introduction D: Biographical Sketch of Edwards	31
Introduction E: Edwards's View of Preaching	45
Chapter 1: An Apology for Pathetic Preaching	51
Chapter 2: Prayer, Fasting and Revival Preaching	66
Chapter 3: Preaching on Hell or "Sulfurous Sermons"	76
Chapter 4: The Role of the Word in Edwards's Revivalistic and Awakening Preaching	84
Chapter 5: The Role of the Holy Spirit in Revival Preaching	95
Chapter 6: The Word/Spirit Blend and Preaching	116
Chapter 7: The Supremacy of God in Preaching	127
Chapter 8: Edwards the Man and Revival Preaching	143
Chapter 9: Correlating Divine Sovereignty and Human Responsibility	154
Chapter 10: The Importance of Application	168
Chapter 11: Spiritual Pride and Revival Preaching	181
Chapter 12: Christocentrism	198
Chapter 13: Application to Preaching Today	210

Appendix 1: What are the Parameters for the Great Awakening? 219
Appendix 2: The Resolutions of Jonathan Edwards 223
Appendix 3: The Defects of Preachers Reproved 239
Appendix 4: What Was the Great Awakening Like? 249
Appendix 5: The Place of Personal Application 251
For Further Reading 257
Bibliography 259

Permissions

Unless indicated otherwise, all quotes from the Bible are from the New International Version (NIV) Holy Bible, New International Version®, NIV® Copyright ©1973, 1978, 1984, 2011 by Biblica, Inc.® All rights reserved worldwide.

Several times the author quotes from the New American Standard Bible (NASB) copyright The Lockman Foundation (www.lockman.org). New American Standard Bible®, Copyright © 1960, 1971, 1977, 1995, 2020 by The Lockman Foundation. All rights reserved.

Several times the author quotes from the New Living Translation (NLT).

Several times the author quotes from the King James Version, (KJV) since this was the version Edwards was familiar with and used. Public Domain.

Several times the author quotes from the New Revised Standard Version (NRSV). New Revised Standard Version Bible, copyright © 1989 the Division of Christian Education of the National Council of the Churches of Christ in the United States of America. All rights reserved

Several times the author quoted from the King James 2021 Version (KJ21). Scripture taken from the New King James Version®. Copyright © 1982 by Thomas Nelson. All rights reserved.

Several times the author quoted from the Contemporary English Bible (CEB) Copyright © 2011 by Common English Bible.

Several times the author quoted from the New King James Version (NKJV) Scripture taken from the New King James Version®. Copyright © 1982 by Thomas Nelson. All rights reserved.

Several times the author quoted from the New American Standard Bible® (NASB1995), Copyright © 1960, 1971, 1977, 1995 by The Lockman Foundation. All rights reserved.

Several times the author quoted from The Holy Bible, English Standard Version. (ESV)® Text Edition: 2016. Copyright © 2001 by Crossway Bibles, a publishing ministry of Good News Publishers.

Several times the author quoted from The Living Bible (TLB) copyright © 1971 by Tyndale House Foundation. Tyndale House Publishers Inc., Carol Stream, Illinois 60188. All rights reserved.

Several times the author quoted from The Holy Bible, English Standard Version. (ESV) ® Text Edition: 2016. Copyright © 2001 by Crossway Bibles, a publishing ministry of Good News Publishers.

This material is also available in Spanish, published by CLIE. https://www.clie.es/la-predicacion-que-aviva-lecciones-de-jonathan-edwards

Biographical Sketch of The Author

THE REVEREND DR. ERNEST (Ernie) Klassen was born December 30, 1954. He has been married to Marilyn (Goerz) since 1976, is the father of two married children Daniel (Jessica) and David (Boyda) and grandfather to Kaden and Owen (sons of Daniel and Jessica). Ernie is the author of "Characteristics of Authentic Revival" (2020) (Teología Para Vivir) (in Spanish). This present work has been published by CLIE in Spanish) (2016). He is a student of the life and thought of Jonathan Edwards (1703–58), especially his writings and sermons on revival. Edwards was a pastor, theologian, philosopher, revivalist, defender, and critic of the First Great Awakening. Ernie currently serves with the Christian & Missionary Alliance of Canada as an International Worker. He and his wife have served together in various Latin American countries including Peru and Mexico for 25 years, serving in pastoral work, teaching, conference speaking, church planting, and evangelism. They have also served an Alliance pastorate in Canada for seven years before returning to the Spanish-speaking world from 2013–19, this time Spain. He recently finished serving as professor at Ambrose University (www.ambrose.edu) where he taught missions, theology and a course on Religious Affections. Ernie earned a D. Min. in 2006 from Asbury Theological Seminary with an emphasis on preaching and has done post-doctoral studies on Edwards under Kenneth Minkema's tutelage at Yale. Ernie is a product of the 1971 revival in western Canada.

If you would like to communicate with the author, he welcomes your inquiries and comments. He can be reached at revernieklassen@gmail.com.

Introduction A

Introducing the Theme

"The best way to revive the church is to restore fire in the pulpit" (Moody)[1].
"If the Lord would come back again He wouldn't cleanse the temple –
He would cleanse the pulpit" (Anonymous).[2]

IF MEN AND WOMEN are going to come to Christ in large numbers, in a great awakening, there must be a previous revival of God's people. Revival and awakening are close to God's heart and He wants these themes to be close to every believer's heart, especially every preacher's heart. Preaching is one of several elements that contributes to or detracts from revival and awakening. In this study we will explore what constitutes effective Revival Preaching. Of all the practitioners who can teach us a great deal about this theme, perhaps none can speak with greater authority than Jonathan Edwards.

When most people think of revival preaching and Edwards, they either draw a blank or their thoughts gravitate to a recollection of a portion of undoubtedly his most famous sermon: Sinners in the Hands of an Angry God. There we find this kind of powerful rhetoric:

> So that thus it is, that natural men are *held in the hand of God over the pit of hell*; they have deserved the fiery pit, and are already sentenced to it; and God is dreadfully provoked, his anger is as great towards them as to those that are actually suffering the executions of the fierceness of his wrath in hell, and they have done nothing in the least to appease or abate that anger,

1. Moody, *Fire*.
2. Christian Post, *Powerful Message*. This is a quote from a compilation of powerful and deeply moving messages on Revival. The reader may want to listen in: http://gnli.christianpost.com/video/christians-preaching-a-powerfull-message-14780.

neither is God in the least bound by any promise to hold 'em up one moment; the devil is waiting for them, hell is gaping for them, the flames gather and flash about them, and would fain lay hold on them, and swallow them up; the fire pent up in their own hearts is struggling to break out; and they have no interest in any mediator, there are no means within reach that can be any security to them. *In short, they have no refuge, nothing to take hold of, all that preserves them every moment is the mere arbitrary will, and uncovenanted unobliged forbearance of an incensed God.* (Sermon: Sinners in the Hands of an Angry God[3]).

O sinner! Consider the fearful danger you are in: 'tis a great *furnace of wrath,* a wide and *bottomless pit,* full of the *fire of wrath,* that you are held over in the hand of that God, whose wrath is provoked and incensed as much against you as against many of the damned in hell; *you hang by a slender thread,* with *the flames of divine wrath flashing about it, and ready every moment to singe it,* and burn it asunder; and you have no interest in any mediator, *and nothing to lay hold of to save yourself, nothing to keep off the flames of wrath, nothing of your own, nothing that you ever have done, nothing that you can do, to induce God to spare you one moment* (Jonathan Edwards) (Sermon: Sinners in the Hands of an Angry God[4]).

Because of this caricature of Edwardsean revival preaching, (and it is a caricature), and because of the somewhat archaic and circuitous ways that Edwards expresses himself, and because we are some 300 years removed from Edwards (1703–58) and from the Great Awakening (1734/35 and 1740/41/42) some may have an aversion to this theme. I trust *you* will explore the theme with me and am convinced that as you push through the challenges and persevere, your mind will be favourable stimulated, your *religious affections* deeply stirred, and you will powerfully be engaged. I trust especially that if you are either a burgeoning preacher, or a more seasoned preacher with an ache for more spiritual vitality and effectiveness in your own preaching, will be motivated to cultivate and develop elements of "revival preaching" that we can learn from Edwards. Many churches today need revival, and the world needs an awakening. May the result of this journey with Edwards into "Revival Preaching" be revived and awakened preachers,

---

3. Edwards, *Works,* 22: 409. (All the works of Jonathan Edwards in English can be accessed at edwards.yale.edu/archive and click on "research.")

4. Edwards, *Works,* 22: 412.

revived and awakened churches, and eventually lead to an awakening of the lost and their salvation, ultimately to the glory of God.

FOCUS

This is *not* a book exclusively about preaching. This is *not* a book exclusively about revival. This is *not* a book exclusively about Edwards. This is a book about where these three intersect.

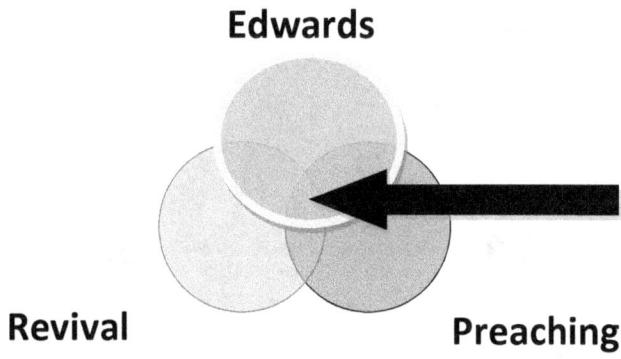

What we mean by preaching will be defined in our opening chapter. What we mean by revival and awakening will also be defined. Then we will consider that we mean by "revival preaching." Because of our focus on Edwards, we will spend some time introducing him to our readers, including his roots in Puritanism and Reformed theology. Because our spotlight will be on those sermons preached by Edwards during the Great Awakening, we will spend some time identifying the nature and parameters of that "surprising work of God" and consider in general terms his views on preaching. Once we have done all that, primarily to "set the stage" for our focus, we will delve into those elements of Revival Preaching that Edwards teaches us. At this stage we simply want to introduce those elements:

Chapter 1—The Heart, The Head, and Preaching

Chapter 2—Prayer and Fasting

Chapter 3—Hellfire

Chapter 4—The Word and Preaching

Chapter 5—The Holy Spirit

Chapter 6—The Word-Spirit Blend and Preaching

Chapter 7—The Supremacy of God in Preaching

Chapter 8—Edwards the Man as Preacher

Chapter 9—The Sovereignty of God and Human Responsibility

Chapter 10—Application

Chapter 11—Personal Humility

Chapter 12—Christo Centrism

Perhaps a way of visualizing this study is to see these themes as slices of a pie, with the "pie" itself being "Revival Preaching—Twelve Lessons from Jonathan Edwards."

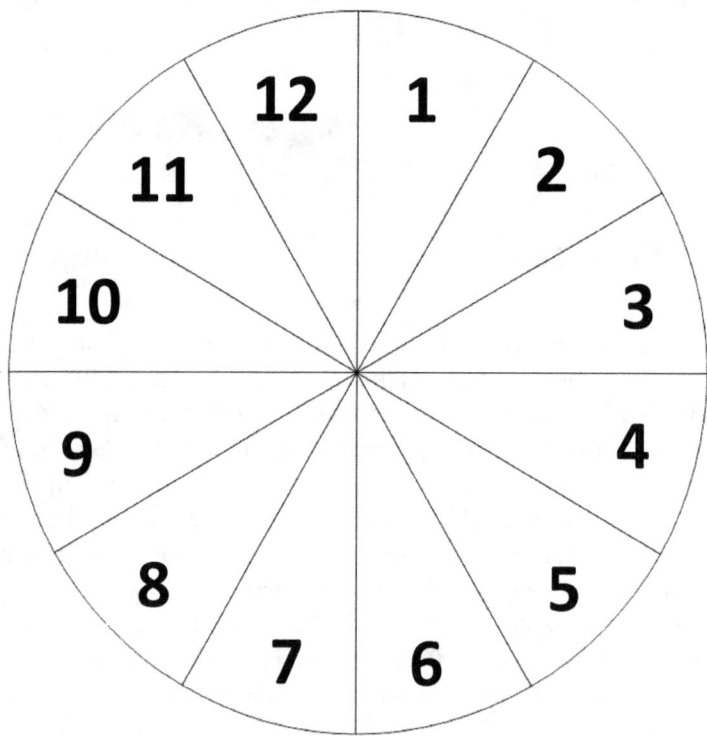

Twelve Aspects of Revival Preaching—Lessons from Jonathan Edwards

After reflecting on these twelve elements of "Revival Preaching" from Edwards, we want to reflect on preaching today and ask some application questions for today's preacher.

1. What correlation exists between preaching and revival? What kind of preaching facilitated revival in the past? What can we learn from Edwards and the Great Awakening that would facilitate awakening in our day? Are there any applications from our study germane to our postmodern milieu?
2. What practical implications and changes and applications does this study have on preachers today in North America, in Spain, and in Latin America?

APPROACH

What we will endeavor to do in this study is approach a particular aspect or element that explains Jonathan Edwards's view of Revival Preaching, and then dissect it by looking at it from various perspectives. There is a *biblical* perspective, where we highlight significant Scriptural texts that show the importance of the point and how it played out in the preaching ministry of biblical characters. Where possible and helpful, we will incorporate Edwards's comments on those passages. We also draw upon the *70 resolutions* of Edwards, if possible and relevant, to show the correlation between the man and his conviction about revival preaching. We will endeavor to provide specific *quotes from Edwards* himself or *quotes by Edwardsean scholars* that enunciate his understanding of revival preaching. We will also endeavor to provide, where possible, relevant *illustrations from the actual sermons of Edwards* to demonstrate the case in point.

Perhaps a word should be said about the rationale behind integrating Edwards's resolutions into the point about revival preaching. There is a fundamental law that "the man is the message" or "the medium is the message." We believe that in the ultimate sense, the truth of God's Word is the message, the truth of the Gospel is the message. Nevertheless, a very important aspect of preaching is that there is a profound interrelationship between what you have lived and are living, and the effect of your ministry in preaching. Effective revival preaching flows through a person who lives and grows in that truth. Consider Paul's references to "my Gospel":

- 16 This will take place on the day when God judges people's secrets through Jesus Christ, as my gospel declares (Romans 2:16) (NIV) and again in

- Romans 16:25 "25 Now to him who is able to establish you in accordance with my gospel, the message I proclaim about Jesus Christ," (NIV) and again in
- 2 Timothy 2:8 where we read "Remember Jesus Christ, raised from the dead, descended from David. This is my gospel . . . " (NIV)

We see that three times Paul refers to the Gospel as "my Gospel." Why? We believe that Paul so identifies with the Gospel and is so profoundly and personally affected by the Gospel, and so fully identified with the divine commissioning to preach the Gospel, that he owns it, and identifies it as "my Gospel." We believe that *this* is an indispensable element in effective Revival Preaching. We cannot transmit effectively what we have not experienced and believe there is a definite correspondence between the degree to which the preacher experiences the message and the degree of effectiveness he has in communicating that message.

Bounds says essentially the same thing: "Paul refers to 'my Gospel' not because of some personal eccentricity or an egotistical appropriation, but rather because there was placed, in his heart and in his soul a personal confidence which is reflected in his Pauline epistles, inflamed and energized by the flaming energy of a soul on fire."[5]

Alluding to the resolutions and personal testimony of Edwards go a long way to clarifying and reinforcing this fundamental premise, which we believe was one of the fundamental convictions that he held to, which so deeply and widely motivated him to be a person of spiritual depth—he knew and believed that he was called to be an example. Edwards himself affirmed " . . . the minister by demonstrating these saintly excellencies teaches his people to imitate Christ in their approach to God"[6]. Edwards had a view of preaching that was very "incarnational." According to Westra, Edwards viewed the minister as "a kind of subordinate savior" (Sermon on Acts 20:28)[7], "their express purpose being to prepare the hearts for the Word and to communicate with utter integrity the vital relationships and connections between words spoken and heard, and their ultimate meanings in the mind and will of God, who is both creative and redemptive Word" (Westra: ix); "In preaching the minister faithfully attempts to externalize the spiritual world of God's will and mind and at the same time to demonstrate an obedient, gracious, personal response to God's infinite perfection and glory."[8]

5. Bounds, *Preacher and Prayer*, 7.
6. Westra, *Minister's Task*, 16.
7. Westra, *Minister's Task*, ix.
8. Westra, *Minister's Task*, x.

As Westra points out "for him [Edwards] the line between his personal and vocational life at times became virtually indistinguishable: the office absorbed the man, the man the office."[9] Edwards has a very strong view on the minister as a model or an example and is called upon to exemplify the truths enunciated. There is to be a fundamental resonance between the message preached and the preacher's life. This is a fundamental issue of spiritual integrity. Revival preaching requires that we live the message that we want to communicate. None of us live it perfectly, but to the degree we exemplify the message, to that degree we influence.

CONCLUSION

So, let us begin our journey by setting the context and establishing our terms. We need to reflect briefly on who Edwards is, what was the First Great Awakening, including its parameters, and then proceed to define what we mean by preaching, what we mean by revival and awakening, what is "Revival Preaching" and then proceed to reflect on what we can learn about "Revival Preaching" from Jonathan Edwards as seen in the First Great Awakening.

---

9. Westra, *Minister's Task*, 3.

Introduction B

Introducing the Thesis of this Book: A Certain Kind of Preaching Is Conducive to Revival

"At Iconium Paul and Barnabas went as usual into the Jewish synagogue. There they spoke so effectively that a great number of Jews and Greeks believed" (Acts 14:1) (NIV).

"An ardent love to Christ and souls warms their breasts and animates their labours. God has made those his ministers active spirits, a flame of fire in his service; and his word in their mouths has been as a fire; and as a hammer that breaks the rock in pieces [Jer 23:29]" (Cooper, in his preface to Edwards's "Faithful Narrative," describing the Great Awakening).

Revival Preaching is preaching that contributes to the revival of the lethargic believer and the awakening and subsequent salvation of the lost.

MULTIPLICITY OF FACTORS THAT CONTRIBUTE TO REVIVAL

We believe that there are many elements that contribute to revival and spiritual awakening, including such elements as historical circumstances, prayer, unusual providential circumstances, cataclysmic social upheaval, economic hardship, political and leadership crises, reports of contemporary revival and awakening from other latitudes, reports of historical revival and awakenings, people feeling powerfully moved to seek God in mysterious ways, the reading of God's Word, powerful worship, the testimony of children youth and adults, and many other factors. These and other important elements bring credibility to the fact that "The wind blows wherever it pleases. You hear its sound, but you cannot tell where it comes from or where it is going. So it is with everyone born of the Spirit" (John 3:8) (NIV).

MYSTERY IN THE SOVEREIGNTY OF GOD

Undoubtedly there is an element of the mysterious in the work of God, and this is especially so when it comes to studying, analyzing, and explaining revival principles. The prophet Isaiah, seeking to understand God's ways, affirms: "Truly, O God of Israel, our Savior, you work in mysterious ways" (New Living Translation). The NASB translates this verse: "Truly, You are a God who hides Himself, O God of Israel, Savior!" (Isa 45:15). The hymnwriter captured this truth when he wrote: 'God moves in a mysterious way His wonders to perform' (William Cowper) (1731–1800). The Scriptures, describing the Exodus under the leadership of men like Moses and Aaron, state: "Your path led through the sea, your way through the mighty waters, though your footprints were not seen" (Ps 77:19) (NIV). Isaiah confirms the mysterious nature of God's designs when God states: "For my thoughts are not your thoughts, neither are your ways my ways, saith the LORD. For as the heavens are higher than the earth, so are my ways higher than your ways, and my thoughts than your thoughts" *(Isa 55:89) (King James Version)*. Endeavoring to understand God's mysterious sovereign designs, the Apostle Paul, that great mind of Christianity, concludes: 33 Oh, the depth of the riches both of the wisdom and knowledge of God! How unsearchable are His judgments and unfathomable His ways! 34 For *who has known the mind of the Lord, or who became His counselor*? (Rom 11:33, 34) (NASB).

While these passages speak to God's ways in general being mysterious, we believe that these same truths are applicable to the study of revivals and awakenings. While we believe that careful study of the Scriptures and church history of revivals, from a sociological, theological, and historical perspective, yield very helpful principles, and we do well to pursue the application of these principles, there remains an element of mystery in the understanding of God's ways, especially of His ways in revival and awakening.

MYSTERY IN THE SOVEREIGNTY OF GOD IN REVIVAL AND AWAKENING

We need to affirm an element of mystery in understanding God's ways in general, which is I believe one of the great lessons of Scripture. God "answered" Job's pain-filled inquiries not with answers, but with 66 questions (see the Divine Discourses, Job chapters 38, 39, 40 and 41). And although our hearts may be pained and grieved by the situation in the church today, and in the world today, we will not always be able to discern the Divine solution in ways that our finite minds can understand. Even with the assistance of the Word of God and the Spirit of God, there are aspects of revival and awakening that defy our understanding. As students of revival and awakening, we do well, like Job, to humble ourselves and remember our limitations. There is one of the 66 questions that God raises with Job that I think is particularly relevant to our study: Job 38:37, 38

> "Who can count the clouds by wisdom,
> Or tip the water jars of the heavens,
> When the dust hardens into a mass
> And the clods stick together?" (NIV)

There is indeed something mysterious about the clouds and the wind and the rain! No one fully understands the dynamic of rain; even the most skilled meteorologists get it wrong! Again, we are reminded of the words of Jesus: "the wind blows where it chooses, and you hear the sound of it, but you do not know where it comes from or where it goes. So, it is with everyone who is born of the Spirit" (John 3:8) (NRSV). And when we give this passage a spiritual application and consider the "landscape" in the church and the world to be like a parched riverbed when the dust hardens into a mass and the clods stick together for lack of rain, we do well to remember that there is an element of mystery in the tipping of the water jars of the heavens. Revival rain is what is needed to bring refreshing to the parched landscape. But as Job needed to learn, there are elements of mystery in the governance of the physical and spiritual world, and all our deliberations and speculations and proposals should be framed by that. God is sovereign. God is sovereign in revival and spiritual awakening. God has always been and always will be sovereign.

PREACHING AND REVIVAL

Having said that, we want to talk about a unique factor that plays a significant catalytic role in revival and spiritual awakening. We mentioned earlier the numerous elements that help to understand the origins of a revival and spiritual awakening. It is a complex matter. However, we dare to take one slice of the pie, remembering that it is only one slice of the pie, and study that slice. We refer to the unique role that preaching has as a catalyst to revival and spiritual awakening.

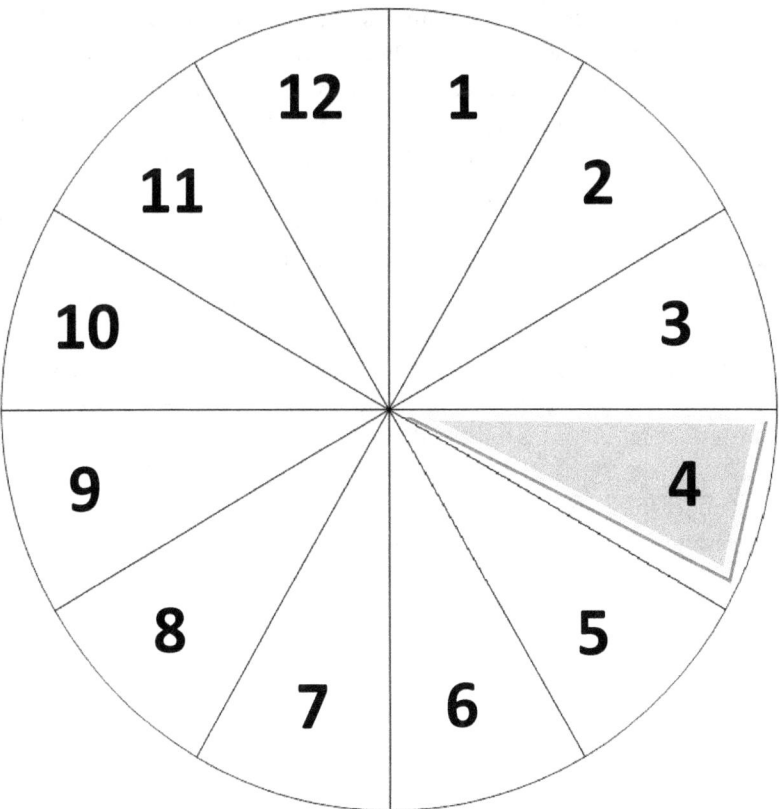

Revival Preaching—Just One Aspect Explaining the Origins of Revival—But a Very Important One

Is there Clear Biblical Evidence Connecting Preaching to Revival?

What is the evidence connecting revival preaching to revival in the Old Testament?[1]

Autrey believes that there was a revival under the spiritual leadership of Moses (Exod 32:1–35 and 33:1–23) that he traces to Moses' preaching of the law.

---

1. Perhaps the two best works tracing Old Testament revivals to preaching are by

Autrey traces the revival under Samuel (I Sam 7:1–17) to his direct preaching (7:3); the classic case of Israel's return to their God after a prolonged period of apostasy was due to the spiritual leadership and proclamation ministry of Elijah (I Kgs 18:1–46); the awakening at Nineveh was due to the preaching ministry of God's reluctant prophet: Jonah. An entire city of spared because of the repentance of the king and "The Ninevites believed God" (Jonah 3:5). There was a remarkable revival under King Asa (II Chr 15) by the confrontational preaching instrumentality of Azariah (II Chr 15:2). The revival was led by King Hezekiah (II Chr 29:1–35; 30:1–27; and 31:1–12) though there was support given by prophets Isaiah and Micah. Autrey affirms that the revival "was no doubt greatly enhanced by great preaching. . ."[2]. The revival under Josiah (II Chr 34:1–33; 35:1–19) was in part due to the prophetic preaching of a prophetess, Huldah (II Chr 34:22–28). Autrey describes the return of the exiles under Nehemiah's leadership and Ezra's preaching as a powerful example of revival (Neh 8:1–18). In addition to Autrey's excellent survey, the Old Testament scholar Kaiser has done a major study on the revivals of the Old Testament. Those additional revivals that he singles out include the revival under the leadership of Zerubbabel with the prophetic involvement of Haggai and Zechariah. A careful study of all these Old Testament revival and awakening movements indicates the strategic role of prophetic preaching.

What is the evidence connecting revival preaching to revival in the New Testament?[3]

Kaiser reworked his original treatment of revivals in the Old Testament in his wonderful book: Revive us Again—Biblical Insights for Encouraging Spiritual Renewal. Kaiser categorizes the following as episodes of Revival in the New Testament: Revival under John the Baptist (Matt 3:1–14); Revival under the Apostle Peter at Pentecost (Acts 2:1–47); Revival under Philip at Samaria (Acts 8:1–25); Revival under the Apostle Peter at Caesarea (Acts 10) and finally Revival under Paul and Silas in Europe (I Thess 1:2–10).[4]

We can see in the book of Acts how the Holy Spirit anointed the preaching of the word to bring about both the awakening of the sinner and the revitalization of the believer, such as the preaching of Peter on the day of Pentecost. Typical of Acts is what happened in Iconium where Paul and

---

Kaiser and Autrey. We highly recommend the study of these two works (see Bibliography).

2. Autrey, *Revivals*, 113.

3. Perhaps the best work tracing New Testament revivals to preaching is also by Kaiser (See bibliography).

4. Kaiser, *Revive Us Again*, 173–228.

Barnabas "entered together into the Jewish synagogue and *spoke in such a way that a great number of both Jews and Greeks believed*" (Acts 14:1) (NASB). The expansion of the kingdom of God in the book of Acts (2:41,47; 4:4; 5:14; 11:24, 12:24, 16:5; 17:4; 17:12; 17:34; 19:20) has a great deal to do with effective preaching (Acts 2:14ad, 2:42; 4:1,2; 5:12; 11:19, 20, 21; 14:1; 16:4; 17:13; 17:10; 17:16–31; 19:8) (We strongly encourage the reader to not skim over these references in Acts, but to reflect on each reference). "For the word of God is alive and active. Sharper than any double-edged sword, it penetrates even to dividing soul and spirit, joints and marrow; it judges the thoughts and attitudes of the heart" (Heb 4:12) (NIV). The fundamental thesis upon which this investigation is built is the premise that Spirit-anointed preaching of the Word is frequently God's instrument for bringing revival and awakening.[5] We want to explore what Spirit-anointed preaching means. We want to explore the preaching during a period when there was a remarkable effusive outpouring of the Spirit in revival and awakening, known by historians as The Great Awakening. We will consider the key role Jonathan Edwards played as a primary protagonist of the Great Awakening, and carefully consider his preaching in relationship to the Great Awakening. It is his example and his appeal to sensible preaching that we will explore, a kind of defence of 'pathetic' preaching (to be defined later).

Is there clear historical evidence connecting preaching to revival?

When it comes to the history of revival preaching and revival preachers, there are so many options, some more known than others. Our focus is on Edwards, but I wanted the reader to be familiar with some of the "champion" revival preachers of history.[6] Here is a list of my favourites: some are more expository preachers, some are evidently revival preachers, (designated with an *) some are more theological preachers, but all are preachers.

---

5. Not all revivals begin with preaching; indeed, not all revivals have a strong preaching component. However, a strong case can be made for the significant role preaching plays in the inception and sustenance of most significant revivals; prayer is critical and foundational, but preaching is also critical and foundational.

6. Some of these are more expositors who may not have been instrumental in facilitating revival and/or spiritual awakening. Much depends on how you define terms. Was the Reformation a revival? Certainly, there were revival elements within the Reformation. For a complete study of the history of preaching, consult "The Wycliffe Handbook of Preaching and Preachers" by Wiersbe and Perry (Moody Press, 1984).

Pre-reformation preachers

Ambrose of Milan (c. 340- 4 April 397); John Chrysostom* (347–407); Augustine of Hippo (354–430); Bernard of Clairvaux (1090—August 20, 1153); St. Francis of Assisi (118–182–October 3, 1226); Thomas Aquinas (28 January 122–527 March 1274); John Wyclif* (1330–84); John Huss*(1373–1415).

Reformation Preachers

Girolamo Savonarola*(1452–98); Ulrich Zwingli (1484–1531); Hugh Latimer (1485–1555); William Tyndale (1494–1536); John Calvin (10 July 1509–27 May 1564); Martin Luther (10 November 1483–18 February 1546); John Knox (1513–72); John Jewel (1522–71); Thomas Cartwright (1535–1603); John Gillespie* (1580–12 Aug. 1627).

Puritan Preachers Most Influential in the Life of Edwards or who ministered in the 16th and 17th Centuries

William Perkins (1558–1602); Joseph Hall (1574–1656); William Greenhill (1581–1677); Thomas Goodwin (1600–80); Thomas Shepard (1605–49); Richard Baxter (1615–91); John Owen (161683); Thomas Manton (1620–77); Thomas Watson (1620–86); John Bunyan (1628–88); Stephen Charnock (1628–80); John Bunyan (1628–88); John Gill (1697–1771); Matthew Henry (1662–1714) Isaac Watts (1674–1748); Griffith Jones (1683–1761).

Preaching Contemporaries of Edwards (17th and 18th Century)

Increase Mather (June 21, 1639–August 23, 1723); Cotton Mather (February 12, 1663–February 13, 1728); Solomon Stoddard (September 27, 1643–February 11, 1729); Timothy Edwards (1668–1759); Nikolaus Ludwig von Zinzendorf* (May 26, 1700–May 9, 1760); Theodore Frelinghuysen* (1691–1747); John Wesley* (28 June 1703–2 March 1791); Charles Wesley* (18 December 1707–29 March 1788); Daniel Rowland* (also spelt Rowlands; 1713–16 October 1790); Howell Harris (1714–73); George Whitefield* (1714–1770); David Brainerd (April 20, 1718–October 9, 1747); Peter Cartwright (September 1, 1785–September 25, 1872); Charles Grandison Finney* (August 29, 1792–August 16, 1875). Christmas Evans (1766–1838); Charles Simeon (1759–1836).

Revival Preachers of the nineteenth century

William C. Burns (1815–1868); Alexander Whyte (1836–1921); George Müller (1805–98); John A. Broadus (1827–95); A. W. Pink (1886–1952); Martyn Lloyd-Jones (1899–1981); D. L. Moody (1837–99); Charles Haddon Spurgeon (1834–92); Alexander Maclaren (1826–1910); Robert Murray McCheyne (1813–43); John C. Ryle (1816–1900), Charles J. Vaughan (1816–97); Joseph Parker (1830–1902); Reuben Archer Torrey (28 January 1856–26 October 1928).

Modern Preachers and Revivalists

John Robert Walmsley Stott (1921–2011); Harry Allan Ironside (1876–1951); Donald Grey Barnhouse (1895–1960); James M. Gray (1881–1935); William Bell Riley (1861–1947); Wallie Amos Criswell (1909–2002); James Denny (1856–1917), George Campbell Morgan (1863–1945); William Graham Scroggie (1877–1958); William Franklin "Billy" Graham, Jr. (1918–2018).

Tracing the Influence of Revival Preaching During the First Great Awakening

We want to explore the preaching during a period when there was a remarkable effusive outpouring of the Spirit in revival and awakening, known by historians as The Great Awakening. We will consider the key role Jonathan Edwards played as a primary protagonist of the Great Awakening, and carefully consider his preaching in relationship to the Great Awakening.

There are so many aspects of the Great Awakening that merit careful study. There are so many aspects of Jonathan Edwards that merit continued study. While his thought has been investigated by many philosophers and theologians and revivalists and historians, not to mention thinking Christians, we believe that there are still significant gems to be discovered and shared with the community of faith. Our focus in this study is Jonathan Edwards view and practice of preaching and revival. More preachers need to read Edwards.[7]

What kinds of sermons were preached before, during and after the Great Awakening? What themes and what texts were preached? What issues

---

7. John Carrick's excellent work on "*The Preaching of Jonathan Edwards*" (Banner of Truth Trust, 2008) provides an excellent foundation on which to build an Edwardsean theology of revival preaching.

were addressed? What was Edwards's approach to preaching in general? What was his philosophy of preaching? What was Edwards's approach to preaching before, during and after the Great Awakening? What lessons are there for us as preachers today? What can we learn from the Great Awakening that would facilitate awakening in our day? What correlation exists between his preaching and revival? What made his sermons so effective? Why did God seem pleased to pour out revival through the agency of these sermons? What about the man Edwards sheds light on the correlation between preaching and revival? While we recognize the complex nature of revivals and awakenings, and the multi-faceted aspects that explain their emergence and their demise, and while we recognize the mysterious nature of revival movements, that the wind blows where it wills, but you cannot tell where it comes from or where it goes, and while we recognize that God is sovereign, and while we recognize that a proper study of revival needs to embrace a careful study of historical context and biographical analysis, nevertheless, with all these caveats, we believe that there is an important correlation between a certain kind of preaching and revival/awakening movements.

There is significant[8] internal evidence that the Great Awakening was brought about by good preaching. In his preface to Edwards's "Faithful Narrative," Cooper comments: "They *preach* the Gospel of the grace of God from place to place with *uncommon zeal and assiduity*. The doctrines they insist on, are the doctrines of the Reformation, under the influence whereof the power of godliness so flourished in the last century. The points on which their *preaching* mainly turns are those important ones of man's guilt, corruption, and impotence; supernatural regeneration by the Spirit of God, and free justification by faith in the righteousness of Christ; and the marks of the new birth. The *manner of their preaching is not with the enticing words of man's wisdom*: howbeit, they 'speak wisdom among them that are perfect' [I Cor 2:4, 6]. *An ardent love to Christ and souls warms their breasts and animates their labours. God has made those his ministers' active spirits, a flame of fire in his service; and his word in their mouths has been as a fire; and as a hammer that breaketh the rock in pieces* [Jer. 23:29]" [Emphasis mine].[9]

Where do we get our ideas from about Edwards's preaching? For primary sources, we look to (1) his manuscripts of his sermons, (2) notes by others of his sermons, a highly developed practice in Colonial America, (3) his assessment of the awakening in his book "Faithful Narrative," (4) his letters, (5) his diary, (6) his writing in general, and (7) his three manuscript

---

8. By significant I mean important. Investigation suggests that preaching often (not always) was the detonate or catalyst which God used to bring about a revival.

9. Edwards, *Works* 4: 217–19.

notebooks, " . . . a kind of literary diary, revealing Edward's thoughts on the sermon and the preacher's duties, week in and week out."[10] We can also be helped by secondary sources who have investigated the Great Awakening, Edwards, and his preaching. Some of the better resources are in the bibliography.

We believe that there is a close connection between preaching and revival. This work is all about that *kind* of preaching that tends towards revival and spiritual awakening. We will carefully examine the view and practice of Edwards on Revival Preaching. We will be looking at various aspects of his preaching. We will be making certain historical allusions and using certain terms. So that we are all on the same page, and not guilty of miscommunication, we do well to establish the historical context and define how we are using certain key and frequently used terms. To do this we have dedicated a preliminary chapter to "Definitions" which we now turn to.

---

10. Kimnach, *Brazen Trumpet*, 29–44.

Introduction C

Defining our Terms

Whenever one writes, it is indispensable to define terms to expedite communication. There are several significant terms and expressions that we will be using throughout this book that require definition. We want to be clear and have precise definitions when we speak about (1) Preaching, (2) Revival, (3) Awakening, (4) The Relationship between Revival and Awakening, (5) Revival Preaching, and finally (6) The First Great Awakening.

DEFINITIONS

1. PREACHING

What follows are several precise definitions by seasoned preachers. They will serve to assist us in arriving at our own definition.

John Stott has a concise definition of preaching: "*To expound Scripture is to open up the inspired text with such faithfulness and sensitivity that God's voice is heard and his people obey him.*" In his masterful work "Between Two Worlds The Art of Preaching in the Twentieth Century," Stott defines preaching as "bridge-building"[1] in which one endeavors to carefully expound the text, in context, of the Scriptures with relevant application to the current setting of the listener, in other words, preaching is building bridges between two worlds, thus the title.

Haddon Robinson states that "Expository preaching is the communication of a biblical concept, derived from and transmitted through a historical, grammatical, and literary study of a passage in its context, which the

---

1. Stott, *Between Two Worlds*, 137.

Holy Spirit first applies to the personality and experience of the preacher, then through the preacher, applies to the hearers."[2]

Martyn Lloyd-Jones wrote a marvelous treatment on preaching, entitled "Preaching and Preachers" wherein he affirms: "Any true definition of preaching must say that that man is there to deliver the message of God, a message from God to those people. If you prefer the language of Paul, he is 'an ambassador for Christ.' That is what he is. He has been sent, he is a commissioned person, and he is standing there as the mouthpiece of God and of Christ to address these people[3].

Martin Luther: Luther affirmed the presence of Christ in the preaching of the Word. Again, Christ is truly present. Thus, Luther had an additional doctrine of the 'real presence'—namely, "the real presence of Christ in proclamation . . . ." This means, according to Fred W. Meuser, "In the sermon one actually encounters God"[4] (Beach: 79).

John Calvin: Because of the influence Calvin had on Puritanism and Edwards, we need to pay careful attention to Calvin's comprehension of preaching. "For, among the many excellent gifts with which God has adorned the human race, it is a singular privilege that he deigns to consecrate to himself the mouths and tongues of men in order that his voice may resound in them."[5] Calvin, like Luther, recognized the union that exists between the work of God and the work of man in biblical preaching. He saw no reason to be squeamish about this union; rather, he believed that believers should be humbled by it. Indeed, what would we do if God's voice thundered from heaven to us, as at Sinai? Who could bear it? Instead, knowing our frailty, God mercifully speaks to His people through human instrumentality. He ministers His words to us in the ministry of the Word—that is, He ministers through the ministry of men, which involves a faithful exposition and application of Holy Scripture. Calvin does not deny that God could have ministered His Word directly; instead, God resolved to minister His Word through the mediation of men. "God might Himself have performed this work [i.e., the work of ministry], if He had chosen; but He has delegated it to the ministry of men. . . .such is the Will of God."[6]

Greg Heisler: A more contemporary treatment of preaching gives this pneumatological definition of expository preaching as ". . .the Spirit-empowered proclamation of biblical truth derived from the illuminating

---

2. Robinson, *Biblical Preaching*, 29.
3. Lloyd-Jones, *Preaching and Preachers*, 53.
4. Beach, *Real Presence*, 77–134.
5. Istafanous, *Calvin's Doctrine of Biblical Authority*, 99.
6. Calvin, *Galatians and Ephesians*, 281.

guidance of the Holy Spirit by means of a verse-by-verse exposition of the Holy Spirit, with a view to applying the text by means of the convicting power of the Holy Spirit, first to the preacher's own heart, and then to the hearts of those who hear, culminating in an authentic and powerful witness to the living Word, Jesus Christ, and obedience, Spirit-filled living."[7]

John Edwards: (not to be confused with Jonathan Edwards). According to Edwardsean scholar Kimnach, who has studied the preaching of Edwards more than any other, Jonathan Edwards was highly influenced by another Edwards (John), who wrote a treatise on preaching that highly influenced Jonathan: John Edwards's *The Preacher* (London, 1705). John Edwards affirms "the Ministers of the Gospel ought to be very Endearing and Affectionate, and to deport themselves with Love and Meekness: for in doing thus, they apply themselves most suitably to Rational Men, who are to be led, not driven, who follow the conduct of Reason rather than of Force." All in all, "a Preacher is one that must have the Gift of Persuading, and this he must do by raising the *Passions* of his Hearers." To preach persuasively, Edwards insists, the preacher must believe and feel intensely what he preaches; he must then communicate his personal feelings with the message so that he preaches experience, . . . "[8] (John Edwards, quoted by Kimnach). We believe that this description/definition of preaching of John Edwards reflects Jonathan Edwards's view of preaching. As Kimnach affirms: ". . .as for *The Preacher*, there are too many echoes of its individualistic expressions throughout Edwards's notebooks to have doubts about its importance to him."[9]

Conclusion: We will see throughout the course of this study various aspects or elements of the preaching of Edwards that will serve to clarify our understanding of Edwards's concept of preaching. A good exercise here would be to reflect on the various elements in the definitions given above, isolate them, describe their importance in the preaching enterprise, and then proceed to create one's own definition of preaching.

2. REVIVAL

When we write about the relationship between Preaching and Revival, or Revival Preaching, we are assuming in that concept of revival that both quickening or revitalization of the regenerate and conversion or awakening of the degenerate are happening. We will identify and define our terms more carefully briefly but suffice it here to say that in revival God uses biblical preaching to impact *both the saved* and *the lost*.

---

7. Heisler, *Spirit-Led Preaching*, 21.
8. Kimnach, *Works* 10: 17.
9. Kimnach, *Works* 10: 16.

Revival: There are many beautiful texts that deal with the nature of revival. One of my favourites is *Isaiah 57:15* "For this is what the high and exalted One says— he who lives forever, whose name is holy: "I live in a high and holy place, but also with the one who is contrite and lowly in spirit, to *revive* the spirit of the lowly and to *revive* the heart of the contrite" (NIV). The nature of the word, both in Hebrew, Greek and English (and other languages) suggests that to revive means to restore "life" and "vitality" to someone (or a group) that has been languishing or fading. A fire tends to go out unless it is replenished with fresh fuel, fresh kindling. As the wood is supplied, and oxygen provided, those flickering and fading embers burst forth into a full flame. When Paul encourages Timothy to "fan into flame the gift of God" (II Tim. 1:6) (NIV) he utilizes a Greek term (αναζωπυρειν) (*anazopurein*) which means precisely and literally to make the fire come to life again (ανα+ζω+πυρειν) (again + life + to burn). In the strictest sense, when we speak of revival, we are referring to those regenerates, those truly born again, those Christians who experience a resurgence or revitalization or renewal of their spiritual life. Revival, in the strictest sense, is for the Christian individual or church that has spiritual life, is genuinely regenerate and born again, but has allowed the flame of spiritual passion to falter and fade.

The biblical references to revival are surprisingly limited. A simple concordance provides seven reverences to the word "revive" (NIV): *Genesis 45:27* But when they told him everything Joseph had said to them, and when he saw the carts Joseph had sent to carry him back, the spirit of their father Jacob *revived*. *Judges 15:19* Then God opened up the hollow place in Lehi, and water came out of it. When Samson drank, his strength returned, and he *revived*. *1 Samuel 30:12* Part of a cake of pressed figs and two cakes of raisins. He ate and was *revived*, for he had not eaten any food or drunk any water for three days and three nights. *Psalm 80:18* Then we will not turn away from you; *revive* us, and we will call on your name. *Psalm 85:6* Will you not *revive* us again, that your people may rejoice in you? *Isaiah 57:15* For this is what the high and exalted One says— he who lives forever, whose name is holy: "I live in a high and holy place, but also with the one who is contrite and *Hosea 6:2* lowly in spirit, to *revive* the spirit of the lowly and to *revive* the heart of the contrite: After two days he will *revive* us; on the third day he will restore us that we may live in his presence. A study of these words suggests a restoration to life, which is what revival literally means: re + viviere = live again. Revival is a revitalization of spiritual life or renaissance or resurgence of spiritual vitality and usefulness.

There are several significant *episodes* of revival recorded in the Scriptures which the reader would do well to investigate, for these historical episodes enrich our understanding of revival (Hezekiah; II Chr 29–30; Josiah; II Kgs 22–23; II Chr 35; Pentecost and beyond: Acts 2ff).

There are also several significant *images* which the Bible employs to convey the concept of revival: The transformation from winter into spring (Song 2:11); the recuperation from a bed of sickness to a place of health and vitality (Job 11:13–20); the revitalization and fruitfulness of vegetation (Hos 14:57); the descent of the rain (1 Kgs 8:35–36); the descent of fire (Acts 2:34); the resurrection of a valley of dry bones (Ezek 37), etc.

There are various *definitions* of revival. What follows are some classic definitions of revival. Each of them is helpful in gaining a sense of what we mean by revival.

    a. The actual word revival means "A restoration to use, acceptance, activity, or vigor after a period of obscurity or quiescence."[10]

    b. "*God's quickening visitation of his people, touching their hearts and deepening his work of grace in their lives*" (J. I. Packer).[11]

    c. "*the sovereign act of God, in which He restores His own backsliding people to repentance, faith and obedience*" (Stephen Olford).[12]

    d. "*Repent, then, and turn to God, so that your sins may be wiped out, that times of refreshing may come from the Lord*" (Acts 3:19) (NIV) (J. Edwin Orr).

    e. "*the return of the Church from her backslidings, and the conversion of sinners.*" "*A new beginning of obedience to God*" (Charles Finney).[13]

    f. "*an extraordinary movement of the Holy Spirit producing extraordinary results*" (Richard Owen Roberts).[14]

    g. "*a community saturated with God*" (Duncan Campbell).[15]

    h. "*the work of the Holy Spirit in restoring the people of God to a more vital spiritual life, witness, and work by prayer and the Word after repentance in crisis for their spiritual decline*" (Earle Cairns).[16]

    i. 'A true Holy Spirit revival is a remarkable increase in the spiritual life of a large number of God's people, accompanied by an

---

10. *American Heritage Dictionary*, 4.
11. Galloway, *Pray for Revival*, Packer.
12. Galloway, *Pray for Revival*, Olford.
13. Finney, *Lectures on Revival*, 1.
14. Galloway, *Pray for Revival*, Roberts.
15. Skinner, *People Saturated*, 1.
16. Muehlenberg, *Revival and Repentance*, 1.

      awesome awareness of the presence of sin with a passionate longing for holiness and unusual effectiveness in evangelism, leading to the salvation of many unbelievers' (Brian Edwards).[17]

  j. Edwards: Edwards clarifies his concept of revival when he makes reference to his revival prayer: " . . . that he would appear in his glory, and favor Zion, and manifest his compassion to the world of mankind, by *an abundant effusion of his Holy Spirit on all the churches, and the whole habitable earth, to revive true religion in all parts of Christendom,* and to deliver all nations from their great and manifold spiritual calamities and miseries, and *bless them with the unspeakable benefits of the kingdom of our glorious Redeemer, and fill the whole earth with his glory . . . ."*[18] [Emphasis mine] (Jonathan Edwards). Edwards viewed the minister as a burning and shining light, and the effects of that light were similar in the spiritual realm as they are in the natural realm: if he is pleased to make you a burning and shining light in this part of his church, and by the influence of your light and heat (or rather by his divine influence, with your ministry) to cause this wilderness to bud and blossom as the rose, and give it the excellency of Carmel and Sharon, and to cause you to shine in the midst of this people with warm and lightsome, quickening and comforting beams, causing their souls to flourish, rejoice and bear fruit, like a garden of pleasant fruits, under the beams of the sun" (Jonathan Edwards).[19] Revival is like springtime for Edwards. What a beautiful figure.

  Conclusion: Revival is primarily the revitalization of the languishing and decaying Christian. But the impact among the saved normally spills over into an awakening of the lost. We turn to consider dimensions of the term "Awakening."

3. AWAKENING

  a. Biblical perspective: We need to take a moment to differentiate between revival and awakening. First, although the Bible does not use the precise term "awakening," it does appeal to the awakening of God, the saved and the lost.

---

17. Nelson, *Evidences*, 1.
18. Edwards, *Works* 5: 321.
19. Edwards, *Works* 25: 99.

1. God Himself as asked by the Psalmist to awaken. In *Psalm 44:23* we read "Awake, why sleepest thou, O Lord? Arise, cast us not off for ever" (NIV). *Psalm 78:65* states "Then the Lord *awaked* as one out of sleep, and like a mighty man that shouteth by reason of wine" (NIV). In a very real albeit metaphorical and anthropomorphic sense the Lord is the One who awakens. The context of Psalm 78:65 strongly suggests a previous period of spiritual decline among God's people (see 78:56–64).

2. *Isaiah 26:19* affirms "Thy dead men shall live, together with my dead body shall they arise. *Awake* and sing, ye that dwell in dust: for thy dew is as the dew of herbs, and the earth shall cast out the dead" (KJ21). Perhaps this was in the mind of those who first crafted the term "awakening," with a clear allusion to the dead receiving life. It appears that this reference to the awakening of the unregenerate is alluded to in Ephesians where Paul exhorts *Ephesians 5:14*: Wherefore he saith, *Awake* thou that sleepest, and arise from the dead, and Christ shall give thee light (KJV).

3. *Romans 13:11* "And that, knowing the time, that now it is high time to *awake* out of sleep: for now is our salvation nearer than when we believed." Believers, it appears from the context, are exhorted to awaken, to wake up" (KJ21).

b. Historically, the term "awakening" has been utilized by historians to describe a period of unusual spiritual fervor or effervescence. J. Edwin Orr distinguishes between a revival (which pertains to languishing believers) and awakening (which pertains to the sleepy and indifferent unbelieving). Historians refer to "the great awakening" or "the first (second) (third) great awakening" because of the general impact that occurs first among God's people and then upon the lost. Frequently the work begins among those who are only nominal Christians (Christian in name only but with no genuine conversion experience) or with those who are, having experienced the grace of conversion, have grown cold, indifferent, or apathetic to the things of God.

c. The term "awakening" is an appropriate term to describe the spiritual reaction of a people that for a period appear to be in a stupor or slumber. It is significant that in the late 17th century and early to mid-18th century most pastors and spiritually minded believers assessed that the state of the church was that of a slumber-party. In describing the period just preceding the great awakening of 1734, Edwards writes "After my grandfather's death, it seemed a time of extraordinary dullness in religion. Licentiousness had for many years too much prevailed among the youth of the town. It was the manner of too many of them to get together, in conventions of both sexes for mirth and jollity, which they called frolics; and they would spend the greater part of the night in them, without regard to order in the families they belonged to"[20]. The churches are described as "slumbering"[21]. "Prior to the 1730's, the state of professing Christians in most parts of the English-speaking world appeared reminiscent of the wise and foolish virgins, 'they all slumbered and slept'"[22]. The response of the people to this surprising work of God could certainly be described as one awakening from spiritual lethargy and slumber.

4. RELATING THE TERMS "REVIVAL" AND "AWAKENING"

What exactly, if any, is the difference between a "revival" and an "awakening"? One modern revival historian and scholar, James Edwin Orr, suggested that the distinction should be made between the revival of the believer and the awakening of the unbeliever. (Believers already have spiritual life, but "revival" is needed when that life becomes dormant, like a tree that has life but is dormant and apparently dead in winter, only to re-vive in spring. Springtime is certainly a powerful analogy to revival). The theological distinction being that believers do not need regeneration, but revival, for they already have life. It is the unregenerate, those without spiritual life, that need more than re-vival. They need "vival"that is, they need the infusion of spiritual life, they need to be born again. Orr refers to the unusual work among believers of spiritual quickening as revival and refers to His unusual work among unbelievers as awakening[23]. But we must be careful not to superimpose a fine distinction elaborated by Orr back into history. We want to ask at this point what understanding Edwards had of "revival" and "awakening."

20. Edwards, *Works* 4: 115.
21. Murray, *Edwards*, 155.
22. Murray, *Edwards*, 125.
23. Lovelace, *Dynamics*, 48.

Edwards's Distinction between God's Work in the Degenerate and His Work in the Regenerate

Certainly, Edwards understood the theological distinction between being degenerate and being regenerate, and understood more clearly than most, if not all, the unique and distinct work that happens in the quickening of the regenerate as well as the unique and distinct work that happens in the quickening of the unregenerate. Nevertheless, the historical documents that refer to this surprising work (The Great Awakening) as an awakening seem to embrace both groups, and sometimes do not seem to differentiate between them. The slumbering saints are awakened. The unregenerate unbelievers are awakened.

Conclusion: The term "awakening" is appropriate to apply to both the revitalization of the saints and the conversion of the unregenerate, although theologically what is happening in conversion is unique and distinct from what is happening in the revitalizing and quickening of the saints. Traditionally, we have understood revival among God's people to lead to the awakening of the lost, portrayed by this graphic:

Revival (of the Saved)

Awakening (of the Lost)

Edwards used these terms with a greater degree of flexibility. He talked about the awakening of the believer as well as the awakening of the unregenerate or nominal (still unregenerate) Christian.

Revival and Awakening (of the Saved)

Awakening (of the Lost)

However, there is a certain symbiotic relationship that exists between revival and awakening. Revival of the languishing believer and the church leads to the awakening and evangelization of the world, true enough, but that evangelistic and missional dynamic produces an impact upon the church, resulting in further revitalization. Perhaps a more precise graphic representation of the relationship between revival and awakening could be portrayed as follows. Also, there is an amazing circular impact in that "awakening preaching" (evangelistic preaching with a focus on the lost, unregenerate) frequently results in the revival and awakening of the Christian. Revival is both the cause of awakening, and the effect of awakening.

Revival (Saved)

Awakening (Lost)

A. *What is Revival Preaching?*

Having defined what is preaching, what is a revival, what is an awakening, and what is the relationship between revival and awakening, we proceed to define what we mean by revival preaching, which is in the title of this book and is at the heart of our study. Revival preaching is that special exposition of the text of Scripture that in its application by the Holy Spirit to the heart of the preacher and through the preacher to his/her audience is intended to, and does indeed result in, the revival of God's people and the awakening of the lost.

Awakening preaching is evangelistic preaching, in the sense that the primary focus is on the conversion of the lost, the unregenerate.

However, historically speaking both "revival preaching" and "awakening preaching" have frequently been blended, so that revival of the languishing Christian individual and church leads to an awakening of the lost.

Conclusion: When we use the term "revival preaching" we are referring to the preaching directed to both the regenerate and the unregenerate, to the saved and the lost. While there may be a primacy to the regenerate, the ultimate end of revival preaching impacts the awakening of the lost.

B. What is The First Great Awakening?

Before we proceed to explore the preaching of Edwards, a few more concepts need to be defined. When we speak of the Great Awakening, we are referring to an unusual time of spiritual fervor on both sides of the Atlantic during the first half of the 18th century. More specifically, for our purposes our focus will be on Northampton, Massachusetts where Edwards was associate pastor from 1727–1729 and then Lead or Senior Pastor until his dismissal in 1750. During his ministry in Northampton there were two periods of unusual spiritual response and activity, from February of 1734 to mid-1735 (about 17 months) and then again from October of 1740 to the end of 1742 (about 27 months). These two periods are commonly referred to as The Great Awakening. For practical purposes, we will refer to these two phases as Chapter One and Chapter Two of the Great Awakening, although some scholars refer to the first move of God as the Little Awakening[24] (Minkema 2009: 9) followed by the Great Awakening.

C. What are the parameters of the First Great Awakening?

Regarding the parameters of the Great Awakening, from the perspective of Northampton, we can speak of 17 months from February of 1734 to June of 1735 and 27 months from October of 1740 to the end of 1742. These dates are fluid, for it is not always easy to define benchmarks or bookends that delineate the parameters of a revival. Nevertheless, they provide a specific frame of reference wherein we can identify specifically those sermons that were preached during and around this specific period.

For a more complete discussion of the criteria, we are using to define these parameters, please consult with Appendix #1.

D. What was so "Great" about the First Great Awakening? Why is it called the First Great Awakening?

Edwards himself gave five characteristics of this unusual move of God that qualified it as great in his mind. 1. Impacted every class and age. 2. 300 souls saved (about 1/4 of the population of Northampton at that time). 3.

24. Minkema, *Great Awakening*, 9.

The surprising and swift nature of the work. 4. Striking depth of emotion 5. The extraordinary extent of the revival, both regionally, nationally, and internationally[25]. How many converted? 25,000–50,000 in New England, which had a population of 250,000 so 10–20% of the population[26]. This does not consider the wider dimensions of the Great Awakening, affecting Moravia (Zinzendorf, et. al.), England (the Wesleys and Whitefield, et. al.) and other latitudes and preachers. Our focus is on Northampton. The First Great Awakening is "great" for several other reasons. It has had and continues to have a significant missiological impact. The First Great Awakening produced, in the crucible of experience, some of the most profound theology on the nature of spirituality and revival (Religious Affections and Distinguishing Marks, both works of Edwards) and philosophy on the nature of the will (Freedom of the Will). It is great that we have so many documents, letters, sermons, and treatises forged on the anvil of the Great Awakening. Finally, we may call it great because of the great preaching. For a sample of Great Awakening preaching, we recommend consulting the web to locate "Sinners in the Hands of an Angry God." Every preacher should read that sermon at least once (see Appendix #4 to find a link to this sermon). For an eye-witness account to the effects of that sermon, please see Appendix #4.

E. Why is it called the First Great Awakening?

There is no doubt that God has been awakening stone-dead sinners and slumbering saints throughout history. There have been other movements where God has awakened several congregants and churches over a wide area. Nevertheless, many historians agree that this is the First Great Awakening because of the unique characteristics that surround this unusual move of God, as described above. Perhaps there is some historical reference to "awakening" in correlation to the Reformation in Europe. Perhaps there is an element of ethnocentricity in assuming that this awakening on both sides of the Atlantic should be categorized as first, just as there is probably an element of ethnocentricity in assuming that Europe is the First World. Something to explore further.

---

25. Haykin, *Edwards*, 17.
26. Haykin, *Edwards*, 17.

F. What does the term "awakening" mean? Why is it called the First Great Awakening?

We have already attempted to define the terms "revival" and "awakening" above. Suffice if here to add the following. The term "awakening" is an appropriate term to describe the spiritual reaction of a people that for a period appear to be in a stupor or slumber. It is significant that in the early 17th century most pastors and spiritually minded believers assessed that the state of the church was that of a slumber-party. The response of the people to this surprising work of God could certainly be described as one awakening from spiritual lethargy and slumber.

Edwards's primary usage of "awakening" has to do with the process of an unbeliever coming out of a state of slumber into a greater state of increasing awareness of his/her need for conversion. To be awakened does not necessarily mean "conversion," although it is meant to culminate in that, and from there to proceed into sanctification. However, "If the minister endeavors to show natural men [unconverted] the dreadful guilt that sin brings, and the dreadfulness of the wrath of God, to awaken them, godly persons need to be awakened as well as them. They also need to be convinced more of the great evil of sin and the dreadfulness of God's wrath."[27]

CONCLUSION

In this chapter we have endeavored to define the following significant terms and concepts (1) Preaching, (2) Revival, (3) Awakening, (4) The Relationship between Revival and Awakening, (5) Revival Preaching, and finally (6) The First Great Awakening. It will be helpful to keep these in mind when we proceed to reflect upon the preaching of Edwards and as we seek to extract from his writings and sermons those principles and practices of preaching that are conducive to the revival and awakening that we seek in our day, in short to pursue the title of our book: Revival Preaching: Twelve Lessons from Jonathan Edwards's Great Awakening Sermons.

---

27. Edwards, *Works* 22: 199.

Introduction D

Biographical Sketch of Edwards

Pastor, Evangelist, Theologian, Revivalist, Philosopher, Educator and Mentor
Primary Source: Jonathan Edwards: A New Biography
(Iain Murray)

A. PRINCIPAL BIOGRAPHICAL INFORMATION

Year	Age	Event
1703		Born in East Windsor, Connecticut, United States (October 5).
1709	06	Learns Latin.
1716	13	Enters Yale University.
1716	13	Writes Scientific Treatise on Spiders (see sermon "Sinners").
1717	14	Studies Locke's "Essay Concerning Human Understanding."
1720	17	Graduates from Yale University.
1722	19	Writes his famous "70 Resolutions" (Appendix #2).
1726	23	Assistant Pastor to his grandfather, Solomon Stoddard.
1727	24	Marries aristocratic Sarah Pierrepont.
1734	31	First Great Awakening breaks out under his ministry.
1740	37	Writes his "Faithful Narrative" of the Surprising Work of God.
1741	38	Whitefield arrives in America and is instrumental in the second phase of the First Great awakening.

1741	38	Gives an address and then writes on "Distinguishing Marks" (Given at the Graduation Exercises at Yale)
1741	38	Preaches his famous sermon "Sinners in the Hands of an Angry God" in Enfield, Connecticut.
1742	39	Writes "Some Thoughts on the present Revival."
1742	39	Writes critically about "Spiritual Pride" as a great danger in the revival.
1746	43	"Religious Affections," probably Edwards's best work on the nature of true spirituality. Absolutely a must read.
1747	44	Brainerd dies in Edwards's home.
1749	46	Writes about Requirement for communion, which proves to be the "final straw" and reason (pretext?) for his dismissal from his pastorate.
1750	47	Finishes his pastorate of 24 years in Northampton.
1751	48	Begins another pastorate and preaching post in Stockbridge.
1754	51	Pulls together "Freedom of the Will" in five months, although percolating years.
1758	54	Dies suddenly from a smallpox inoculation gone wrong (March 22).

B. PRINCIPAL WORKS (IN MY OPINION) (WORKS ESPECIALLY SIGNIFICANT IN UNDERSTANDING EDWARDS AS A REVIVALIST AND THEOLOGIAN OF REVIVAL).

- A Humble Attempt to Promote Explicit Agreement and Visible Union of God's People, in Extraordinary Prayer, for the Revival of Religion and the Advancement of Christ's Kingdom on Earth, Pursuant to Scripture Promises and Prophecies Concerning the Last Time.
- "Faithful Narrative of a Surprising work of God in the conversion of hundreds of souls in Northampton."
- "Distinguishing Marks."
- "Religious Affections."
- "Freedom of the Will" (What Perry called a monument of American philosophy).

C. CONTRIBUTIONS TO REVIVAL

- Confronted and challenged the loss of spiritual power which characterized the renewal movement of Puritanism.
- Spearheaded a prayer movement through his writings, especially "Humble Attempt" and through his personal example.
- Stood up to and opposed the invasion of humanistic enlightenment.
- Was one of the principal protagonists in the First Great Awakening.
- Was both a primary apologist of the revival, as well as one of its most incisive critics.
- Knew how to keep head and heart hand in hand, both practically and theologically.

INTRODUCTION

Jonathan Edwards is a remarkable man of God. His life and thought have affected me more than any other person outside of the biblical record. In this biographical sketch, we will focus on his life, thought and significance with particular attention given to his contribution to theological reflection on revival.

THE LIFE AND TIMES OF JONATHAN EDWARDS

Edwards must be understood in the wider context of reformed Calvinistic Puritanism. Born in New England 83 years from the arrival of the Puritan Pilgrims, Edwards grew up in a context of seeing a "spirit of slumber" overtake the religious community of his time. The puritan "dream" of a slice of heaven on earth in the new world was fast becoming a nightmare. The initial fervor of the "puritans" had been eclipsed by relative peace, prosperity, and freedom from persecution[1]. Arminian and liberal thought were fast encroaching. Evangelical and evangelistic fervor waned.

God appears to have providentially "groomed" this choice servant to be one chief instrument in the First Great Awakening "for such a time as this." Part of that providential preparation included his heritage. His father was most influential in his formation, perhaps because he was the only son with ten sisters (sixty feet of daughters). With a strong emphasis on education,

---

1. Murray, *Edwards New Biography*, 4.

Jonathan was learning Latin when seven and immersed in John Locke's "Essay Concerning Human Understanding" when fourteen. This intellectual prodigy was exposed to a warm evangelical formation at home[2] which laid the foundation of the future. However, as an undergraduate student he realized the blight of pride and vanity was deeply entrenched in him[3] and he realized his needs for a personal deliverance.

CONVERSION

A deep encounter with I Tim. 1:17 resulted in his conviction wherein "there came into my soul, and was as it were diffused through it, a sense of the glory of the Divine Being. . ." Nevertheless, he did not understand this to be of a saving virtue, although there was infused into his being a tremendous hunger to meditate on Christ and in particular:

> ". . .on the beauty and excellency of his Person"[4]. "The sense I had of Divine things, would often of a sudden kindle up, as it were, a sweet burning in my heart; an ardor of soul, that I knew not how to express."[5] This led to a pursuit of God which culminated in "so sweet a sense of the glorious majesty and grace of God. . . the appearance of everything was altered . . . I had vehement longings of soul after God and Christ, and after more holiness, wherewith my heart seemed to be full and ready to break. . . I was almost constantly in ejaculatory prayer, wherever I was. . ... the delights which I now felt in those things of religion, were of an exceeding different kind from those before mentioned, that I had when a boy. . .[6].

It was 1722 and Edwards was 19. Indeed, Edwards exemplified that he also taught, that the individual believer must be affectionately in pursuit of God:

"The Scriptures everywhere represent the seeking, striving, and labour of a Christian as being chiefly after his conversion, and his conversion as being but the beginning of his work. And almost all that is said in the New Testament, of man's watching, giving earnest heed to themselves, running the race that is set before them, striving and agonizing, wrestling not with flesh and blood but with principalities and power, fighting, putting on the whole

---

2. Murray, *Edwards New Biography*, 12.
3. Murray, *Edwards New Biography*, 33.
4. Murray, *Edwards New Biography*, 36.
5. Murray, *Edwards New Biography*, 36.
6. Murray, *Edwards New Biography*, 37.

armor of God, and standing, pressing forward, reaching first, continuing instant in prayer, crying to God day and night; I say, almost all that is said in the New Testament of these things is spoken of and directed to the saints"[7].

THE 70 RESOLUTIONS

Edwards worked towards finishing his Master's degree at Yale. It was at this time that he penned the greatest portion of his famous "70 resolutions" (See Appendix #2). After a brief tenure as pastor in New York City, where he experienced ardent hunger after God, he then proceeded to finish his degree (1723) and was elected to be a tutor[8]. He continued to study Locke, from whom he derived more pleasure "then the most greedy miser finds when gathering up handfuls of silver and gold"[9]. At this time, he was invited to be the assistant to the venerated Solomon Stoddard, Senior Pastor of Northampton's Congregational church, who proved to be a powerful mentor [Stoddard experienced five "harvests" (1679, 1683, 1697, 1712 and 1718)] and so inculcated the value of religious revivals in Edwards. (Stoddard believed that "provided people possessed Christian knowledge and lived upright lives, they need not be required to profess anything about themselves before becoming communicants"[10], also known as the "half-way covenanters").[11] Edwards would eventually espouse a position of "believer's communion" which caused him much strife and eventually the loss of his pastorate. Edwards is ordained in 1726, married in 1727 and assumed the Senior Pastor position in 1729 after Stoddard's demise.

HIS RELATIONSHIP WITH HIS BELOVED WIFE SARAH

Regarding his "uncommon union"[12] with Sarah Pierrepont much can be said. Frequently the role of the woman of God in the biography of such a preeminent figure is easily eclipsed. This is most unfortunate in the case of Jonathan and Sarah. Her heritage was from the more aristocratic class, and there is cogent evidence to suggest that she was the stronghold of the home since he gave thirteen hours every day to theological reflection and sermon

---

7. Murray, *Edwards New Biography*, 260.
8. Murray, *Edwards New Biography*, 55.
9. Murray, *Edwards New Biography*, 64.
10. Murray, *Edwards New Biography*, 89.
11. Hardman, *Seasons of Refreshing*, 36.
12. Tuttle, *Edwards*, 15.

preparation. Sarah herself was profoundly affected by the Great Awakening and scholars believe that Jonathan used her example as a case study to show forth the virtues of authentic revival. In all the literature I have read describing religious experience and revival, very little equals the description of Sarah's spirituality and walk with God. Small wonder that the last recorded words we have of Jonathan Edwards are a touching tribute to his wife: "Give my kindest love to my dear wife and tell her that the uncommon union which has so long subsisted between us has been of such a nature as I trust is spiritual and therefore will continue forever."[13]

PERSONAL CRISIS OF EDWARDS

While pastoring his second church, Edwards entered a deep "valley of humiliation" wherein he came to realize in a deeper way his utter personal depravity. He uses the word "abhorrence" to describe his self-estimation. "The very thought of any joy arising in me, on any consideration of my own amiableness, performances or experiences or any goodness of heart and life, is nauseous and detestable to me. And yet I am greatly afflicted with a proud and self-righteous spirit, much more sensibly that I used to be formerly"[14]. It appears that this was the darkest hour before the dawning of the first great awakening, when God broke the "spirit of slumber."

THE FIRST GREAT AWAKENING

Edwards and others complained of the paucity of spirituality in their congregants and communities[15]. There was a considerable degree of contention and bickering among the saints. "Contention is directly against that which is the very sum of all that is essential and distinguishing in true Christianity, even a spirit of love and peace. No wonder, therefore, that Christianity cannot flourish in a time of strife and contention among its professors. No wonder that religion and contention cannot live together[16]. Dead preaching was producing deader congregants. There was much light, but little heat. In this context God send the Great Awakening, with a harvest in 1735 (see Narrative of Surprising Conversions) and again in 1740 and 1741. Whitefield proved to be the key evangelist that sparked numerous "awakenings" of the

---

13. Tuttle, *Edwards*, 17.
14. Murray, *Edwards New Biography*, 104.
15. Murray, *Edwards New Biography*, 125.
16. Murray, *Edwards New Biography*, 372.

unconverted, wherein many believers were likewise quickened in their faith. It was in this context that Edwards "re-preached" his famous sermon "Sinners in the Hands of an Angry God."[17] Jonathan's own wife is powerfully revived and deepened in her spiritual walk and granted an unusual assurance of intimacy with God.[18] However, significant criticism arose concerning the revival. In apologetic fashion, Edwards wrote "The Distinguishing Marks of a Word of the Spirit of God" (1741) to address Yale's commencement graduates. Later came "Some Thoughts Concerning the Present Revival of Religion in New England" (1742) and then a third critique of revival which many consider his opus, "A Treatise Concerning Religious Affections" (1746). No one gave more thorough theological reflection to the theme of the psychology of religion, especially in revivals, than Edwards. Essentially, Edwards, a philosophical genius of the first order, highly trained and skilled in rational theology and philosophy, called for a defense of experimental religion, which is primarily a matter of both head and heart. The two must be held together, in proper juxtaposition.

During the development of his theology of conversion, Edwards came to the conviction that only genuine regenerate believers should participate in the Lord's Supper. The church's former patriarch, Stoddard, had taught differently, and this discrepancy troubled the indifferent nominalists. This proved to be the "lightning rod" when the storm broke over the divided church. It cost him a great deal of grief and pain. In his farewell message, Edwards referred to this, affirming "Let the late contention about the terms of Christian communion, as it has been the greatest, be the last."[19]

Edwards accepted a call to be a missionary to Stockbridge, ministering to a community of Indians. It was in these twilight years that Edwards produced some of his greatest theological treatises, including "Freedom of the Will." He was also in the process of writing a massive theology combined with an in-depth historical analysis entitled "The History of Redemption." Unfortunately, his life was cut short, and Edwards died of a smallpox vaccination that brought complications.

EDWARDS THEOLOGICAL THOUGHTS

It is difficult to overestimate the depth and breadth of the thought of Edwards. Those who drew up his epitaph stated that "in the acuteness of his intellect his sagacious judgment and his prudence second to none among

---

17. Murray, *Edwards New Biography*, 168.
18. Murray, *Edwards New Biography*, 19596.
19. Tuttle, *Edwards*, 4.

mortals. In his knowledge of science and the liberal arts remarkable. In sacred criticism eminent and a theologian distinguished and without equal."[20]

In philosophy he has been deemed "The profoundest reasoned, and the greatest divine, in my opinion, that America has produced (Davies). A more current opinion by a giant intellectual, Warfield, states "Jonathan Edwards, saint and metaphysician, revivalist and theologian, stands out as the one figure of real greatness in the intellectual life of colonial America (Warfield).[21]

Personally, no one has given as much incisive thinking on the psychology of religion from an evangelical and biblical perspective than Edwards. He had a huge intellect that was matched by his heart. Indeed, it would be difficult to ascertain whether Edwards's spiritual fervor and passion, tempered with his prudence and wisdom, were excelled by his theological perspicuity and philosophical intuition. Edwards combined head and heart[22]. To gain an appreciation for his prolific and fertile cerebrum and heart, we recommend that the reader peruse: <http://edwards.yale.edu/research>.

His reflections on the criteria for discerning the true from the false merit special reflection. His message/treatise on "The Distinguishing Marks of a Work of the Spirit of God" give us a fine example of his wisdom, prudence, amplitude of spirit and discerning criteria for evaluating to discern is a manifestation of revival is from God or not. He spoke of "no signs" which was the New England eighteenth century shorthand for saying "false criteria." Edwards was critical of those who immediately endorsed or immediately rejected a move (supposedly) of God based on, in his opinion, extrabiblical criteria. He affirmed that the "no signs" simply did not provide an adequate paradigm for either rejecting or endorsing a revival. Therefore, he designated as a "no sign" that there was an extraordinary work, physical manifestations, excitement, vivid imaginations, contagious testimonies, extremes, delusions, apostasies, and fervent preaching. All these "phenomena" are not conclusive indicators, one way or the other, in determining the nature of the work. Edwards then proceeds to delineate what he considered to be the "yes signs" or valid criteria for ascertaining whether a particular work was of God or not. He maintained that when you have the exaltation of Jesus, the thwarting of the kingdom of darkness, an increased love for the Scriptures, a manifestation of the Spirit of truth and an effusion of love, then you have sufficient evidence to substantiate that a supposed revival is in fact an authentic work of God, with or without the accompanying of the "no

---

20. Gerstner, *Rational Theology*, 1920.
21. Murray, *Edwards New Biography*, xvii.
22. Tuttle, *Edwards*, 35.

signs." The genius of Edwards is his ability to discern, and guide ministers in this discerning process, a science and an art so desperately needed in the ministry, especially during times of revival and church renewal.

INFLUENCE OF EDWARDS

Edwards has had an incalculable influence on English-speaking evangelicalism. It was a gift of [Edwards's wirings] from Erskine to English Baptists which molded the thought of the men who from 1784 gathered in prayer 'for the general revival and spread of religion'. It was these Baptists of the English midlands who reissued Edwards's 'Humble Attempt to Promote... Extraordinary Prayer' in 1790, and who sent William Carey to India in 1793. At least one volume of Edwards went with Carey on that historic voyage.[23]

David Brainerd spent his last days in Edwards's home, and entrusted Edwards with his journals and letters, saying, to quote Edwards, "I might dispose of them as I thought would be most for "God's glory and the interest of religion."[24] Edwards published them in "An Account of the Life and Ministry of the Late Reverent Mr. David Brainerd."[25] According to his biographer, "if the 'Humble attempt' promoted intercession, few books have done so much to prompt prayer and action as 'The Life of Brainerd.'"[26] A. J. Gordon was profoundly impacted by reading the life of Brainerd and "when we shut the book, we are not praising Brainerd but condemning ourselves, and resolving that, by the grace of God, we will follow Christ more closely in the future"[27]. In missionary circles, the example of Brainerd has been incalculable, and we are indebted to Edwards for that written legacy.

Edwards has left his imprint on American Reformed Calvinistic thought, which continues to exercise a considerable influence upon many of the leading evangelical theologians. To study American theology without understanding Edwards would be a great oversight indeed. His philosophical and theological contribution to the understanding of the will continues to be felt in this twenty-first century.

The First Great Awakening has, in many senses, deeply influenced the evangelical understanding of revivalism. As God continues to revive His church, Edwards is making a significant contribution, especially in religious phenomenology and the psychology of religion. Edwards's classic work on

23. Murray, *Edwards New Biography*, 457.
24. Murray, *Edwards New Biography*, 307.
25. Murray, *Edwards New Biography*, 307.
26. Murray, *Edwards New Biography*, 307.
27. Murray, *Edwards New Biography*, 309.

"Distinguishing Marks" has been republished in modern English recently (2000) by Crossway Books. Both protagonists and critics of contemporary revival movements appeal to Edwards. It is crucial that Edwards be studied in the light of his historical context, otherwise his thought can be twisted and "eisegeted" to substantiate one's own personal bias. However, a careful historically informed reflection on those biblical principles that Edwards expounded (on I John) would do incalculable good to our contemporary evangelical communities. In many latitudes where aberrations of revival abound creating a skepticism towards the unusual working of the Holy Spirit during revivals among certain evangelicals, we would do well to rediscover the wisdom of this prophetic voice to the eighteenth and twenty-first centuries.

SUMMARY

Who Was Jonathan Edwards?

Pastor

Edwards pastored a congregational church with a Calvinistic profile in the town of Northampton, in the western part of the state of Massachusetts, on the eastern seaboard of the United States. He pastored from 1727 (24 years old) until his forced departure in 1750 (at the age of 47). During his pastoral ministry, he was both witness and protagonist of a revival movement known by historians as the First Great Awakening. He was happily married to Sarah, through whose 'uncommon union' they produced 8 daughters and 3 sons.

Evangelist

The ministers during his time not only pastored in their local church, but also visited the churches of the district and surrounding area, especially because of his recognized spiritual authority. Many of Edwards's sermons demonstrate a passionate evangelistic fervor. Probably his most famous sermon is powerfully evangelistic: 'Sinners on the Hands of an Angry God'.

Missionary

Edwards, after serving for 23 years as a Pastor, at the age of 47, accepted a call to serve as a missionary in Stockbridge, ministering to a community of Indians as well as some English-speaking congregants. We see a man with remarkable intellectual and academic capability humbly serving humble people with limited capabilities. During this time, Edwards wrote some of his most significant academic works, including his monumental philosophical work: Freedom of the Will.

Philosopher

Edwards was a child prodigy. At the age of 6 he was studying Latin and became of disciple of John Locke at the age of fourteen. Some of Edwards's biographers, (including Perry from Harvard) suggest that Edwards was the most brilliant mind that the United States ever produced. His philosophical writings, especially his treatment of the will, are superlative and continue to be consulted and respected today.

Theologian

Edwards is one of the most brilliant theological minds the world has ever seen, along with Augustine and Calvin. He had the unique ability to integrate philosophy, psychology, and history with Scripture to enrich our understanding of theology. First and foremost, Edwards was a man of the Word, profoundly shaped by and versed in the Scriptures and the theological writings of ancient and contemporary church history.

Writer

Edwards's literary output is really amazing. Almost all his writings and sermons are recorded for posterity by the Jonathan Edwards Study Center. <http://edwards.yale.edu/archive>. What a treasure trove! Glancing over the amount of his writings, and then delving into the depth of his thought and spiritual insight, persevering in the sometimes-intricate thought, one is handsomely rewarded. In my estimation, his treatment on revival theology and psychology are unequaled. His classic on "Religious Affections" is a masterpiece on the spirituality of the heart. Edwards dedicated 13 hours of his day to the research and writing of his sermons and manuscripts.

Academic and Educator

Jonathan Edwards was the third president of the College of New Jersey (Princeton Seminary), one of the best-known universities of his day, and indeed one of the most important universities in the development of thought in the United States. Edwards also played a significant role as mentor to several emerging pastors.

Puritan

It is difficult to understand Edwards without appreciating his spiritual heritage as a child of the Reformation, Calvinism and Puritanism. Edwards's strong commitment to the primacy of Scriptures, the sovereignty of God, the centrality of Christ, the empowering of the Spirit, the absolute necessity of justification by faith, personal regeneration, and a robust spirituality where head and heart go hand in hand define him as vintage Puritan as do his emphasis on prayer, his spirituality of the heart and his moral ethic.

Man of God

In the writings of Edwards, one finds a blend of spirituality of the heart with a powerful rational or cognitive element that place him in a unique category. Edwards has a passion for the glory of the Triune God, as well as a profound and passionate desire for communion with that Triune God. Edwards's spiritual life, his familiarity with Scripture, his involvement and evident success on the work of the Lord both locally and internationally (through his writings), as well as the warmth and spirituality of his relationship to his wife in their "uncommon union" all combine to demonstrate a quality of spirituality and integrity.

Defender and Critic of the Great Awakening

Edwards had a heart for God, and a heart and passion for the work of God in a church purified and evangelistic, which lies at the heart of Puritanism. Edwards was both a protagonist and witness of the First Great Awakening. When critics questioned the extremes of the Revival and undermined its theological integrity, Edwards rose to the occasion and dedicated his brilliant mind and passionate heart to a thorough and rigorous biblical analysis of revivalism. We are profoundly indebted to him! He applied his knowledge of Scripture, history, and biblical psychology to the events and phenomenology of the Great Awakening to defend and justify the legitimacy of the revival. Later, Edwards himself criticized some of the excesses but was remarkable capable of sifting through and separating the genuine from the spurious. His perspective, his hermeneutic, his argumentation and his reasoning ability provide us with significant insights into evaluating revival movements and contemporary spirituality today. He seemed providentially prepared with his spiritual depth, pastoral experience, theological awareness, intellectual rigor, and psychological health to speak to revivalism then, and now.

Legacy

Edwards's influence can be measured in many ways. Let us reflect on his family legacy. "An American educator, A.E. Winship decided to trace the descendants of Jonathan Edwards almost 150 years after his death. Jonathan Edwards' legacy includes: 1 U.S. Vice-President, 1 Dean of a law school, 1 dean of a medical school, 3 U.S. Senators, 3 governors, 3 mayors, 13 college presidents, 30 judges, 60 doctors, 65 professors, 75 Military officers, 80 public office holders, 100 lawyers, 100 clergymen, and 285 college graduates. How may this be explained? Edwards was a godly man, but he was also hard working, intelligent and moral. Furthermore, Winship states, "Much of the capacity and talent, intensity and character of the more than 1,400 of Edwards' family is due to Mrs. Edwards."[28] The Edwards family is a compelling example of the biblical principle "Start children off on the way they should go, and even when they are old, they will not turn from it" (Prov. 22:6) (NIV).

Mentor

Finally, Edwards is my mentor. I first "discovered" him when I bought "Religious Affections" for 25 cents at a used bookstore. (The book was uncut—I had to use a penknife to open the book) (Unfortunately, for many Edwards remains a closed book). What a great read! What a healthy biblical psychology. His insight into the revival and his balanced approach to some of the revival phenomenology convinced me of his insight into revival. Edwards is very open to the supernatural. He is balanced like few I know. His ability to integrate various disciplines into the discussion is second to none.

> Epitaph of Jonathan Edwards
> Located in Princeton, New Jersey
> 17031758

---

28. Ballard, Multigenerational Legacies. (See also Hedberg, *A Life Well Lived*, chapter 3.)

Conclusion

Who really was Jonathan Edwards? Perhaps the best summary is that written on his gravestone: "Wouldst thou know, oh Traveller, what manner of person he was whose mortal part lies here? A man indeed, in body tall yet graceful, attenuated through acidity and abstinence and studies most intense; in the acuteness of his intellect, his sagacious judgment and his prudence second to none among mortals; in his knowledge of sciences and the liberal arts remarkable, in sacred criticism eminent, and a theologian distinguished without equal; an unconquered defender of the Christian Faith and a preacher grave, solemn, discriminating; and by the favor of God most happy in the success and issue of his life. Illustrious in his piety, sedate in manners, but towards others friendly and benignant, he lived to be loved and venerated, and now, alas! To be lamented in his death. The bereaved college mourns for him, and the church mourns, but Heaven rejoices to receive him: Abi, Viator, El Pia Sequere Vestigia (Go hence, oh traveller, and his pious footsteps follow).[29]

---

29. Gerstner, *Rational Theology*, 20.

Introduction E

Edwards's View of Preaching

BEFORE WE EXPLORE THE actual lessons learned from Edwards's Preaching during the Great Awakening, we do well to reflect briefly on Edwards's View of Preaching in General.

As we have seen from our introduction, Edwards was Reformed and Puritan in his theology. He followed in the tradition of Paul, Augustine (354-430), and Calvin (1509-64).

When we focus in on the Puritan formation that Edwards enjoyed, we have to focus in on such names as William Perkins (1558-1602); Joseph Hall (1574-1656); William Greenhill (1581-1677); Thomas Goodwin (1600-80); Thomas Shepard (1605-1649); Richard Baxter (1615-91); John Owen (1616-83); Thomas Manton (1620-77); Thomas Watson (1620-86); John Bunyan (1628-88); Stephen Charnock (1628-80); John Gill (1697-1771); Matthew Henry (1662-1714) Isaac Watts (1674-1748); and Griffith Jones (1683-1761). All these men shaped, to one degree or another, the view that Edwards had on preaching.

We need to remember that Edwards's father Timothy was a preacher and teacher, and Edwards was undoubtedly influenced by him more than any other single influence. Minkema observes the influence of his father on Edwards: "As a scion of a powerful extended family within the New England ministerial elite, Edwards was inculcated with a fervent conversionist piety and a penchant to take particular notice of any signs of awakening within individuals and groups. His father, the Reverend Timothy Edwards, though now virtually unknown, was at the time one of the most successful revivalists in Connecticut, having overseen no less than five episodes in his church at East Windsor" (Minkema).[1] Finally, Edwards's maternal grandfather,

---

1. McClymond, *Encyclopedia*, 151.

Solomon Stoddard (September 27, 1643 February 11, 1729) was considered "the pope" over the Connecticut Valley, was the Senior Pastor of the Northampton Congregational Church and was instrumental in seeing five remarkable "harvests" during his 60-year pastorate in Northampton (1679, 1683, 1696, 1712 and 1718), and since Stoddard was the Senior Pastor of the church which Edwards took over, there is a remarkable spiritual legacy that Edwards received from him. Stoddard wrote a significant book for preachers entitled "Defects of Preachers Reproved" which was part of his spiritual formation at Yale.[2] Edwards's background under his father and maternal grandfather "certainly contributed more to the character of Edwards's sermons than any rhetoric or homiletics texts that he may have studied at Yale College."[3] All these streams feed into Edwards's view of preaching. What can we say in summary fashion about the views of these spiritual mentors regarding preaching?

"Edwards also looks vocationally on himself as, among other things, a shepherd, a trumpet, a spiritual father, God's mouth or voice, God's ambassador, keeper of God's oracles, officer in God's kingdom, the people's mouth to God, the church's proxy husband, the church's physician, God's watchman, and a burning and shining light."[4]

The Apostle Paul considered the preaching of the Word to be paramount. Consider his exhortation to Timothy: "I solemnly charge *you* in the presence of God and of Christ Jesus, who is to judge the living and the dead, and by His appearing and His kingdom: 2 *preach the word*; be ready in season *and* out of season; reprove, rebuke, exhort, with great patience and instruction" (II Tim. 4:1,2) (NASB). It is the word that is God-breathed and profitable for teaching, for reproof, for correction and for training in righteousness so that the man of God may be adequate, *equipped for every good work* (II Tim. 3:16, 17) (NASB). *This was Edwards's view of preaching*. He had a keen sense of being "charged" with a solemn responsibility to preach God's Word, with the underlying conviction that God's inspired Word, applied by the same Spirit that inspired it, effects God's sovereign will among the listeners.

In the first edition of his *Institutes*, concerning ministers Calvin wrote, "Their whole task is limited to the ministry of God's Word, their whole wisdom to the knowledge of his Word: their whole eloquence, to its proclamation." *This was Edwards's view of preaching*. Calvin states: "Since it is almost

---

2. See Appendix #3 for a summary of Stoddard's points on defects of preachers and a brief reflection on Edwards's preaching, point by point, according to the list of defects elaborated by Stoddard.

3. Kimnach, *Trumpet*, 32.

4. Westra, *Minister's Task*, 11.

his only task to unfold the mind of the writer whom he has undertaken to expound, he misses his mark, or at least strays outside his limits, by the extent to which he leads his readers away from the meaning of his author."[5] He delineates the preacher's task of speaking for God in his comment on Isa 55:11: "The Word goeth out of the mouth of God in such a manner that it likewise 'goeth out of the mouth' of men; for God does not speak openly from heaven, but employs men as his instruments, that by their agency he may make known his will."[6] *This was Edwards's view of preaching.* To preach was to be the voice of God unto the people. To preach the Bible is to be the voice of God to that people.

In his excellent article entitled "A Classical Analysis of Puritan Preaching," Joseph Steele makes the following observation: Just as essential as phonics is for teaching a child how to read, so too the Bible was the sine qua non of Puritan preaching. The Puritans were not just Theo-centric, they were Word-centric. The full-orbed implications of the Reformation maxim sola scriptura was writ large upon the face of Puritan preaching. The lives of the Puritans were uniformly shaped by the revealed will of the Triune God contained in sixty-six books which they believed were divinely preserved for the good of God's people. Accordingly, the Puritans "loved, lived, and breathed Scripture, relishing the power of the Spirit that accompanied the Word. They viewed Scripture as God speaking to them as their Father, giving them the truth, they could trust for all eternity"[7]. "The puritan conviction about the centrality of the Bible in preaching was reinforced by the practice of largely or exclusively limiting the details of the sermon to biblical material." Puritan preaching was expository in nature, meaning that the entire sermon was to be inextricably tied to the text. The mere establishment of a connection between the sermon and the text was not sufficient for Puritan preachers. Quite the contrary, for, according to the Puritans, "The sermon is not just hinged to Scripture; it quite literally exists inside the Word of God; the text is not in the sermon, but the sermon in the text . . . Put summarily, listening to a sermon is being in the Bible"[8] (Steele). *This was Edwards's heritage. This was his view of preaching.*

According to Richard Baxter, "Of all preaching in the world, (that speaks not stark lies) I hate that preaching which tends to make the hearers laugh, or to move their minds with tickling levity, and affect them as stage-plays used to do, instead of affecting them with a holy reverence of the name of God.

---

5. Masters, *What the Reformers Really Said.*
6. Calvin, *Isaiah.*
7. Steele, *Classical Analysis,* 1.
8. Steele, *Classical Analysis,* 2.

Jerome says, 'Teach in thy church, not to get the applause of the people, but to set in motion the groan; the tears of the hearers are thy praises.'"[9] *This was Edwards's view of preaching.* One of his college resolutions was "Resolved, to live with all my might while I live." He also wrote resolution #38: Resolved, never to speak anything that is ridiculous, sportive, *or matter of laughter on the Lord's day.* Sabbath evening, Dec. 23, 1722. It appeared that he took this very much to heart, not just to his demeanor outside of the church, but within. As Piper notes "His preaching was totally serious from beginning to end. You will look in vain for one joke in the 1200 sermons that remain."[10] More than an aversion to humor, Edwards was captivated by the solemnity of the preaching office. Prince, historian, said of Edwards that he always exuded a "habitual and great solemnity, looking and speaking as in the presence of God, and with a weighty sense of the matter delivered"[11].

Edwards's Ordination Sermon, entitled "The True Excellency of a Minister of the Gospel," was preached in 1744, and provides his most clear and compelling vision of the preacher in a single document. It is significant that his text was "*He was a burning and a shining light*" from John 5:35. As Kimnach comments: "His text's light is "burning and shining," corresponding to ardor and intelligence—or will and understanding. For Edwards, the important thing is that the two dimensions of light be balanced equally and united in a functional whole. Thus, the minister must be both learned in the Scripture and familiar with the "inward operations" of the Holy Spirit; likewise, the doctrine he preaches must be both "bright and full," or purely inspiring and rich in content. The minister must address his flock discreetly yet present true religion authentically."[12]

WE WILL EXTRACT SEVERAL POINTS FROM THIS SERMON WHICH HIGHLIGHT HIS VIEW OF PREACHING.

1. It is significant that Edwards used John as a paradigm of Christian ministry. It was John who affirmed: "He must *increase*, but I must *decrease*" John 3:30 (NASB) (Emphasis mine). The nature of the ministry is to point to Christ, not self. As Paul affirmed "for we do not preach ourselves but Christ Jesus as Lord, and ourselves as your bondservants

---

9. Baxter, *Reformed Pastor*, point 11.
10. Piper, *God's Passion*, 47.
11. Westra, *The Minister's Task*, 17.
12. Kimnach, *Works*, 25: 82.

for Jesus' sake" (II Cor. 4:5) (NASB). Undoubtedly Edwards selected John the Baptist as a model for the minister because of this predominant feature in John; His Christ-centeredness and his renunciation of self. This goes to the quintessential nature of ministry in general, and of the preaching ministry in particular.

2. The role of the preacher is *to diffuse light*. Edwards states: "Ministers are set to be lights to the souls of men in this respect, as they are to be the means of imparting divine truth to them, and bringing into their view the most glorious and excellent objects, and of leading them to, and assisting them in the contemplation of those things that angels desire to look into; the means of their obtaining that knowledge is infinitely more important and more excellent and useful, than that of the greatest statesmen or philosophers, even that which is spiritual and divine. They are set to be the means of bringing men out of darkness into God's marvelous light, and of bringing them to the infinite fountain of light, that in his light they may see light. They are set to instruct men and impart to them that knowledge by which they may know God and Jesus Christ, whom to know is life eternal" (Jonathan Edwards).[13]

3. The role of the preacher *is to beautify the truth*, as light beautifies. "Another use of light is to *refresh* and delight the beholders. Darkness is dismal: the light is sweet, and a pleasant thing it is to behold the sun. Light is refreshing to those who have long sat in darkness" (Jonathan Edwards).

4. The minister is a *guide to the truth*. "Ministers have the record of God committed to them that they may hold that forth, which God has given to be to man as a "light shining in a dark place" (2 Peter 1:19) (NASB), to guide them in the way through this dark world to regions of eternal light" (Jonathan Edwards).[14]

5. Preachers are called to be *men of prayer*. "Ministers, in order to their being burning and shining lights, should walk closely with God, and keep near to Christ; that they may ever be enlightened and enkindled by him. And they should be much in seeking God, and conversing with him by prayer, who is the fountain of light and love. And knowing their own emptiness and helplessness should be ever dependent on Christ; being sensible with Jeremiah that they are children, should sit as children at Christ's feet to hear his word, and be instructed by him; and being sensible with Isaiah that they are men of unclean lips should

---

13. Edwards, *Works*, 25: 90.
14. Edwards, *Works*, 25: 91.

seek that their lips may be as it were touched with a live coal from the altar, as it were by the bright and burning seraphim" (Jonathan Edwards).[15]

CONCLUSION

This view of the preacher by Edwards provides us with an excellent template within which we pursue the particulars of a revival preacher. It is to be noted that the concepts of light and heat, so central to his view of the preaching ministry, are vitally linked to revival and awakening. Light and heat go together to bring life and growth, revival and awakening. I thought it important to set the observations of revival preaching derived from Edwards within this larger framework of his view of preaching in general.

---

15. Edwards, *Works*, 25: 100.

Chapter 1

An Apology for Pathetic Preaching

"Our people don't so much need to have their heads stored as to have their hearts touched and they stand in the greatest need of that sort of preaching that has the greatest tendency to do this" (Jonathan Edwards).[1]

"THERE IS TODAY AN evangelical rationalism not unlike the rationalism taught by the scribes and Pharisees. They said the truth is in the word, and if you want to know the truth, go to the rabbi, and learn the word. If you get the word, you have the truth. . . .. But revelation is not enough! There must be illumination before revelation can get to a person's soul. It is not enough that I hold an inspired book in my hands. I must have an inspired heart. There is the difference, despite the evangelical rationalist who insists that revelation is enough. . . . ."[2]

We are at a point where we can begin to explore the sermons and writings of Edwards to ascertain and extract important lessons on Revival Preaching. As we have indicated earlier, we will ask certain key questions: What kinds of sermons were preached before, during and after the Great Awakening? What themes and what texts were preached? What issues were addressed? What was Edwards's approach to preaching in general? What

---

1. Edwards, *Works*, 4: 388.
2. Tozer, *Faith Beyond Reason*, 23–24.

was his philosophy of preaching? What was Edwards's approach to preaching before, during and after the Great Awakening? What lessons are there for us as preachers today? What can we learn from the Great Awakening that would facilitate awakening in our day? What correlation exists between his preaching and revival? What made his sermons so effective? Why did God seem pleased to pour out revival through the agency of these sermons? What about the man Edwards sheds light on the correlation between preaching and revival?

As we have raised these questions in our research, we have recognized certain salient truths related to Edwards's Revival Preaching. We believe that these truths provide valuable lessons for us today who have a preaching ministry and responsibility. We will look at 12 of the most significant.

What we have endeavored to do in this study is approach a particular aspect or element that explains Jonathan Edwards's view of Revival Preaching, and then (1) *define it*, dissect it, and look at it from various perspectives. There is a (2) *biblical* perspective, where we highlight significant Scriptural texts that show the importance of the point and how it played out in the preaching ministry of biblical characters. We endeavor to provide specific (3) *quotes from Edwards* himself or (4) *quotes by Edwardsean scholars* that enunciate his understanding of revival preaching. We have also endeavored to provide, where possible, relevant (5) *illustrations from the actual sermons of Edwards* to demonstrate the case in point. Where possible and helpful, we incorporate Edwards's comments on those passages. We also draw upon the (6) *70 resolutions* of Edwards, if possible and relevant, to show the correlation between the man and his conviction about revival preaching. Finally, we will endeavor to reinforce this fundamental aspect of "Revival Preaching" from (7) *other authors*. Finally, we will give our (8) *conclusion* to the matter.

WHAT CAN WE LEARN ABOUT REVIVAL PREACHING FROM EDWARDS?

Edwards on the Place for Passion in Preaching

Edwards believed in the importance of passionate preaching. He said something on his view of preaching that arrested my attention and triggered this study. Although I quoted it at the outset of this chapter, it merits repetition here. Edwards said: "Our people don't so much need to have their heads stored as to have their hearts touched and they stand in the greatest need of that sort of preaching that has the greatest tendency to do this"

(Jonathan Edwards).³ Revival Preaching is preaching that touches the heart. If this quote were taken out of context, one could deduce that Edwards was denigrating the more rational or cognitive aspect of preaching, in favor of a more emotional and passionate appeal, an appeal to the heart instead of the head. Anyone who has read Edwards's sermons, knows that was certainly not his practice! It is not a question of either/or; it is a question of both/and. We do not and should not have to choose between head or heart, we must keep both in perspective. There is solid evidence in Edwards to indicate that he believed that the way to the heart was through the head; what he appears to be saying in the above quote is that preachers should not simply or merely be satisfied with a dry, dispassionate intellectual approach. There was evidence in his ministry and in the ministry of others that good orthodoxy was abundant in the pulpits of New England, but that this was not effecting change.

1. DEFINING THE CONCEPT

An Apology for Pathetic Preaching

A key word that comes close to capturing this aspect of revival preaching is what I would call "pathetic preaching." Words change their meanings over time. Take the title of this chapter: An Apology for Pathetic Preaching. The word "apology" can mean either explanation, written in defense of, *or* something much like the exact opposite: admission of guilt, request for forgiveness, regret, confession, act of contrition, and/or expression of shame. In similar fashion, the word "pathetic" can either mean "poor, wretched, dismal, sad, pitiable, weak, useless, feeble, and something which is to be shirked and abandoned as horrible and miserable. . . *or*, in the classic and more traditional sense, "pathetic" can mean passionate, moving, heartfelt, fervent, earnest, avid, warm, ardent, touching, zealous, heartbreaking, sensible, affecting, loving, poignant, and stirring, as in preaching "with pathos." So, I ask the question: does my title mean

a. Asking Forgiveness for Poor Preaching *or*

b. Asking Forgiveness for Passionate Preaching *or*

c. In Defense of and Appealing for Poor Preaching *or*

d. In Defense of and Appealing for Passionate Preaching?

---

3. Edwards, *Works*, 4: 388.

This chapter is primarily about #4, a defense of and appeal for passionate, moving, heartfelt, fervent, earnest, avid, warm, and ardent, touching, zealous, heartbreaking, affecting, loving, poignant, and stirring preaching. In a very real sense this chapter and entire book is motivated by and about #1, asking forgiveness for poor preaching, and then promoting #4. Good, stimulating, moving, relevant preaching is hard to find, and this absence is, in the opinion of many, a primary cause of the decline of church attendance and general religious disillusionment in our world today. In many parts of the world today we see the fulfillment of the prophecy in *Amos 8:11* "Behold, the days come," saith the Lord *God*, "that I will send a *famine* in the land, not a *famine* of bread, nor a thirst for water, but of hearing the *words* of the Lord" (KJV). Even "orthodox" preaching can come under this indictment, as Edwards will explain shortly.

We as preachers need to be revived in our preaching ministry. Revival will come as we as preachers are revived personally, leading to a revival of our preaching. Then our churches will be revived, and the lost awakened. Edwards himself states: "If a minister has light *without heat*, and entertains his [hearers] with learned discourses, *without a savour of the powers of goodliness, or any appearance of fervency of spirit, and zeal for God and the good of souls*, he may gratify itching ears, and fill the heads of his people with empty notions, but *it will not be very likely to teach their hearts, or save their souls*" (Jonathan Edwards).[4] But all this needs to be carefully explained. Edwards can help us considerably at this juncture.

Sensible Preaching

Although the primary thrust is for pathetic preaching, we must add the words rational and biblical. By "rational" we mean intellectual, reasonable, logical, *sensible*, based on reason, sound, judicious, insightful, relevant, and coherent. By "biblical" we mean rooted in Scripture. Edwards was a Calvinist/Reformed/Puritan preacher with a Lockean twist. I will unpack that later. If he was anything, he was a preacher, son of a good preacher (Timothy Edwards), grandson of a great preacher (Stoddard). He was steeped in Puritan homiletics, and deeply grounded in Reformed theology. With that kind of heritage, it should go without saying that he was a *biblical* preacher. But the way he preached the Bible, with a rational and pathetic approach, is what we want to explore.

If you have read carefully, you will notice that the word *"sensible"* applies to describing both "pathetic" and "reasonable" preaching. If we take

---

4. Edwards, *Works*, 25: 84–104.

these two nuances together, I think we have one key word that describes the preaching of Edwards: sensible. Sensible in the sense of reasonable, and sensible in the sense of affecting the affections. Edwards's preaching is where head and heart go hand in hand. Edwards himself used the term "sensible" in this two-pronged manner.

As we will see, Edwards's view of the person involves the religious affections as a fundamental integration of "strong and vigorous inclinations that manifest themselves in thought, feeling and action"[5]. Another way of expression this fundamental integration is the fusion of orthodoxy, "orthopathos" and orthopraxis,[6] that is, where right belief is blended with right emotions leading to upright living. As we shall see, the kind of preaching that characterized Edwards during his preaching ramping up to and during the Great Awakening is a preaching that emphasized the integrity of the person, with a very strong emphasis on the application of the text and doctrine. But the point we are trying to make in this chapter is that for the sermon to affect the behaviour, the life, the actions of the congregant, the message must be *both* cognitive and emotional, in a word: sensible. The will can only be engaged when the head and the heart are addressed. Revival preaching addresses the will by engaging the heart. Neglect this blend, and we will have pathetic (modern sense) preaching; cultivate and develop this blend and we will have pathetic (classic sense) preaching.

2. BIBLICAL INSIGHTS

We gain a better idea of what "pathetic preaching" or "sensible preaching" is all about by considering some of the revival preachers in the Biblical record.

> a. Jeremiah: Jeremiah is not our best example of "revival preaching" but certainly the principle of "sensible preaching" is exemplified in his ministry: powerful arguments combined with compassion and tears. *Jeremiah 20:9* "But if I say, 'I will not remember Him or speak anymore in His name,' Then in my heart it becomes like a burning fire shut up in my bones; And I am weary of holding *it* in, And I cannot endure it" (NASB). It is this fire in the bones that is, we believe, the quintessential element of revival preaching. That fire has to do with God's call upon the preacher's life (Jeremiah 1:4, 5) but is primarily the effect of the Spirit birthing

---

5. Haykin, *Edwards*, 125.

6. I am indebted to R. Paul Stevens of Regent College for this concept: The Other Six Days: Vocation, Work and Ministry in Biblical Perspective (Eerdmans: 2000).

God's Word in the heart and convictions of the preacher. The context indicates clearly that Jeremiah is referring to the fire of God's Word: "Because for me the word of the Lord has resulted in reproach and derision all day long" (Jeremiah 10:8). *Jeremiah 5:14* "Therefore, thus says the Lord, the God of hosts, "Because you have spoken this word, behold, I am making My words in your mouth fire And this people wood, and it will consume them'" (NASB). God's Word becomes like a fire in the audience when it is first and foremost a fire in the heart of the preacher. So when we read *Jeremiah 23:29* 'Is not My word like fire?' declares the Lord, 'and like a hammer which shatters a rock?' (NASB) it follows that previous reference in Jeremiah 20 to the prophetic word burning within. That fire produces a powerful conviction. Sometimes, like Jeremiah 5:14 above confirms, revival preaching is confrontational. Jeremiah is the "poster-boy" when it comes to confrontation. In fact, the term "jeremiad" is derived from his name. The Merriam Webster Dictionary defines a jeremiad as "a prolonged lamentation or complaint; *also*: a cautionary or angry harangue." Edwards and his contemporaries clearly demonstrate the importance of the correlation between "jeremiads" and revival. This will be developed more fully in another chapter but is germane here because of the element of "emotion" and "passion" necessary for an effective jeremiad.

b. Isaiah: Isaiah's effective prophetic role as a revival preacher can be traced back to that Theophany (technically a Christophany: see John 12:41) when the prophet's lips were touched with a live coal from the altar (Isaiah 6:6). What a powerful metaphor for passionate preaching, and certainly Isaiah exemplifies the Edwardsean concept of "sensible preaching" which we are defining as reasonable and affecting.

c. Peter at Pentecost: We have defined "sensible preaching" with a double nuance: sensible in the sense of, and sensible in the sense of *affecting the affections*. Edwards's preaching is where *reasonable* head and heart go hand in hand. It is amazing how the Holy Spirit can take a fisherman like Peter and gift and anoint him to have such penetrating and reasonable insights and explanations of both Scripture and contemporary events, and then enable the preacher to explain and proclaim in a highly affecting fashion that men's hearts are pierced (Acts 2:37) and 3000+ cry out "Brethren, what shall we do?" Now that's revival preaching, and it is sensible preaching, preaching that appeals to both the mind and the heart.

d. The Apostle Paul: When one traces the "revival preaching" ministry of the Apostle Paul in the Book of Acts, as well as his epistles, one is struck with the unique and convincing blend of head and heart that he exhibits. In fact, the very vocabulary that Dr. Luke employs in describing the public speaking ministry of Paul confirms that Paul was a "sensible" preacher, in the way we are defining "sensible." When, for example, in Acts 17, describing Paul's preaching ministry in Athens on Mars Hill, Luke very precisely utilizes terms like "provoked" (παρωξυνετο), (*paroxuneto*) (16); " reasoning" (διελεγετο), (*dielegeto*) (17); "conversing" (συνεβαλλον), (*suneballon*) (17); "proclaimer" (καταγγελευς), (*kataggeleus*) (18); and "preaching" (ευηγγελιζετο) (*euaggelizeto*) (18). It makes for a fascinating study to explore the various unique vocabulary applied to Paul's communication of the Gospel. Here in the span of three verses Luke employs 5 unique and varied rich terms to accentuate the unique blend of intelligence and passion that formed an essential part of Paul's "sensible" "Revival Preaching."

e. Apollo: There is a marvelous text in Acts 18:24ff which perfectly sums up the preaching ministry of Apollo and so beautifully and concisely summarizes this quality of "revival preaching." There we read: 24 "And a certain Jew named Apollo, born at Alexandria, an eloquent man and mighty in the Scriptures, came to Ephesus. 25 This man was instructed in the Way of the Lord; and being fervent in the Spirit, he spoke and taught diligently the things of the Lord, though he knew only the baptism of John. 26 And he began to speak boldly in the synagogue." Although needing further enlightenment, Apollo illustrates well the kind of blended preaching that I have been calling for.

Conclusion: The Biblical examples of men who preached with biblical integrity and passion are numerous. Jeremiah and Isaiah in the Old Testament, Peter, Paul, and Apollo in the New Testament illustrate the model, the paradigm of sensible preachers that are often the catalysts to revival and spiritual awakening.

3. QUOTES FROM EDWARDS

To develop and refine the concept of "pathetic preaching," I want to draw in more quotes and explanations from Edwards.

One of the criticisms against the revival was the high degree of emotional preaching. As Edwards expressed the criticism: " 'Tis no argument that a work is not from the Spirit of God, that it seems to be promoted by ministers insisting very much on the terrors of God's holy law, and that *with a great deal of pathos and earnestness*" [*emphasis* mine] (Jonathan Edwards).[7] Confronting this accusation head on, as is his style, Edwards defends his kind of emotional preaching with a very powerful analogy:

> "If there be really a hell of such dreadful, and never-ending torments, as is generally supposed, that multitudes are in great danger of, and that the bigger part of men in Christian countries do actually from generation to generation fall into, for want of a sense of the terribleness of it, and their danger of it, and so for want of taking due care to avoid it; then *why is it not proper for those that have the care of souls, to take great pains to make men sensible of it?* Why should not they be told as much of the truth as can be? If I am in danger of going to hell, I should be glad to know as much as possibly I can of the dreadfulness of it: if I am very prone to neglect due care to avoid it, he does me the best kindness, that does most to represent to me the truth of the case, that sets forth my misery and danger *in the liveliest manner* (Jonathan Edwards).[8]

Notice here the justification and defense of "pathetic hellfire preaching." His reasoning is clear: Hell is a serious matter. We must do all we can to rescue men and women from such a plight, and we as preachers must do so "in the liveliest manner" and with great pathos and passion.

Edwards proceeds to give a homely illustration or analogy from the real world:

> I appeal to everyone in this congregation, whether this is not the very course they would take in case of exposedness to any great temporal calamity? If any of you that are heads of families, saw one of your children in an house that was all on fire over its head, and in eminent danger of being soon consumed in the flames, that seemed to be very insensible of its danger, and neglected to escape, after you had often spake (old English)

---

7. Edwards, *Works*, 4: 247.
8. Edwards, *Works*, 4: 246–47.

to it, and called to it, would you go on to speak to it only in a cold and indifferent manner? *Would not you cry aloud, and call earnestly to it, and represent the danger it was in, and its own folly in delaying, in the most lively manner you was (sic) capable of?* Would not nature itself teach this, and oblige you to it? If you should continue to speak to *it only in a cold manner*, as you are wont to do in ordinary conversation about indifferent matters, would not those about you begin to think you were bereft of reason yourself? This is not the way of mankind, nor the way of any one person in this congregation, in temporal affairs of great moment, that require earnest heed and great haste, and about which they are greatly concerned, to speak to others of their danger, and warn them but a little; and when they do it at all, *do it in a cold indifferent manner: nature teaches men otherwise.* If we that have the care of souls, knew what hell was, had seen the state of the damned, or by any other means, become sensible how dreadful their case was; and at the same time knew that the bigger part of men went thither; and saw our hearers in eminent danger, and that they were not sensible of their danger, and so after being often warned neglected to escape, *it would be morally impossible for us to avoid abundantly and most earnestly setting before them the dreadfulness of that misery* they were in danger of, and their great exposedness to it, and warning them to fly from it, and even *to cry aloud to them* (Jonathan Edwards).[9] [Emphasis mine].

Edwards here is subtly (or perhaps not so subtly) criticizing preachers who are not more passionate in their reference to hell, or who neglect the theme entirely. He as much as says so in the following quote:

When ministers preach of hell, and warn sinners to avoid it, in a cold manner, though they may say in words that it is infinitely terrible; yet (if we look on language as a communication of our minds to others) *they contradict themselves*; for actions, as I observed before, have a language to convey our minds, as well as words; and at the same time that such a preacher's words represent the sinner's state as infinitely dreadful, his behavior and manner of speaking contradict it, and shew that *the preacher don't (sic) think so*; so that *he defeats his own purpose; for the language of his actions, in such a case, is much more effectual than the bare signification of his words* (Jonathan Edwards).[10]

9. Edwards, *Works*, 4: 247.
10. Edwards, *Works*, 10: 247.

This quote is significant for several reasons. First, it is one of the clearest statements of Edwards defending "pathetic (passionate) preaching" and conversely criticizing dispassionate preaching. Secondly, this quote points to Edwards's view of preaching as drama. We know that significant scholarship has been dedicated to describing the preaching of Whitefield as drama. Stout has written an excellent study on Whitefield as "The Divine Dramatist" because of the dramatic and vivid nature of his extemporaneous preaching (Whitefield grew up on the stage and allowed his formation to influence his style of preaching). Unfortunately, and inaccurately, Edwards is portrayed as plain, dead, dull, and boring. For example, Gideon Clark, (1722–1807) contemporary of Edwards, portrays Edwards's preaching style as boring and dull: "He looked on the bell rope until he looked it off." However, we see from this quote by Edwards that he, at least in theory, argues for a "language of his actions," a correspondence and symmetry between what the preacher says and how he says it. Form and substance need to complement each other, otherwise our style can undermine our words, and betray our lack of conviction and true belief about what we "say" we believe.

This blending of head and heart is reflected in Edwards's Master's dissertation: Edwards, defending the Reformed doctrine of justification by faith alone, affirms "receiving Christ and his benefits takes place by the faith of the entire soul; it is not merely the intellect's reception by assent, nor merely the will's reception by choosing him, not only the affections' reception in love, nor merely the capacities we have for action receiving him in obedience. Rather, it is a reception of the entire soul, which includes all of these."[11] Here we see his early emphasis on the blending of head, heart, will and action.

Edwards not only preaches with these convictions; he demonstrates these same convictions in his own beliefs. Edwards himself talks about the evolution in his understanding of certain great truths, such as, for example, his evolving belief in the sovereignty of God. "But I have oftentimes since that first conviction, had quite another kind of sense of God's sovereignty, then I had then. I have often since, not only had a conviction, but a *delightful* conviction (Jonathan Edwards).[12] This evolution from "conviction" to "delightful conviction" reflects his belief in the need for a more fully emotional acceptance and affirmation of the truth, as opposed to a mere intellectual cognizant affirmation.

Edwards affirms: "Thus there is a difference between having an opinion that God is holy and gracious, and having a sense of the loveliness and beauty of that holiness and grace. There is a difference between having a

---

11. Minkema, *Works*, 14: 60–61.
12. Edwards, *Works*, 16: 792.

rational judgment that honey is sweet and having a sense of its sweetness. A man may have the former, that knows not how honey tastes; but a man cannot have the latter, unless he has an idea of the taste of honey in his mind."[13] The blending of "opinion" and "sense"; between "rational judgment" and "a sense of" is quintessential Edwardsean understanding on the nature of belief, and he firmly believed that the style of preaching which combined both intelligence and affection was that kind of preaching most likely to produce that kind of integrated belief.

While we will deal with the issue of hellfire preaching and its relationship to revival and awakening, it is appropriate here to quote Edwards on the issue of what we could call a "preaching disassociate dissonance disorder." Let me explain. Sometimes there is a dissonance between the intellectual or reasonable or cognitive aspect of the sermon, and the more affective, emotional, feeling aspect of the sermon. It is like the preacher is only half there. There may be orthodoxy, but there is no orthopathos, and as a result there is no orthopraxis. This dissonance is picked up on by the congregant, and the message is lost. This is what is happening in today's evangelical world. Our neglect of the theme of hell, or the dispassionate way in which we approach the matter, betrays our fundamental lack of conviction regarding the truthfulness of what we say we believe. To put it in Edwards's words, the preacher's dispassionate manner of preaching ". . . shew that the preacher doesn't think so . . ." (Jonathan Edwards)[14] or to paraphrase Edwards in a more congenial modern English, the preacher's modern neglect of hell or the way the preacher preaches about hell "shows that the preacher doesn't really believe it." This lack of conviction regarding hell is one of the primary causes of lack of revival in the twenty-first century.

This reflects Edwards's philosophy of preaching. There is a profound correlation, in Edwardsean thought, between the preacher himself and the sermon. The man *is* the message. While Edwards believed that the B-I-B-L-E is the message, there is a profound sense in which he believed that the minister must incarnate the truth for that message to be faithfully transmitted. The emotions of the person must be linked with the reasons of the person, and both must be rooted in the Word of God. More on this when we come to Edwards the man and his preaching.

13. Edwards, *Works*, 17: 414.
14. Edwards, *Works*, 4: 248.

4. QUOTES BY EDWARDSEAN SCHOLARS

Considerable research has been done by Edwardsean scholars showing the influence of Locke on Edwards. Sereno Dwight tells us that "in the second year of his collegiate course, while at Wethersfield, Edwards read Locke on the Human Understanding with peculiar pleasure. . . . From his own account of the subject, he was inexpressibly entertained and delighted with that profound work, when he read it at the age of fourteen; enjoying a far higher pleasure in the perusal of its pages, 'than the most greedy miser finds, when gathering up handfuls of silver and gold, from some newly discovered treasure.'"[15]

Of particular interest to us at this juncture is the influence of Locke on Edwards's view of preaching, especially of this kind of "sensible" preaching. John Smith, in his work "Jonathan Edwards, Puritan, Preacher, Philosopher" affirms "Edwards had a genius, brought into play by his study of Locke, for presenting ideas in the most vivid way."[16] Fundamental to understanding Edwards's view of preaching is his understanding of the Religious Affections, a concept so integral to Edwardsean thought that he wrote 368 very carefully structured pages to show the nature and importance of the affection in the spiritual life. As Smith observes "Edwards's position will never be understood correctly by anyone who comes to it with some form of a heart/head dualism at hand"[17]. Edwards believed that reason and emotion must be so blended because of the very essence of knowledge, to which he is indebted to Locke as well as Calvin and ultimately, to the Scriptures.

Smith affirms that "he was meticulous in his choice of words to achieve the greatest accuracy in the ideas they were meant to convey and, above all, he was concerned to make these ideas 'sensible' through vivid images, metaphors and dramatic comparisons"[18] and again "his sermons are always models of carefully reasoned discourse, a fact acknowledged even by those not entirely in sympathy with his doctrine. The issue is in any case *not an opposition between affections and thought. Religious Affections was dedicated to overcoming any such opposition*but rather in differences of rhetorical style" [emphasis mine].[19]

---

15. Ramsey, *Works*, 1: 47.
16. Smith, *Edwards: Puritan Preacher*, 29.
17. Smith, *Edwards: Puritan Preacher*, 31.
18. Smith, *Edwards: Puritan Preacher*, 139.
19. Smith, *Edwards: Puritan Preacher*, 140.

5. ILLUSTRATIONS FROM THE ACTUAL SERMONS OF EDWARDS

When one consults with Edwards's sermon on a "Divine and Supernatural Light immediately imparted to the soul by the Spirit of God" (sermon title) we find a marvelous blend of Scripture and Reason, of Biblical reference and reference to Locke, which fits with the title which continues "shown to be both a *Scriptural* and a *Rational* Doctrine." When one explores the sermon, one sees this further blend of intellectual conviction and delightful embracing of the truth.

When one reads the sermons of Edwards, one is struck with this compelling combination of intelligence and emotional and passionate appeal. The "rhetoric of sensibility" is so combined with the "persuasiveness of logic" that one is captivated in both mind and heart, and so drawn compellingly to the truth. For example, in his sermon "The Unreasonableness of Indetermination in Religion" he not only presents cogent arguments calling for a decision for faith, but one "senses" the rhetoric of sensation, especially in the conclusion. Upon reading the sermons, the impact is similar today because of these twin elements.

In Edwards's classic sermon on "False Light and True," he clarifies for us his understanding of the difference between notional and sensible knowledge. Edwards states: "Spiritual light han't [has not] its seat only in the head, but mainly in the heart. It primarily consists of a sense of the excellency of divine things in the heart. There is a twofold knowledge of good that God has made the mind of man capable of, viz. (1) that which is merely speculative, whereby men have only a notion of divine things in their heads. Thus, a natural man may have a notion that God is just, and that he is good, and that he [is] holy, and that Christ is one of wonderful love. But (2) the other is that which consists in the sense of the heart, whereby men have in their hearts a sense of the excellency of these things, and they seem sweet, and glorious, and delightful to him. He has not only a notion in his head of the attributes of God; but he has a sense of the excellency of them in his heart that delights his heart, and draws his heart, and changes his heart. 'Tis [It is] accompanied with a relish of these things in the heart" (Jonathan Edwards).[20]

---

20. Edwards, *Works*, 19: 140.

6. 70 RESOLUTIONS

Edwards was a man who lived with both head and heart. Our focus here is on the heart. Resolution #6 states: "Resolved, to live *with all my might*, while I do live." Here is a man with heart. Edwards has a reputation for being cerebral, intellectual, hyper analytical and rational. And all this is true. However, it is not the whole truth. He was a passionate man, with a passion for God and for people. John Piper refers to "God's Passion for His Glory" and subtitles his book "Living the Vision of Jonathan Edwards" because Edwards was passionate for God's glory. We shall develop this more when we consider the emphasis on the glory of God as a motivation for living and serving, which forms a fundamental and essential motivation for Edwards's preaching. However, the point we make here is that this ultimate and transcendent motive, the glory of God, was for him a passion. It was indeed his life's vision.

We can see this evidently in his magnum opus, Religious Affections, where he explains his understanding of the nature of man and the nature of spiritual life.

7. OTHER AUTHORS

Hart has a book entitled *Preaching, the Secret to Parish Revival* in which he talks about the importance of ministering from the heart to the heart. He uses a Latin phrase "cor ad cor" and "Cor ad cor loquitur" which is the Latin expression of speaking from the heart to the heart[21] (Hart: 3). The young Oxford don and preacher, Newman, dedicated his Fifth Oxford University Sermon to this very topic: *Personal Influence, the Means of Propagating the Truth*. He claims in this sermon that no one can be won for Jesus Christ and His Church merely by means of arguments. Credible witnesses are more important than words. The truth of the Gospel "has been upheld in the world not as a system, not by books, not by argument, nor by temporal power, but by the personal influence of such men. . ., who are at once the teachers and the patterns of it."[22]

Whitefield alludes to the importance of preaching with heart and experience of the truth when, in his journal, he describes the preaching ministry of Tennent, whom one scholar speculates Whitefield considered "the best preacher of the Great Awakening"[23]: "He convinced me more and more that

---

21. Hart, *Preaching*, 3.
22. Newman, *Fifteen Sermons*, 91–92.
23. Conrad, *Importance of Preaching*, 115.

we can preach the Gospel of Christ no further than we have experienced the power of it *in our own hearts* [Emphasis mine]. Being deeply convinced of sin, by God's Holy Spirit, at his first conversion, Mr. Tennent has learned experimentally to dissect the heart of the natural man."[24] Undoubtedly Whitefield would have said the same about Edwards. Whitefield affirms about Edwards "Mr. Edwards is a solid, excellent Christian. I think I have not seen his fellow [equal] in all New England."[25]

John Stott refers to this balance between Head and Heart in his masterful treatment on preaching: "Between Two Worlds": "What is needed today is the same synthesis of reason and emotion, exposition and exhortation, as was achieved by Paul."[26] Quoting G. Campbell Morgan, Stott affirms "The three essentials of a sermon, he said, are 'truth, clarity, and passion.'"[27]

Martyn Lloyd Jones asks the question 'what is preaching?' and proceeds to answer "Logic on fire. Eloquent reason! Are these contradictions? Of course, they are not. Reason concerning this truth ought to be mightily eloquent, as you see it in the case of the Apostle Paul and others. It is theology on fire. And a theology which does not take fire, I maintain, is a defective theology. Preaching is theology coming through a man who is on fire."[28]

8. CONCLUSION

Edwards was an effective revival preacher because of the way in which he maintained in biblical juxtaposition the head and the heart. The school theme for Asbury Seminary, where I am writing this chapter, is "Where head and heart go hand in hand." Wesley the Arminian and Edwards the Calvinist were both effective preachers because they were pathetic preachers, sensible preachers, and biblical preachers! While we strongly favour Edwards the Calvinist, the appeal here is to integrate head and heart if we are to have effective revival preaching. Certainly, this is something both Arminians and Calvinists can agree on.

---

24. Conrad, *Importance of Preaching*, 115.
25. Conrad, *Importance of Preaching*, 114.
26. Stott, *Between Two Worlds*, 283.
27. Stott, *Between Two Worlds*, 284.
28. Lloyd-Jones, *Preaching and Preachers*, 97.

Chapter 2

Prayer, Fasting and Revival Preaching

"And he said unto them, this kind can come forth by nothing, but by *prayer and fasting*" (Mark 9:29) (KJV).

"...graceful, attenuated through acidity and abstinence and studies most intense."[1]

"When God has something very great to accomplish for his church, it is his will that there should precede it the extraordinary prayers of his people" (Jonathan Edwards).[2]

INTRODUCTION

In this chapter we will explore Edwards's understanding of the importance of prayer and fasting as it relates to effective revival preaching. What exactly is the correlation between prayer and revival, between fasting/prayer and revival?

---

1. Gerstner, *Rational Theology*. 1: 19.
2. Edwards, *Works*, 4: 516.

1. DEFINE IT

It is not rocket science. We know as preachers what it means to pray; to be on our knees before God, recognizing our utter dependence upon God. Prayer is asking and receiving. That is it! Of course, there are many nuances to prayer, intercession, confession, thanksgiving, praise, but the essence of prayer is "asking and receiving." Edwards states: "Prayer is but a sensible acknowledgment of our dependence on him to his glory" (Jonathan Edwards).[3]

Fasting is prayer on steroids. Fasting is voluntary abstinence of food for the explicit purpose of concentrated prayer. Fasting seems to be a way that the Scriptures teach us to reinforce the sense of seriousness and desperation of our situation.

2. BIBLICAL PERSPECTIVE

First, we need to focus on the place of prayer in the life of the preacher. The Scriptures abound with placing a priority on prayer for the preacher. The two classic texts in Acts 6:2, 4 affirm categorically: "It is not fitting that we should leave the Word of God to serve tables. . . .4 But we will give ourselves continually to prayer and to the ministry of the Word." The Apostles were zealous for guarding the priority of prayer in relationship to the ministry of the Word.

Examples of preachers praying for the revival of their people and the awakening of the lost abound in Scripture. *Psalm 39:3* "My heart was hot within me, while I was musing the fire burned: then spake I with my tongue" (KJV). The fire of God's Word and God's Spirit is kindled and fanned into full flame while we muse[4] in prayerful meditation, thinking prayerfully about the truth that we have been entrusted to communicate.

God frequently takes his servants aside for a prolonged season of prayer and meditation before he thrusts them only the more public stage of revival preaching. Elijah spent three years in prayerful meditation (I Kgs 17) before confronting the prophets of Baal and seeing a breakthrough with the descent of rain from heaven (I Kgs 18). Another classic case linking prayer and revival by a prophet is Habakkuk's classic prayer: "O Lord, revive thy work in the midst of the years, in the midst of the years make known; in wrath remember mercy" (Hab 3:2) (KJV).

---

3. Haykin, *Edwards*, 139.

4. The issue of amusement in today's culture and among preachers is significant. Amuse means literally the negation of musing: "a" "muse." We can easily be distracted from deep prayerful thinking by amusements.

There is an abundance of evidence showing the correlation between effective revival preaching and combining prayer with fasting. All Christians are called to pray and fast (Mat 6:16–18). Jesus affirmed that certain kinds of situations are so severe and difficult and intense that in addition to prayer, we should approach them with fasting: *Mark 9:29* "And he said unto them, This kind can come forth by nothing, but by *prayer and fasting*" (KJV). The apostles were not able to exorcise the demonized through simple prayer, and as we see the situation in many churches in the English and Spanish-speaking world, we see the need for a serious call to prayer and fasting so that we can exorcise the demons that hold back individuals and churches and resist the demons that keep multitudes in their clutch.

Nehemiah: Nehemiah was a leader with a significant leadership role during a period of restoration and revival (See for example, 2:17; 4:14; 5:12, etc.). We read in Nehemiah one: 4 When I heard these words, I sat down and wept and mourned for days; and I was fasting and praying before the God of heaven. 5 I said, "I beseech You, O Lord God of heaven, the great and awesome God, who preserves the covenant and loving-kindness for those who love Him and keep His commandments..." (Neh 1:4, 5) (NASB). There is a profound correlation between his passion, born and nurtured in prayer and fasting, and his effective leadership. (As a baby can only be born through the process of the 9 months gestation and the pain of giving birth, so prayer and fasting will bring about the works of God that can only be 'born' through the process of prayer and fasting.)

The apostle Paul and prayer/fasting for revival in relationship to preaching: In 2 Corinthians 11:23–27 Paul says: "Are they ministers of Christ? . . . I am more . . . " Paul then proceeds to elaborate and provide detail: In verse 27 he says: "In weariness and painfulness, in watchings often, in hunger and thirst, in fastings often . . ." Here again Paul joins 'watching' closely with 'fasting'. The plural form, 'in fastings often,' indicates that Paul devoted himself to frequent periods of fasting. 'Hunger and thirst' refer to occasions when neither food nor drink was available. 'Fastings' refers to occasions when food was available, but Paul deliberately abstained for spiritual reasons."[5]

3. QUOTES FROM EDWARDS

What evidence is there to demonstrate Edwards's belief in prayer and fasting for revival?

---

5. Cauchi, *Fasting*, 3.

First, we know that he practiced prayer and fasting for resolving matters related to personal melancholy and depression. Writing a friend, he counsels: "With regard to the case of extraordinary temptation, and buffeting of Satan, which you mention, I don't very well know what to say further. I have often found my own insufficiency as a counsellor in such like cases, wherein melancholy and bodily distemper have so great a hand, and give Satan so great advantage, as appears to me in the case you mention: If the Lord do not help, whence should we help? If some Christian friends of such afflicted and (as it were) possessed persons, would, from time to time, pray and fast for them, it might be a proper exercise of Christian charity, and the likeliest way I know for relief" (Jonathan Edwards).[6]

Edwards believed in praying for the Spirit to come, as is evident by his numerous positive references to the practice[7] (WJE 5: 347, 348, 356). Edwards wrote a treatise calling for Humble Attempt to Promote Unity in Concerted Prayer for Revival, "... extraordinary, speedy, fervent, and constant prayer" for a "great effusion of the Holy Spirit that will dramatically advance the kingdom of Christ" (Jonathan Edwards).[8]

Samuel Hopkins, writing from the perspective of a young minister who spent eight months as a type of pastoral intern in the Northampton pastor's home during the early 1740s, noted that while much of Edwards's personal piety was concealed from onlookers, he knew that Edwards "often kept days of fasting."[9]

Jonathan Edwards comments that when God has something very great to accomplish for His church, it is His will that there should precede it the extraordinary prayers of His people, quoting from Ezekiel 36:37,—"I will yet for this be inquired of by the house of Israel, to do this for them." In Zechariah 12:10 it is revealed that, when God is about to accomplish great things for His church, He will begin by a remarkable pouring out of "the Spirit of grace and supplication." It is the invariable constitution of the Kingdom of Heaven that blessings of great magnitude are not imparted except to prayers of the deepest urgency[10].

Whitney observes that Edwards himself connects prayer and fasting to the revival in his treatment on the Great Awakening. Edwards believed that ministers, as they were to be examples to the flock, should especially feel responsible to discipline themselves to observe fast days. He said as

6. Edwards, *Works*, 2: 511.
7. Stein, *Works*, 5: 347–56.
8. Edwards, *Works*, 5: 321.
9. Whitney, *Jonathan Edwards's "Fast Days,"* 1.
10. Hulse, *Extraordinary Prayer*, 1.

much in *Some Thoughts Concerning the Present Revival*, when he wrote, "I should think ministers, above all persons, ought to be much in secret prayer and fasting, and also much in praying and fasting with one another." In his "Blank Bible" notes on Matthew 17:21, Edwards summarized succinctly, "fasting is a part of Christian worship."[11]

J. Edwin Orr, that famous revival historian, wrote an article entitled "Prayer and Revival" wherein he documented the relationship between the two. He affirms: "There was a Scottish Presbyterian minister in Edinburgh named John Erskine, who published a Memorial (as he called it) pleading with the people of Scotland and elsewhere to unite in prayer for the revival of religion. He sent one copy of this little book to Jonathan Edwards in New England. The great theologian was so moved he wrote a response which grew longer than a letter, so that finally he published it is a book entitled 'A Humble Attempt to Promote Explicit Agreement and Visible Union of all God's People in Extraordinary Prayer for the Revival of Religion and the Advancement of Christ's Kingdom on Earth, pursuant to Scripture Promises and Prophecies . . . '. Orr goes on to challenge us all as believers and particularly as preachers: "Is not this what is missing so much from all our evangelistic efforts . . . ?"[12]

4. QUOTES BY EDWARDSEAN SCHOLARS

Commenting on his famous sermon "Sinners in the Hands of an Angry God," one scholar comments: "Edwards held the manuscript so close to his eyes that his listeners could not see his face. Nevertheless, upon concluding the discourse the whole great auditorium was moved. One man ran towards him proclaiming, 'Mr. Edwards, have mercy!' Others grabbed a hold of the pew thinking that they would fall into hell. I watched how they grabbed a hold of the church pillars to support themselves, thinking that the final judgment had arrived." "The power of that sermon still continues to impact the world today. Nevertheless, it is important to point out some details on the history of the sermon that are generally suppressed. For three days Edwards had not taken any food, and for three nights he had not slept. He had been praying to God without ceasing: 'Give me New England!' After rising from prayer, as he made his way to the pulpit, one of those present there said that his countenance was like he who, for some time, had been contemplating

---

11. Whitney, *Jonathan Edwards's "Fast Days,"* 1.
12. Orr, *The Role of Prayer*, Video.

the face of God. Even before opening his mouth to pronounce his first word, the conviction of the Holy Spirit fell upon the auditorium" (Chapman) .[13]

The place of fasting for revival is illustrated in the following reference: "In April 1734, two young persons in the town, a man and a woman, died suddenly. While their young companions were still greatly sobered by these deaths, the preacher quickly seized his opportunity, organized the young people into small groups for private meetings, *appointed fasts*, and in various other kept religion in the foreground during the week as well as on Sunday" [Emphasis mine][14].

The epitaph of Edwards describes him as a man who was much given to prayer and fasting. There is a phrase in his epitaph which describes him as "In person he was tall and slender, thin with intense study, *abstinence* and application."[15]

Edwards practiced fasting and participated in public fasts and practiced fasting regularly in his own private life. Indeed, in a sermon entitled "Fast Days in Dead Times," while lamenting and denouncing the abuses of fasting, Edwards points to the legitimate place for fasting as a sign of repentance.[16]

5. ILLUSTRATIONS FROM THE ACTUAL SERMONS OF EDWARDS

There are numerous occasions in which Edwards is described as preaching at a "fasting" Sunday. We would be safe to assume that Edwards participated in the fast on those occasions.

There are times when Edwards explicitly appeals for fasting. For example, in a sermon preached in the winter of 1730, Edwards affirms "if a people in a time of sore drought acknowledge God, and turn from their sins which procure this judgment, and go to God through Christ by *prayer and supplication*, 'tis the way for them both to obtain the temporal blessing they need, and also to obtain great spiritual blessings that are far better" which scholars believe was probably a fast sermon (Jonathan Edwards).[17]

---

13. Boyer, *Biografías*, 5.
14. Winslow, *Edwards*, 159.
15. Gerstner, *Rational Theology*, 20.
16. Edwards, *Works*, 19: 67.
17. Edwards, *Works*, 17: 447.

6. 70 RESOLUTIONS

What is there in the resolutions that reinforces the concept of prayer and fasting in the life of Edwards? Considerable material indeed:

24. Resolved, whenever I do any conspicuously evil action, to trace it back, till I come to the original cause; and then, both carefully endeavor to do so no more, and to *fight and pray with all my might* against the original of it.

Edwards was not content to identify the external actions, he was diligent to "trace it back" to the "original cause," the heart issue and then to address the matter through diligent prayer *("with all my might")*. Edwards was determined to address the heart issues in his life through prayer.

29. Resolved, never to count that a *prayer*, nor to let that pass as a *prayer*, nor that as a petition of a *prayer*, which is so made, *that I cannot hope that God will answer it*; nor that as a confession, which I cannot hope God will accept.

Edwards not only was committed to a life of prayer, but he worked hard at addressing the quality of his prayer life. Here we see him addressing the issue of unbelief. I would paraphrase this vow: Resolved never to pray without believing that God will answer it. Resolved never to confess my sins without believing that God will grant me forgiveness. If we were to be just as candid and implement such a strategy to our prayer lives, and to our manner of confessing our sins, would that not result in a major revolution in our spiritual lives?

64. Resolved, when I find those "groanings which cannot be uttered" (Rom 8:26) (KJV), of which the Apostle speaks, and those "breakings of soul for the longing it hath," of which the Psalmist speaks, Psalm 119:20, that *I will promote them to the utmost of my power*, and that I will not be wear' [weary] of *earnestly endeavoring to vent my desires, nor of the repetitions of such earnestness. July 23,* and *August 10, 1723.*

Edwards here is resolved to follow through on those promptings of the Spirit and longings of the soul, and "promote them to the utmost of my power" or, in other words, to cultivate and develop and foster that spirit of prayer. When he speaks of "will not be wear', of earnestly endeavoring to vent my desires, . . . " he is saying that he will not give up, he will not be weary, he will not be lazy or slothful, but will "vent my desires" and give full expression to his prayers, not to be weary in the "repetitions of such earnestness." Here is a young man committed to prayer, who set early in his life and ministry the priority of prayer, and we have solid reason to believe that he followed through on these resolutions to cultivate a life of prayer.

In regard to fasting, there is only inference made to fasting in the resolutions. We can infer from the following that Edwards practiced fasting on a regular basis:

4. Resolved, *never to do any manner of thing, whether in soul or body, less or more, but what tends to the glory of God; nor be, nor suffer it, if I can avoid it.*

20. Resolved, to maintain *the strictest temperance in eating and drinking*. (Undoubtedly the maintenance of the strictest temperance in eating and drinking implied that frequently Edwards practiced fasting).

40. Resolved, to inquire every night, before I go to bed, *whether I have acted in the best way I possibly could, with respect to eating and drinking.* Jan. 7, 1723. Every night Edwards inquired as to whether he had in the best possible way. Eating and drinking properly were so important to him.

7. OTHER AUTHORS

E. M. Bounds has written extensively on the relationship between the Preacher and Prayer. I strongly encourage each preaching pastor to read that little booklet at least twice a year, to help keep the priority of prayer in place. His treatment of revival also deals effectively with the place of prayer.

History demonstrates this principle. The common precursor to revivals has been prevailing prayer. Pentecost, which was the first Christian revival, followed ten days of intense prayer characterized by whole-hearted unity (Acts 1:14, 2:14). Before the Second Great Awakening (late 1850s), Jeremiah Lamphier called a prayer meeting in downtown New York. Within six months 10,000 businessmen were praying for revival, and within two years about 2,000,000 people were added to the churches. The same pattern is found before the 1859 revival in Ulster, Ireland. James McQuilkin and three others began to meet in a schoolhouse every week for prayer and Bible study. They kept themselves warm with armfuls of peat gathered on the way to the schoolhouse every Friday evening. While peat warmed their bodies, the Spirit kindled the fire in their hearts. By the end of 1858, the participants at the prayer meeting had grown to fifty. Intercession without distraction to other subjects was made for an outpouring of the Holy Spirit on themselves and the country. Their prayers [and possibly those of many more] were wonderfully answered in 1859 when an estimated 100,000 were added to the churches in Ulster. These accounts and many others illustrate prayer as the genesis of revival. The beginning of a time of revival invariably has been marked by quickening of the ordinary prayer meetings, resulting in new vitality, more participation, more sense of the presence of the Holy Spirit, and more unction in intercession. Therefore, in times of special need and of the church's weakness, there is a biblical and historical warrant to resort to extraordinary prayer for revival. Isn't spiritual apathy and powerlessness in the church today a crisis which calls for urgent prayer?[18]

J. Edwin Orr, in his work "Prayer and Revival" writes, "Most people have heard of the Welsh Revival which started in 1904. It began as a movement of prayer. Seth Joshua, the Presbyterian evangelist, came to Newcastle Emlyn College where a former coal miner, Evan Roberts aged 26, was studying for the ministry. The students were so moved that they asked if they could attend Joshua's next campaign nearby. So, they cancelled classes to go to Blaenanerch where Seth Joshua prayed publicly, 'O God, bend us.' Evan Roberts went forward where he prayed with great agony, 'O God, bend me.' "That was the beginning of the Welsh Revival."

Describing the kind of preaching that will produce revival, Keevil affirms: " . . . it will be filled with power. Revival preaching will be bathed in prayer. Prayer is the energy of true effectual preaching, and without it the sermon is nothing more than words spoken into the air. Prayer is essential for both preacher and people. When both are prepared through prayer, an atmosphere is created conducive to expectations of blessing. The reformed synthesis of Word and Spirit means that without the Spirit, the Word is a dead letter"[19]. As one of my reviewers of this book commented: "This really is so very important, but how does one get people not only to hear this and nod agreement, but to bend the knees and pray—pray—pray?"

8. CONCLUSION

The relationship between prayer and revival has been clearly established by many biblical scholars and historians. Dr. A. T. Pierson once said, "There has never been a spiritual awakening in any country or locality that did not begin in united prayer." J. Edwin Orr's studies on prayer and revival are second to none. His classic study on Prayer and Revival affirms that whenever you have revival "it began through a movement of prayer" (J. Edwin Orr). There is considerable evidence that prior to the great awakening, there was a strong sense of need and spiritual lethargy that prompted the more spiritually minded to implore God for a Great Awakening. In the preface to Edwards famous "Faithful Narrative" of the Great Awakening, we have this significant observation by Cooper, who wrote the preface. After describing the spiritual decline and lethargy, Cooper affirms "Accordingly, it has been

---

18. Hulse, *Extraordinary Prayer*, 1.
19. Keevil, *Preaching in Revival*, 163–64.

a constant petition in our public prayers from Sabbath to Sabbath, that God would 'pour out his Spirit upon us and revive his work in the midst of the years'" [Joel 2:28; Hab 3:2] (William Cooper).[20]

More particularly, we would do well to reflect on the place of prayer in the life of the revival preacher. Just as there is a correlation between prayer and revival, there is a special correlation between God stirring the heart of the preacher, his prayer life, and personal and subsequent corporate revival. Orr documents how men were moved to prayer, and to call others to prayer. Men like William Carey, Andrew Fuller and John Sutcliffe. Orr affirms: "In New England, there was a man of prayer named Isaac Backus, a Baptist pastor, who in 1794, when conditions were at their worst, addressed an urgent plea for prayer for revival to pastors of every Christian denomination in the United States" (Orr). "There was a Scotch-Irish Presbyterian minister named James McGready. . . [he] was such a man of prayer that not only did he promote the concert of prayer every first Monday of the month, but he got his people to pray for him at sunset on Saturday evening and sunrise Sunday morning. Then in the summer of 1800 came the great Kentucky revival"[21].

God calls us as preachers to prayer for revival. We need to pray for our own spiritual vitality, and that of our family, and then for the spiritual vitality of the people of God under our care. What could happen if preachers sought God earnestly for revival and awakening, beginning in their own hearts, their own homes and in their own parishes? The Scriptures and the annals of history are replete with documented evidence of what can happen. Lord, we need another Great Awakening. We as pastors humble ourselves and pray and seek Your face and turn from our wicked ways, so that you might have mercy, hear our prayers, and heal our churches and awaken our land (II Chr 7:14). Amen.

---

20. Edwards, *Works*, 4: 217.
21. Orr video.

Chapter 3

Preaching on Hell or "Sulfurous Sermons"[1]

Burning indignation has seized me because of the wicked,
Who forsake Your law (Ps 119:53) (NASB).

Eyewitness Account of the Sermon
"Sinners in the Hands of an Angry God"
"We went over to Enfield where we met dear Mr. Edwards of Northampton who preached a most awakening sermon from these wordsDeut. 32:35 and before [the] sermon was done—there was a great moaning and crying out through ye [the] whole House—What shall I do to be saved?—Oh I am going to Hell—Oh what shall I do for Christ,... (Eyewitness account).[2]

"Some talk of it as an unreasonable thing to think to fright persons to heaven; but I think it is a reasonable thing to endeavor to fright persons away from hell...'tis a reasonable thing to fright a person out of a house on fire" (Jonathan Edwards).[3]

---

1. Edwards, *Works*, 10: 132.
2. Winslow, *Jonathan Edwards*, 192.
3. Edwards, *Works*, 4: 248.

INTRODUCTORY COMMENTS

Is there a correlation between revival and an emphasis on hell? Is there evidence from the First Great Awakening that the revival of the sluggish saints and the awakening of the slumbering sinners can be traced to that kind of a preaching that emphasized the fire of hell and eternal condemnation?

1. DEFINE IT

What do we mean by "preaching on hell" or "hell-fire preaching"? Hell-fire preaching refers to that kind of preaching which calls attention to the final destiny of the impenitent. There may be degrees of emphasis, and there may be degrees of extent to which hell is emphasized in the sermon. According to Houdmann, there are those who view God as so loving and kind that the concept of hell is barbaric, then, on the other hand are " . . . those who see a perpetually angry, wrathful, and vengeful God who condemns people to hell for the sheer enjoyment He gets from it. Both these views of God's character and of hell are biblically insupportable."[4] From a historical perspective, " . . . hellfire preaching has come to be associated with preachers of the 18th and 19th centuries in Europe and America. The image of Puritan preachers is often one of bewhiskered, black-frocked theological terrorists pounding their pulpits and continually threatening their congregations with eternal burning. Perhaps the epitome of the image of the hellfire preacher is Jonathan Edwards, whose sermon 'Sinners in the Hands of an Angry God' depicted the realities of hell so clearly that it was said the hearers could smell the sulfur burning."[5] However, is this understanding of hellfire preaching a caricature of Edwards? We believe that while Edwards did preach on hell, it did not characterize or predominate his preaching. Nevertheless, hell-fire preaching was a significant element within Edwards's preaching, and a significant element and stimulus to the awakening.

To clarify, Edwards's concept of hell was a place of conscious eternal torment. Gerstner sums up his concept of hell: "Hell is a spiritual and material furnace of fire where its victims are exquisitely tortured in their minds and in their bodies eternally, according to their various capacities, by God, the devils, and damned human beings including themselves, in their memories, and consciences as well as in their raging, unsatisfied lusts, from which

---

4. Houdmann, *Hell-Fire Preaching*.
5. Houdmann, *Hell-Fire Preaching*.

place of death God's saving grace, mercy, and pity are gone forever, never for a moment to return."[6]

2. BIBLICAL PERSPECTIVE

There can be no doubt: The Bible teaches clearly that hell is real. The Synoptic *Gospels* contain 15 references to the word "hell" as employed by Jesus. There is a definite correlation between the preaching of Jesus and his usage of hell. The two references to hell in the book of *Acts* (2:27; 2:31) are more related to Christ not remaining in hell, and not so much used in a minatory[7] manner. Although the actual term "hell" is not employed by *Paul* in his epistles, he refers, in 2 Corinthians 5:11 to the terror of the Lord and links that fact to preaching and evangelism: "Knowing *therefore* the terror of the Lord, we persuade men; but we are made manifest unto God; and I trust also are made manifest in your consciences." The only other times that the term "hell" is employed in the epistles are James 3:6 and II Peter 2:4. The James reference is not really used in the sense of warning non-believers of the danger that it imminently theirs, but II Peter does make reference to hell and points to the certain end of the unrighteous who are kept "under punishment for the day of judgment" (II Pet 2:9) (NASB). Nevertheless, taking into consideration the broader question of justice and Divine judgment, there can be no doubt that in Pauline thought the concept of judgment is a powerful motivator in evangelism and missions (see Rom 2:5,8,9). The author to the Hebrews speaks (Hebrews 10:31) that "It is a fearful thing to fall into the hands of the living God" (NIV).

3. QUOTES FROM EDWARDS

In responding to the critics of the revival who accused ministers of using scare tactics, Edwards reasoned: "To say anything to those who have never believed in the Lord Jesus Christ, to represent their case any otherwise than exceeding terrible, is not to preach the Word of God to 'em; for the Word of God reveals nothing but truth; but this is to delude them. *Why should we be afraid to let persons that are in an infinitely miserable condition, know the truth, or bring 'em into the light, for fear it should terrify them? 'Tis light that must convert them, if ever they are converted. The more we bring sinners into the light, while they are miserable, and the light is terrible to them, the more likely it is that by*

---

6. Gerstner, *Edwards on Heaven and Hell,* 53.
7. Minatory means "in a threatening manner."

and by the light will be joyful to them. The ease, peace and comfort, that natural men enjoy, have their foundation in darkness and blindness; therefore as that darkness vanishes, and light comes in, their peace vanishes and they are terrified: but that is no good argument why we should endeavor to hold their darkness, that we may uphold their comfort" [Emphasis mine] (Jonathan Edwards).[8]

Regarding the issue of balancing law and Gospel, or hell and heaven, Edwards was careful to note: "Not that I think that the law only should be preached: ministers may preach other things too little. The Gospel is to be preached as well as the law, and the law is to be preached only to make way for the Gospel, and in order to an effectual preaching of that; for the main work of ministers of the Gospel is to preach the Gospel: it is the end of the law; Christ is the end of the law for righteousness [Romans 10:4]. So that a minister would miss it very much if he should insist so much on the terrors of the law, as to forget his end, and neglect to preach the Gospel; but yet the law is very much to be insisted on, and the preaching of the Gospel is like to be in vain without it" (Jonathan Edwards).[9]

Regarding the nature of hell itself, Edwards states: "As God's favour is infinitely desirable so 'tis a part of his infinite awful majesty that his displeasure is infinitely dreadful which it would not be if it were contrary to the perfection of his nature to punish eternally. If God's majesty were not infinite and his displeasure were not infinitely dreadful he would be less glorious" (Edwards).[10]

What evidence is there connecting revival to hell-fire preaching? Edwards himself, in his famous "Faithful Narrative" clearly identifies those kinds of messages that were most instrumental in bringing revival. He states: "I think I have found that no discourses have been more remarkably blessed, than those in which the doctrine of God's absolute sovereignty about the salvation of sinners, and his just liberty with regard to answering the prayers, *or succeeding the pains of natural men*, continuing such, have been insisted on. I never found so much immediate saving fruit, in any measure, of any discourses I have offered to my congregation, as some from those words, Romans 3:19, "That every mouth may be stopped"; endeavoring to show from thence that *it would be just with God forever to reject and cast off mere natural men*" [Emphasis mine] (Jonathan Edwards).[11] There can be no doubt that when Edwards refers to "the pains of natural men" and "forever to reject and cast off mere natural men" he is referring to eternal condemnation in

---

8. Edwards, *Works*, 4: 391.
9. Edwards, *Works*, 4: 247.
10. Gerstner, *Edwards on Heaven and Hell*, 79.
11. Gerstner, *Edwards on Heaven and Hell*, 168.

hell. That emphasis, states Edwards, is what led to the revival. As Edwards expresses it, a person ". . . must be shown the danger of his present condition and the impending doom that is hanging over his head."[12]

4. QUOTES BY EDWARDSEAN SCHOLARS

According to Edwardsean scholar at Yale, Stout, "Satan's kingdom was hell, a place without goodness or God; a physicality of pain and suffering where flames licked at sinners with relentless ferocity. Where many medieval writers favored images of hell that played on infinite darkness, Edwards preferred images of furnaces and fire. In a "Miscellanies" entry he wrote, "Hell is represented by fire and brimstone. . . . Lightning is a stream of brimstone; and if that stream of brimstone which we are told kindles hell be as hot as streams of lightning, it will be vehement beyond conception" (Jonathan Edwards).[13] What made this infinite stream of fire even more agonizing was the fact that God permitted the damned to view the alternative paradise of the saints in heaven, and vice versa. And, like Calvin's, Edwards's God allowed no second chance after death. Hell was eternal and irreversible. With relentless logic Edwards insisted that because God hates sin "it is suitable that he should execute an infinite punishment" (Jonathan Edwards).

Possibly no other Edwardsean scholar has investigated the theme of Edwards's hellfire preaching more than Gerstner (see bibliography). It is instructive to notice the frequency with which Edwards preaches on hell. Gerstner, in his excellent concise work entitled "Jonathan Edwards on Heaven and Hell" suggests that "Edwards's distribution of sermons. . .may not run three to one in favour of minatory [expressing, uttering, or conveying a threat] to comforting themes (as the Bible itself seems to do), but it certainly favours such an emphasis. As a rough sample check we found that, among the 140 sermons on Matthew, 13 are devoted explicitly to heaven, 23 to hell. Of the 43 Mark sermons there were 7 on heaven and 4 on hell. Luke had 10 on heaven and 13 on hell. It is to be remembered furthermore that Edwards does not use texts as pretexts or even as mere points of departure for a topical development. He almost always begins with a contextual introduction and then proceeds to expound the meaning of his text, which he then states in the form of a "doctrine." So, when Edwards devotes these sermons to hell, he believes that the texts deal with that subject and this it is incumbent on his as a steward of the mysteries of God to do the same."[14]

12. Gerstner, *Edwards on Heaven and Hell*, 52.
13. Edwards, *Works*, 13: 376.
14. Gerstner, *Edwards on Heaven and Hell*, 52–53.

Frequency of the word "hell" in Edwards's sermons
(Includes Editorial and Introductory Comments/Just Edwards)

PERIOD OF TIME	"HEAVEN"	"HELL"
WJE, Volume #10 Sermons and Discourses 1720–23	250/189	120/80
WJE, Volume #14 Sermons and Discourses 1723–29	217/206	185/166
WJE, Volume #17 Sermons and Discourses 1730–33	227/216	62/55
WJE, Volume #19 Sermons and Discourses 1734–38	319/303	98/94
WJE, Volume #22 Sermons and Discourses 1739–42	259/155	210/99
WJE, Volume #25 Sermons and Discourses 1743–58	319/287	74/63
TOTALS	1591/1356	749/557

Of course, it is a bit misleading to determine emphasis based exclusively on usage of terminology. There are other significant factors, such as the development of the theology of justice, punishment, and condemnation. Nevertheless, the component of "hell-fire" or "terror" preaching, and the frequency of those terms, is a significant aspect of the revival preaching of Edwards.

5. ILLUSTRATIONS FROM THE ACTUAL SERMONS OF EDWARDS

Here are a few of the more compelling quotes to substantiate that Edwards was indeed a hell-fire preacher.

"O sinner! Consider the fearful danger you are in: 'tis a great *furnace of wrath*, a wide and *bottomless pit*, full of the *fire of wrath*, that you are held over in the hand of that God, whose wrath is provoked and incensed as much against you as against many of the damned in hell; *you hang by a slender thread, with the flames of divine wrath flashing about it,* and ready *every moment to singe it,* and burn it asunder; and you have no interest in any mediator, *and nothing to lay hold of to save yourself, nothing to keep off the flames of wrath, nothing of your own, nothing that you ever have done, nothing that you can do, to induce God to spare you one moment*" (Jonathan Edwards) (Sermon: Sinners in the Hands of an Angry God)[15].

"God may set up your souls as flaming monuments of his displeasure, and severity, in hell forever" (Jonathan Edwards).[16]

---

15. Edwards, *Works*, 22: 412.
16. Edwards, *Works*, 10: 173.

"There is nothing that keeps wicked men at any one moment out of hell, but the mere pleasure of God" (Jonathan Edwards).[17]

"It is an awful thing to think of that there are now some persons in this very congregation, here and there, in one seat and another that will be the subjects of that very misery that we have now heard of as dreadful as it is though it be so intolerable and though it be eternal" (Jonathan Edwards).[18]

6. 70 RESOLUTIONS

The first reference to "hell" in the Resolutions is #10: "Resolved, when I feel pain, to think of the pains of martyrdom, and of hell." This points to the consciousness that Edwards had on the reality and pain of hell and implies his determination to cultivate a consciousness and sensitivity to this reality so that it would infiltrate and permeate his preaching and writing, indeed his whole ministry. We can see that this did in fact happen, by the strong emphasis that Edwards gives to the theme in his sermons.

The second reference to "hell" in the Resolutions is found in Resolution # 55: "Resolved, to endeavor to my utmost to act as I can think I should do, if I had already seen the happiness of heaven, and hell torments." *July 8, 1723.*We can infer from this resolution that part of Edwards's motivation on preaching on hell was his desire to be faithful to this resolution; undoubtedly, he believed that by preaching on hell, he was acting "as I can think I should" in the light of seeing "hell torments." This is especially true when we consider from the rest of Edwards's writing his firm and solid belief in the place of hell.

7. OTHER AUTHORS

Is there clear and compelling evidence that other preachers believe or believed in the importance of hellfire preaching to revival and awakening? Perhaps Houdmann has the best summary when he affirms, "Is there a place for hellfire preaching today? Not only is there a place for teaching about the fires of hell and the only way to escape them, but true preaching of the gospel of Christ is not complete without it. If today's pastors and preachers are to be consistent with the Scriptures, preaching and warning their flocks about the fires of hell must be part of their message" (Houdmann). "When thou diest, thy soul will be tormented alone; that will be a hell for it, but at the day of judgment thy body will join thy soul, and then thou wilt have twin hells, thy soul sweating drops

---

17. Edwards, *Works*, 10: 208.
18. Gerstner, *Edwards on Heaven and Hell*, 52.

of blood, and thy body suffused with agony. In fire exactly like that which we have on earth thy body will lie, asbestos-like, forever unconsumed, all thy veins roads for the feet of pain to travel on, every nerve a string on which the devil shall forever play his diabolical tune of 'Hell's Unutterable Lament' (Charles Spurgeon)." The late Bishop J.C. Ryle, who died in 1900, said: "If you would promote faith, defeat the devil and save souls, preach Hell!"

8. CONCLUSION

Just how much should hell-fire preaching form a part of our preaching today? We must take our cues from Scripture, not church history. I would say that while hell is clearly taught in the Scripture, the practice of "hell-fire" preaching in the Scripture is limited. Certainly, within our duty to preach "the whole counsel of God" (Acts 20:27) we are under orders to set forth the solemn truth of hell, along with the hopeful truths of grace and deliverance through Christ. But we must not preach hell with a vindictive spirit. I leave you with a quote referring to how two leaders felt about hell: "An evangelist tells the story of visiting Francis and Edith Schaeffer in their Switzerland home in L'Abri. After dinner one night the conversation ranged over several profound theological subjects, and suddenly someone asked Dr Schaeffer: 'What will happen to those who have never heard of Christ?'. Everyone around the dinner table was waiting for some great theological answer, a weighty intellectual response—and none came. Instead, he bowed his head and wept . . . R. Dale once said of D.L. Moody that 'he had the right to preach about hell, because he so clearly did so from a weeping heart'. Do we have weeping hearts when we attempt to speak to others about their need of Christ?" (David Legge).[19]

"But Edwards the preacher was about far more than fire and brimstone. Yes, hell was a real place in Edwards's mind, and therefore worthy of continual warning to avoid it at all costs. But this was emphatically not the subject that preoccupied his thoughts and visions. "Heaven" and "love" were the two most important words in Edwards's sermons, and he struggled weekly to bring those realities into the consciousness of his hearers. Edwards was far more concerned that his congregation come to a saving knowledge of God through an awareness of the beauty of God's great and powerful redemptive love for them. Even a cursory scan of the titles of Edwards's sermons will make this point forcefully."[20, 21]

19. Legge, *Preach the Word*.
20. Edwards, *Works*, 14: 412.
21. Bibliographic Recommendation: Chan, *Erasing Hell*, Colorado Springs: David Cook, 2011.

Chapter 4

The Role of the Word in Edwards's Revivalistic and Awakening Preaching

The unfolding of Your words gives light;
It gives understanding to the simple
Psalm 119:130 (NASV).

The Lord's voice unleashes fiery flames.
Psalm 29:7 (CEB).

"Let us labour in a very particular, convincing and awakening manner to dispense the Word of God; so to speak as tends most to reach and pierce the hearts and consciences, and humble the souls of them that hear us" (Jonathan Edwards).[1]

Regarding the Word of God Edwards writes, "Be assiduous in reading the Holy Scriptures. This is the fountain whence all knowledge in divinity must be derived. Therefore, let not this treasure lie by you neglected" (Jonathan Edwards).[2] "God's minister's chief work is to mill the precious kernels of biblical truths,

---

1. Edwards, *Works*, 10: 15.
2. Edwards, *Works*, 2: 54.

removing them from the obscure husks or 'veils' of their historic, cultural matrix. The preacher in this way makes God's truths palatable and nourishing for the salvation of the souls in his keeping."[3]

"My method of study, from my first beginning the work of the ministry, has been very much by writing; applying myself, in this way, to prove every important hint; pursuing the clue to my utmost, when anything in reading. . .."[4]

INTRODUCTORY COMMENTS: GOD'S WORD is absolutely foundational to revival. The Psalmist David wrote: "Your *word* has *revived* me" (Ps 119:50) (NASB). The Psalmist appealed "*Revive* me according to Your *word* (NASB), and again "I am exceedingly afflicted; *Revive* me, O Lord, according to Your *word*" (Ps 119:107) (NASB). Sustained revival and awakening will always be rooted in the Word. What role does the preaching of the Word have in revival and awakening? What can Edwards teach us about this dynamic?

Revival Preaching is Word-Based preaching. But this raises a question. Why is so much orthodox preaching ineffective? Word-based preaching is not synonymous with revival preaching. After the best sermon ever preached, it was said "28 When Jesus had finished saying these things, the crowds were amazed at his teaching, 29 because he taught as one who had authority, and not as their teachers of the law" (Matt 7:28, 29) (NIV). The scribes and Jesus were both Word-based preachers, but Jesus' preaching was with authority. Prior to the Great Awakening, there was a lot of orthodox preaching, but there was no revival. Edwards preached the Word, but there was a spiritual authority with it that effected revival. Today as well there is a plethora of "orthodox" preaching, but we pine for revival and awakening. What makes Word-based preaching authoritative? What happens to transform Word-based preaching into Revival Preaching? This chapter will endeavor to answer these questions.

1. DEFINE IT

The preaching of the Word means the proclamation of the very Word of God, whether that be in expository fashion or more thematic. Expository preaching is defined by Haddon Robinson, contemporary king of expository preaching and homiletics, as "the communication of a biblical concept, derived from and transmitted through a historical, grammatical, and

---

3. Westra, *The Minister's Task*, 25–26.
4. Westra, *The Minister's Task*, 59.

literary study of a passage in its context, which the Holy Spirit first applies to the personality and the experience of the preacher, then through the preacher applies to the hearer"[5] (Robinson / Larson: 58). *Expository preaching* in a technical sense "requires that it expound Scripture by deriving from a specific text main points and sub-points that disclose the thought of the author, cover the scope of the passage, and are applied to the lives of the listeners."[6] Revival and awakening are seen as a by-product of the Spirit of God taking the Word of God passed through the prism of the personality of the man/woman of God who proclaims the truth of God. The Word and the Spirit work together in revival preaching.

2. BIBLICAL PERSPECTIVE

Are there clear biblical examples of revival connected to the preaching of the Word of God? Absolutely. Is there clear biblical teaching correlating revival to the preaching of the Word? Again, absolutely.

We know that Scripture clearly establishes a relationship between conversion and the Word. "Of his own will he brought us forth *by the word of truth*" (Jas 1:18) (NKJV) [Emphasis mine]. "For since in the wisdom of God the world through its wisdom did not know him, God was pleased *through the foolishness of what was preached to save those who believe*" (I Cor 1:21). It is not through foolish preaching that we are saved, but rather through the foolishness of preaching. There is abundance biblical evidence that connects the instrumentality of the Word with regeneration and quickening. Psalm 19 reminds us: "7 The law of the Lord is perfect, *converting* the soul: the testimony of the Lord is sure, making wise the simple.8 The statutes of the Lord are right, *rejoicing the heart*: the commandment of the Lord is pure, enlightening the eyes." (Ps 19:7, 8) (KJV) [Emphasis mine]. Both the conversion of the soul (awakening) and the revitalization and rejoicing of the heart (revival) are brought about by the Spirit of God utilizing the Word of God. When Jesus said, "It is the spirit that *quickeneth*; the flesh profiteth nothing: the *words* that I speak unto you, they are spirit, and they are life" (KJV) (John 6:63), he clearly established the efficacy of the Word by the Spirit.

Psalm 119, which exalts and eulogizes the Bible, shows repeatedly the instrumentality of the Word in quickening the spiritual life (verses 25, 37, 40, 50, 88, 93, 107, 149, 154, and 156). Consider the power of these phrases, all but two of them prayers for revival, and all of them, as every verse in Psalm 119, related to and specifically mentioning some synonym for the

---

5. Robinson, *Art and Craft*, 58.
6. Johnson, *The Glory of Preaching*, 57.

Bible. There is no more compelling "proof text" to clearly establish the relationship between the instrumentality of the Word and revival. (All the texts below are from the NASV, and they all translate the Hebrew with the word "revive." The KJV uses the word "quickening.")

- Turn away my eyes from looking at vanity, And *revive* me in Your ways (Ps 119:37)
- Behold, I long for Your precepts; *Revive* me through Your righteousness (Ps 119:40).
- This is my comfort in my affliction, That Your word has *revived* me (Ps 119:50).
- *Revive* me according to Your loving-kindness, So that I may keep the testimony of Your mouth (Ps 119:88).
- I will never forget Your precepts, For by them You have *revived* me (Ps 119:88).
- I am exceedingly afflicted; *Revive* me, O Lord, according to Your word (Ps 119:107).
- Hear my voice according to Your loving-kindness; *Revive* me, O Lord, according to Your ordinances (Ps 119:149).
- Plead my cause and redeem me; *Revive* me according to Your word (Ps 119:154).
- Great are Your mercies, O Lord; Revive me according to Your ordinances (Ps 119:156).
- Consider how I love Your precepts; *Revive* me, O Lord, according to Your loving-kindness (Ps 119:159).

Several of the biblical accounts of revival particularly emphasize the role of Spirit-anointed preaching of the Word. Autrey believes that there was a revival under the spiritual leadership of Moses (Exod 32:1–35 and 33:1–23) that he traces to *Moses' preaching of the law*. Autrey traces the revival under Samuel (I Sam 7:1–17) to his *direct preaching* (7:3); the awakening at Nineveh was due to *the preaching ministry of God's reluctant prophet: Jonah*. There was a remarkable revival under King Asa (II Chr 15) by the confrontational preaching instrumentality of Azariah (II Chronicles 15:2). *The revival led by King Hezekiah* (II Chr 29:1–36; 30:1–27; and 31:1–12) was supported and reinforced by prophets like Isaiah and Micah. Autrey affirms that the revival "was no doubt greatly enhanced by great preaching. . ."[7]. Perhaps the

---

7. Autrey, *Revivals in the Old Testament*, 113.

clearest example linking the reading and preaching of the Word to revival is the biblical account of revival during King Josiah's reign, where the Word of the Lord was discovered (II Kgs 22:8), read (II Kgs 22:10), and produced an immediate effect in the heart of the king (II Kgs 22:11). Under the preaching and tutelage of Huldah the prophetess, (II Kgs 22:14–20), the king implemented a major reformation (II Kgs 23). The best succinct summary of that revival highlights the role of the word: "There was no king like him before or after [Josiah], who turned to the Lord with all his heart and all his soul and all his might, *according to all the law of Moses*" [Emphasis mine] (II Kgs 23:25). This revival under Josiah (II Chr 34:1–33; 35:1–19) was in part due *to the prophetic preaching of a prophetess*, Huldah (II Chr 34:22–28).

3. QUOTES FROM EDWARDS

"You all have by you a large treasure of divine knowledge, in that you have the Bible in your hands; therefore, be not contented in possessing but little of this treasure. God hath spoken much to you in the Scriptures; labour to understand as much of what he saith as you can. God hath made you all reasonable creatures; therefore, let not the noble faculty of reason or understanding lie neglected. Content not yourselves with having so much knowledge as is thrown in your way, and received in some sense unavoidably by the frequent inculcation of divine truth in the preaching of the word, of which you are obliged to be hearers, or accidentally gain in conversation; but let it be very much your business to search for it, and that with the same diligence and labour with which men are wont to dig in mines of silver and gold" (Jonathan Edwards).[8]

"His [the preacher's] fervent zeal, which has its foundation and spring in that holy and powerful flame of love to God and man, that is in his heart, appears in the fervency of his prayers to God, for and with his people; and in *the earnestness, and power with which he preaches the word of God*, declares to sinners their misery, and warns them to fly from the wrath to come, and reproves, and testifies against all ungodliness; . . . " (Jonathan Edwards in his famous Ordination Sermon "The True Excellency of a Minister of the Gospel").[9]

What does Edwards say about revival preaching and the role of the Word? We know from the general survey we made of Edwards's background as a Reformed Puritan just how important the proclamation and explanation of the Scriptures was to him (See Introductory Chapter E dedicated to

---

8. Edwards, *Works*, 2: 54.
9. Edwards, *Works*, 25: 92.

Edwards's View on Preaching). We know from his ordination sermon "The True Excellency of a Minister of the Gospel" that Edwards placed a high emphasis on the Word: "He must be one that is *able to teach*, not one that is raw, ignorant or unlearned, and but little versed in the things that he is to teach others; not a novice, or one that is unskillful in the word of righteousness; he must be one that is well studied in divinity, well acquainted with the written Word of God, mighty in the Scriptures, and able to instruct and convince gainsayers (Jonathan Edwards).[10]

In instructing the congregation at the ordination ceremony of a minister, Edwards states: "And particularly when your minister shows himself to be a burning light by burning with a proper zeal against any wickedness that may be breaking out amongst his people and manifests it by *bearing a proper testimony against it in the preaching of the word*"[11] (Jonathan Edwards). Edwards believed the minister needed to confront wickedness by preaching against it with the Word. He exemplified this counsel with his approach to encroaching Arminianism, and this proved to be instrumental in the unleashing of revival fire.[12]

Obviously, for the minister to be an expository preacher, he must dedicate time to the study of the Scripture. Edwards, in his famous ordination sermon, addressed the importance of the study of God's Word: "And particularly, *ministers should be very conversant with the Holy Scriptures*; making it very *much their business*, with the utmost *diligence and strictness, to search those holy writings*. For they are as it were the beams of the light of the Sun of Righteousness; they are the light by which ministers must be enlightened and the light they are to hold forth to their hearers; and they are the fire whence their hearts and the hearts of their hearers must be enkindled. *They should earnestly seek after much of the spiritual knowledge of Christ*, and that they may live in the clear views of his glory. For by this means they will be changed into the image of the same glory and brightness, and will come to their people, as Moses came down to the congregation of Israel, after he had seen God's backparts in the mount, with his face shining.

10. Edwards, *Works*, 25: 92–93.

11. Edwards, *Works*, 25: 101.

12. Edwards himself affirmed: "I think I have found that no discourses have been more remarkably blessed, than those in which *the doctrine* of God's absolute sovereignty with regard to the salvation of sinners, and his just liberty with regard to answering the prayers, or succeeding the pains of natural men, continuing such, have been insisted on. I never found so much immediate saving fruit, in any measure, of any discourses I have offered to my congregation, as some from *those words*, Romans 3:19, "That every mouth may be stopped";" (Jonathan Edwards) (Goen, *Works* Vol. 4, 168). The timely and confrontational exposition of the Word was instrumental in the inception of the Great Awakening.

If the light of Christ's glory shines upon them, it will be the way for them to shine with the same kind of light on their hearers, and to reflect the same beams, which have heat, as well as brightness" (Jonathan Edwards) (from the Sermon "The True Excellency of a Minister of The Gospel").[13]

Edwards was a wonderful model and example of this counsel. We know that he spent an average of 13 hours every day in his study. Here is a sampling of his experiential knowledge of the Scriptures: "I had then, and at other times, the greatest delight in the Holy Scriptures, of any book whatsoever. Oftentimes in reading it, every word seemed to touch my heart. I felt a harmony between something in my heart, and those sweet and powerful words. I seemed to see so much light exhibited in every sentence, and such a refreshing ravishing food communicated that I could not get along in reading. Used oftentimes to dwell long on one sentence, to see wonder contained in it; and yet almost every sentence seemed to be full of wonders" (Jonathan Edwards)[14]. The Bible states that "A good man out of the good treasure of his heart brings forth good; and an evil man out of the evil treasure of his heart brings forth evil. For out of the *abundance of the heart* his mouth speaks (Luke 6:45) (KJV). Revival started in the heart of Edwards as he had a personal encounter with God in the Word, as this quote demonstrates. Then he preached from a blazing heart. Edwards preached "out of the abundance of the heart." As the Psalmist puts it: "My heart was hot within me, While *I was musing* the fire burned; *Then* I spoke with my tongue" (Ps 39:3) (NASB). Personal musing and meditation on the Word, resulting in a flaming engagement with the Living Word, must precede preaching if it is to become revival preaching instead of just orthodox preaching. As Carrick rightly observes: " . . . this feeling of passion, which belongs to the essence of true preaching, is inextricably related to the spirituality or piety of the preacher's heart."[15]

4. QUOTES BY EDWARDSEAN SCHOLARS

Samuel Hopkins, Edwards's first biographer, states that Edwards managed to study the Bible "more than all other books."[16] According to Hopkins, "Edwards's significance as a religious thinker was to be measured in great part by his interpretive acumen.[17] According to Hopkins, Edwards "cast

---

13. Edwards, *Works*, 25: 100.
14. Edwards, *Works*, 16: 797.
15. Carrick, *Preaching of Edwards*, 54.
16. Brown, *Edwards and the Bible*, 4.
17. Brown, *Edwards and the Bible*, 4.

much light on many parts of the Bible, which has escaped other interpreters. And by which his great and painful attention to the Bible, and making it the only rule of his faith, are manifest."[18]

"By God's Word the world exists and continues."[19] " . . . the words of the minister, as he is God's instrument and voice, are powerfully active, and as such demand notice and response."[20] Faithful preaching is never inconsequential or ineffective; it is a power, for good or for ill, to those that hear it. Just as Edwards believed in the continuous creation by the immediate agency of God through His creative Word, so God is continuously creating spiritual life through the mediation of His living and powerful Word (Heb 11:3; Heb 1:3).

In his approach to the Scriptures, Edwards was indebted to John Locke. Brown affirms: "Locke in fact proved to be a helpful resource to Edwards in his own thinking about the Bible. One finds, for example, that he often cites Locke's commentary on the New Testament epistles regarding the historical-grammatical meaning of words and phrases in his Scripture notes. Edwards's epistemological *critique of natural religion* also bears striking parallels with that found in Locke's "Reasonableness of Christianity," a work he owned and used constructively."[21] Edwards's understanding of the Word was enriched by his study of other scholars, not just studying what they said about certain texts, but by studying what they said about approaching the text in general.

With other Puritans Edwards believed that "as God's collaborator, actively speaking with the authority of a divine officer," the minister's word "even in imprecatory sermons—breathes with the same performative force that God's glorious word breathes . . . ".[22] This is highly significant. When the Spirit speaks through the speaker, what God says is what the preacher says, with that same creative and performative (enabling, enacting) force.

Edwards had a remarkable gift in blending reason and Scripture together. Reason was always subject to revelation. He believed in a ministerial versus magisterial role of reason—reason is meant to serve hermeneutics, not lord it over the Scriptures. When we consult Edwards's sermon on a "Divine and Supernatural Light immediately imparted to the soul by the Spirit of God" (Sermon Title) we find a marvelous blend of Scripture and Reason, of biblical reference and reference to Locke, which fits with the

18. Brown, *Edwards and the Bible*, 4.
19. Westra, *Minister's Task*, 7.
20. Westra, *Minister's Task*, 7.
21. Brown, *Edwards and the Bible*, 82.
22. Geschiere, *Taste and See*, 50.

title which continues "shown to be both a *Scriptural* and a *Rational* Doctrine." The interrelationship between Scripture (always first) and reason as complementary and not contradictory is one of the hallmarks of Edwards's sermons, and for that complementarity we see Locke's influence.

"The preacher of the Gospel must be a truly converted and deeply pious man—all other attainments are useless without these qualities. *He must preach the Word, the whole Word, nothing but the Word—warm, pure, and holy.* He must preach constantly, always seizing favourable opportunities as they present themselves; if no favourable times and seasons appear on the horizon, the preacher must make the most of the unfavourable ones. He must preach plainly and simply, so that hearers, regardless of their intellectual levels, may understand. He must preach practical sermons, not cold, dry soul-starving discourses on the one hand, or mere ranting declamations on the other hand, but the solid trusts of the Bible, presented in a practical manner. He must preach faithfully, keeping back no part of the Gospel because of fear, favor, or regard for the opinions of influential persons. These were some of the major means employed by the leaders of the Great Awakening to make Christ known to the American colonists."[23]

5. ILLUSTRATIONS FROM THE ACTUAL SERMONS OF EDWARDS

It is obvious from even a superficial study of Edwards's sermons that the place of the text was preeminent. Every sermon started with a text, and in typical Puritan fashion, Edwards proceeded to expound on the meaning of that text, extracting doctrine from it, and then applying it to the listener.[24]

23. Conrad, *Importance of Preaching*, 118.

24. Did Edwards really practice expository preaching? If not, how to square that fact with the call for expository preaching today? First, was Edwards an expository preacher? That is debatable, depending upon your definition and understanding of "expository preaching," and depending upon your interpretation of Edwards's sermons. Edwards always started with a text, and in true Puritan style endeavored to explore the meaning of the text within the immediate context, and then from there to proceed to the doctrine derived from the text. In that sense, Edwards was an expository preacher. Kimnach, the world's leading authority on Edwards as a preacher, affirms: " . . . the main literary emphasis was upon instruction through clear, systematic exposition" (Jonathan Edwards) (Kimnach, *Works* Vol. 10, 104).

However, if we understand expository preacher to include the verse-by-verse development of biblical thought, allowing the passage itself, and not merely the "stand alone" key verse, to be the message, then I would humbly suggest that Edwards was not an expository preacher. Sometimes expository preaching exalts the text without having a corresponding dependence upon the Spirit, resulting in dead orthodoxy, a kind of Bibliolatry. Edwards's strength in preaching was his blend of both the Word and the Spirit.

It is also remarkable how many texts of Scripture comprise his sermons. Entire verses and passages are quoted at length and frequently, reinforcing the view that it is God's Word, and not our exposition of that Word, which is life-transforming.

Edwards once preached the following: "2. What means do you expect to be awakened by? As to the awakening awful things of the Word of God, those you have had set before you times without number, in the most moving manner that the dispensers of the Word have been capable of" (Jonathan Edwards).[25]

6. 70 RESOLUTIONS

11. "Resolved, when I think of any theorem in divinity to be solved, immediately to do what I can towards solving it, if circumstances do not hinder." Edwards' world was primarily theological. He brought his academic rigor and biblical awareness to everything, and this greatly enhanced his understanding of the Word and truth in general.

28. "Resolved, to study the Scriptures so steadily, constantly and frequently, as that I may find, and plainly perceive myself to grow in the knowledge of the same." Revival was born in the heart of Edwards. He studied the Scriptures, gaining both a notional and an experiential knowledge of the same, and ministered the Word out of that richness. Hopkins claimed: "He commonly spent thirteen hours, every day, in his study." One can trace the evolution of his thought from his miscellanies to his sermons to his discourses. If ever anyone grew in the knowledge of Scripture, it was Edwards. We must qualify that knowledge for Edwards means more than intellectual knowledge. It includes that, and then proceeds to a fuller emotional and experiential knowledge of the Word. This growth in knowledge of the Word made Edwards uniquely qualified to preach with authority.

7. OTHER AUTHORS

Edwards was deeply influenced by the Reformed adage of "Sola Scriptura."[26]

---

25. Lesser, *Works*, 19: 299.

26. Foord, *Sola Scriptura*. Meaning of "Sola Scriptura." *Sola scriptura* (Latin ablative, "by scripture alone") can be described / defined as "Firstly, *sola scriptura* meant Scripture was the supreme authority over the church. It did not mean Scripture was the only authority. Luther, Calvin, and the other reformers used other authorities like reason and tradition. They developed arguments using logic (reason) and learned from the writings of past Christians (tradition) as they explored the Bible. Yet the Bible was

What role does the Bible play in revival? Especially revival preaching? Keevil has made an extensive study on the history of preaching in revival, which he documents in his masterful book: *Preaching in Revival: Preaching and a Theology of Awakening*. In regard to the centrality of the Word in preaching, here are his conclusions: "There are certain characteristics which emerge from the study of sermons preached during seasons of revival. The sermon that brings revival will usually be pointed. It will be clear and transparent. It will ordinarily be delivered with intensity and passion."[27] "Revival preaching is associated with that anointing of the Holy Spirit without which all passion and intensity is merely feigned religious sentiment. Language carries its own intensity and its own power."[28] "Revival preaching will be *orthodox*. It will proclaim and defend the truth. *It will be exposition of the Word*. Illustrations will illustrate and not detract from the truth proclaimed. It will be filled with power. Revival preaching will be bathed in prayer. Prayer is the energy of true effectual preaching, and without it the sermon is nothing more than words spoken into the air. Prayer is essential for both preacher and people. When both are prepared through prayer, an atmosphere is created conducive to expectations of blessing. *The reformed synthesis of Word and Spirit means that without the Spirit, the Word is a dead letter.*"[29]

8. CONCLUSION

At the outset of this chapter, I asked what the difference is between orthodox preaching and effective and authoritative Word-based revival preaching. In summary I would say that the preacher's personal engagement with and obedience to the Word, combined with the Spirit's anointing upon the prayerful preacher and God's Word are those elements which convert orthodoxy into effective revival preaching.

---

the supreme authority that ruled reason and tradition because Scripture alone was infallible precisely because it is God's word. All other authorities (including church leadership) were fallible and must submit to Scripture."

27. Keevil, *Preaching in Revival*, 163.
28. Keevil, *Preaching in Revival*, 164.
29. Keevil, *Preaching in Revival*, 163–64.

Chapter 5

The Role of the Holy Spirit in Revival Preaching

The Holy Spirit is "...the preacher's privilege" (Jonathan Edwards).[1]

Our message needs to be both Spirit born and Spirit borne.
'I have, many times, had a sense of the glory of the Third Person in the Trinity, and his office as Sanctifier; in his holy operations, communicating divine light and life to the soul. God in the communications of his Holy Spirit, has appeared as an infinite fountain of divine glory and sweetness; being full, and sufficient to fill and satisfy the soul; pouring forth itself in secret communications; like the sun in its glory, sweetly and pleasantly diffusing light and life. And I have sometimes an affecting sense of the excellency of the word of God as a word of life; as the light of life; a Sweet, excellent, life-giving word; accompanied with a thirsting after that word, that it might dwell richly in my heart' (Jonathan Edwards).[2]

"I desire your fervent prayers for us may yet be continued, that God would

---

1. Edwards, *Works*, 4: 438.
2. Edwards, *Works*, 16: 801.

not be to us as a wayfaring man, that turns aside to tarry but a night, but that he would more and more pour out his Spirit upon us, and no more depart from us; and for me in particular, that I may be filled with His Spirit, and may become fervent, as a flame of fire in my work, and may be abundantly succeeded, and that it would please God, however unworthy I am, to improve me as an instrument of his glory, and advancing the kingdom of God" (Jonathan Edwards).[34] Written December 14, 1740. (Just after Whitefield was there in Northampton and preached under the anointing).

INTRODUCTORY COMMENTS

We turn our attention to another significant element in Edwards: The Holy Spirit's Role in Revival Preaching. There can be no doubt about it: The Holy Spirit is the "open secret" to revival. The Holy Spirit lives in perpetual revival Himself, within the Triune Godhead, enjoying unabated perpetual harmony and vibrancy. The Holy Spirit is the author of life. The Spirit moved over the surface of the deep (Gen 1:2) and together with the Word (Gen 1:3, 6, 9, 14, 20, 24, 26) brought about the created order. We see this Spirit/Word dynamic throughout the Scriptures (Ezek 37; Acts 2; etc.). God's Spirit breathed into Adam and caused him to become a living being. The Psalmist David cries out for personal revival (Ps 51) and focuses particularly upon the Spirit of God and his personal revival (51:10–12) and subsequent influence in the awakening of the lost (Ps 51:13). The Holy Spirit convicts both the believer and the lost (John 16:8–10) and conviction of sin is the quintessential element of revival and awakening. The anointing and empowering of the preacher are frequently mentioned and highlighted as an essential precursor to revival and awakening (judges, prophets, preachers, etc.). Small wonder that Martyn Lloyd Jones states: "The essence of a revival is that the Holy Spirit comes down upon a number of people together, upon a whole church, upon a number of churches, districts, or perhaps a whole country. That is what is meant by revival. It is, if you like, a visitation of the Holy Spirit, or another term that has often been used is this—an outpouring of the Holy Spirit . . . " (Lloyd Jones).

---

3. Edwards, *Works*, 16: 87.
4. Haykin, *Edwards*, 41.

1. DEFINE IT

Definition of terms: When we refer to the role of the Holy Spirit in Revival Preaching, there are several terms that come to bear on the theme.

- a. The Holy Spirit: This is the third person of the Trinity, who according to Alliance doctrine we describe as follows. *"The Holy Spirit is a divine Person, sent to indwell, (John 14:16–17) guide, teach and empower the believer, and to convince the world of sin, of righteousness and of judgment (John 16:7–11; 1 Cor 2:10–12)"* (Statement of Faith Article #3).[5]

- b. The Fullness of the Spirit: The Alliance Canada Statement of Faith affirms: "It is the will of God that in union with Christ each believer should be sanctified thoroughly (1 Thess 5:23) thereby being separated from sin and the world and fully dedicated to God, receiving power for holy living and sacrificial and effective service toward the completion of Christ's commission (Acts 1:8). *This is accomplished through being filled with the Holy Spirit which is both a distinct event and progressive experience in the life of the believer* (Rom 12:12; Gal 5:16–25)."[6]

- c. Anointing: The anointing of the Spirit can be more easily described than defined. It is that Divine afflatus, that special "smear" (literally) of oil that symbolizes the Spirit's enabling and empowering. It has to do with unction. It is that "something special" that lifts ordinary into extraordinary, the natural into the supernatural. Various preachers have sought in vain to describe or define it.

John MacArthur states "I can't measure it. I cannot quantify it. I cannot feel it. I don't know what it is the Holy Spirit is doing; I don't know when He's doing it and when He's not. In fact, I've said this, but there are times when you feel . . . you know this, there's a great freedom when you preach and you feel like something's kind of carrying you along and you're better than you should be, right? And you just feel like it was cohesive and it came together and it worked . . . He illumines the Word in my mind, and empowers my passion."[7]

---

5. Alliance Canada, *Statement of Faith*.
6. Alliance Canada, *Statement of Faith*.
7. Heisler, *Spirit-Led Preaching*, 1.

Spurgeon states is this way: "One bright benison[8] which private prayer brings down upon the ministry is an indescribable and inimitable something, better understood than named; it is a dew from the Lord, a divine presence which you will recognize at once when I say it is 'an unction from the Holy One.' What is it? I wonder how long we might beat our brains before we could plainly put into words what is meant by *preaching with unction*; yet he who preaches knows its presence, and he who hears soon detects its absence; Samaria in famine, typifies a discourse without it; Jerusalem, with her feasts of fat things full of marrow, may represent a sermon enriched with it. Everyone one knows what the freshness ofc the morning is when orient pearls abound on every blade of grass, but who can describe it, much less produce it of itself? Such is the mystery of spiritual anointing; we know, but we cannot tell others what it is. It is as easy as it is foolish to counterfeit it, as some do who use expressions which are meant to betoken fervent love, but oftener indicate sickly sentimentalism or mere cant. "Dear Lord!" "Sweet Jesus!" "Precious Christ" are by them poured out wholesale, till one is nauseated, if not profane."[9]

Biblical Perspective

2. REVIVAL AND THE HOLY SPIRIT

It was when the fire of God (symbol of the Spirit) fell that the people of Israel were restored in their faith (I Kgs 18:38, 39).

It was when the Spirit of God anointed the judges that they were qualified and enabled to lead their people into spiritual renewal (Judg 3:10; 6:34; 11:29; 13:25; 14:6,19; 15:14).

God's Spirit and God's Word work together in revival. In Kaiser's treatment of revivals in the Old and New Testament[10], he selects the Revival under Jehoshaphat as an example of how God works in revival. It is important to note in that revival that the Spirit of God came upon Jahaziel (II Chr 20:14) and through him came a prophetic word for the people.

The essence of revival is illustrated in II Chronicles 34:19 when King Josiah responded in brokenness to the Word of God read. We read in Isaiah 57:15 "For this is what the high and exalted One says— he who lives forever,

---

8. Benison and its synonym "benediction" share more than a common meaning; the two words come from the same root, the Latin *benedicere,* meaning «to bless.» («Benedicere» comes from the Latin *bene dicere*—"to speak well of"—a combination of the Latin *bene,* meaning «well,» and «dicere," to say.) Of the two words, "benediction" is more common today, but "benison" has a longer history in English. https://www.merriam-webster.com/dictionary/benison.

9. Spurgeon, *Lectures*, 50.

10. Kaiser, *Revive Us Again.*

whose name is holy: 'I live in a high and holy place, but also with the one who is contrite and lowly in spirit, to revive the spirit of the lowly and to revive the heart of the contrite.'" The response of King Josiah to the Word, and God's Reviving work as described in Isaiah 57:15, are undoubtedly the work of the Holy Spirit.

The stirring of the spirit of man is undoubtedly the work of the Spirit of the Lord. And it is this initial stirring in the hearts of the leadership (first here—see reference below) and the people that prepares the way for revival. Haggai 1:14 (NIV) 14 So the Lord stirred up the spirit of Zerubbabel son of Shealtiel, governor of Judah, and the spirit of Joshua son of Jozadak, the high priest, and the spirit of the whole remnant of the people. They came and began to work on the house of the Lord Almighty, their God . . . "

The Book of Acts: Luke is careful to link the revitalization of the church, the expansion/growth of the church and the Holy Spirit. The Holy Spirit was promised (Acts 1:5); the empowering of the Spirit and the expansion of the church was linked (Acts 1:8); the Holy Spirit's initial outpouring and fullness in the life of the disciples resulted in a great revival of the believers and an awakening of the lost; Peter relates the unusual phenomenon of revival to the Spirit (Acts 2:17, 18, 33); the ongoing fullness enabled the apostles to be bold, which is a form of ongoing revitalization or revival, and He enabled them to preach the Gospel with subsequent awakening of the lost (Acts 4:8; 4:31); the evangelistic impetus and strategizing is primarily in the hands of the Spirit (Acts 8:29); the greatest evangelist (Paul) was filled with the Spirit, enabling him to minister with great effect (Acts 9:17,20); the expansion of the church is correlated to the comfort and strengthening of the Spirit (Acts 9:31); the expansion of the Gospel into the Gentile community (the house of Cornelius) was accompanied by the outpouring of the Spirit (Acts 10:44-47).

3. REVIVAL, PREACHING AND THE HOLY SPIRIT

The role of the Holy Spirit in revival preaching is absolutely paramount and indispensable. This point is the theme of Heisler's masterful book *Spirit-led Preaching* (see Bibliography). We need to remember what preaching is, what revival is, what the Scriptures are, and the role of the Holy Spirit in each, to realize how critical His role is in Revival Preaching. These references and comments reinforce this point:

  a. *Numbers 11:25* Then the Lord came down in the cloud and spoke with him, and he took some of the power of the Spirit that was on him and put it on the seventy elders. When the Spirit rested on them, they prophesied. . ." (NIV). The capability to "prophesy" effectively was dependent upon the Spirit's empowering and resting upon.

b. *Micah 3:8* On the other hand I am filled with power—With the Spirit of the Lord—And with justice and courage To make known to Jacob his rebellious act, Even to Israel his sin" (NASB). Revival Preaching includes an element of courageous confrontation, which can only effectively be accomplished in the power and enabling of the Spirit.

c. *Luke 4:16–18* 16 And He came to Nazareth, where He had been brought up; and as was His custom, He entered the synagogue on the Sabbath, and stood up to read. 17 And the book of the prophet Isaiah was handed to Him. And He opened the book and found the place where it was written, 18 *"The Spirit of the Lord is upon Me, Because He anointed Me to preach the gospel to the poor. He has sent Me to proclaim release to the captives, And recovery of sight to the blind. . ."* (NASB1995). This is a description of the preaching ministry of our Lord, a fulfillment of that Messianic prophecy found in Isaiah 61:1 "The Spirit of the Lord God is upon me, Because the Lord has anointed me to bring good news to the afflicted; . . ." (NASB1995). Jesus preached effectively by full reliance upon the Spirit of God. Heisler affirms "Our Lord's communion with the Holy Spirit was established before he took on his public ministry of teaching and preaching"[11]. Jesus commissioned us to go, to preach, in a definite fashion: He stated: Again Jesus said, "Peace be with you! As the Father has sent me, I am sending you" (John 20:21) (NIV). When we realize that we are commissioned to go, to preach in this same Spirit-anointed fashion, and follow through in obedience and full dependence upon the Spirit's anointing, our lives and ministries will be transformed. Jesus affirmed frequently that the effectiveness of his teaching and preaching rested upon the Spirit's enabling. John 6:63 affirms "The Spirit gives life; the flesh counts for nothing. The words I have spoken to you—they are full of the Spirit and life" (NIV). "Even the living Word used the written Word under the anointing of the Holy Spirit as an authentication of the authority and power of his preaching."[12] Can we do any less?

---

11. Heisler, *Spirit-Led Preaching*, 27.
12. Heisler, *Spirit-Led Preaching*, 27.

d. *Acts 1:8* "But you will receive power when the Holy Spirit comes on you; and you will be my witnesses in Jerusalem, and in all Judea and Samaria, and to the ends of the earth." When this promise was fulfilled on the day of Pentecost, Peter preached in the fullness and freshness and anointing of the Spirit. We believe that Pentecost is a paragon for revival and awakening, and it certainly reinforces the role of Spirit-anointed preaching and establishes its correlation to revival and awakening. This same truth is reinforced throughout the book of Acts. See *Acts 4:8* "Then Peter, filled with the Holy Spirit, said to them: "Rulers and elders of the people!" Acts 4:31 (NIV) affirms: "After they prayed, the place where they were meeting was shaken. And they were all filled with the Holy Spirit and spoke the word of God boldly."

e. *Romans 1:16* "For I am not ashamed of the gospel, because it is *the power of God* that brings salvation to everyone who believes: first to the Jew, then to the Gentile" (NIV). The Gospel is the power of God, and the means of communicating that Gospel is also the power of God. Paul knew that the medium needed to be consistent with the message. "Paul's doctrine of salvation as a work of the Spirit through the proclamation of the Word drove his biblical theology of preaching."[13]

f. *1 Corinthians 1:17*—"For Christ did not send me to baptize, but to preach the gospel—not with wisdom and eloquence, lest the cross of Christ be emptied of its power" (NIV). The Apostle Paul's reliance upon the Spirit of God, and not upon human rhetoric, was counter-intuitive and counter-cultural, but Paul's mandate for preaching was not rooted in his intuition or in the culture, but rather in the Scriptures and in the template provided by His Lord and ours. See also 1 Corinthians 1:23–24.

g. *1 Corinthians 2:4, 5* "My message and my preaching were not with wise and persuasive words, but with a demonstration of the Spirit's power, 5 so that your faith might not rest on human wisdom, but on God's power" (NIV).

h. *1 Corinthians 2:13* "This is what we speak, not in words taught us by human wisdom but in words taught by the Spirit, explaining spiritual realities with Spirit-taught words" (NIV). "Spirit-empowered preaching is the result of proclaiming the Spirit-taught word that gives a Christ-centred witness and calls

---

13. Heisler, *Spirit-Led Preaching*, 31.

for a Spirit-filled response. Consequently, the Holy Spirit not only empowers the message; he provides the source and abundance of the message in the Scripture that he has inspired."[14]

i. *1 Thessalonians 1:5* "because our gospel came to you not simply with words but also with power, with the Holy Spirit and deep conviction. You know how we lived among you for your sake" (NIV). The Gospel was communicated, preached, "not simply with words" but in and with the power of the Spirit, and the reason is clear.

Summary: There are numerous other references that reinforce (both explicitly and implicitly) the concept that the Holy Spirit's role in Revival Preaching is indispensable. For further Biblical study, consider Deut. 18:18, I Samuel 10:6, I Samuel 19:23, Ezekiel 37:1–12; Joel 2:28, II Samuel 23:2, Psalm 51:11–13, II Tim. 1:7; I Corinthians 14:1; and I Peter 1:12 along with many others that forcefully compel the reading preacher to recognize his/her utter dependence upon the fullness and enabling of the Spirit of God in order to preach for revival. What then shall we say to these things, and how should they impact our approach to ministry? What did Edwards say? What did Edwards do? How did Edwards preach?

4. QUOTES FROM EDWARDS AFFIRMING THE ROLE OF THE SPIRIT IN REVIVAL PREACHING

Edwards described, in his "Faithful Narrative" the work of God in such a way as to give credit to the Holy Spirit: "This work of God, as it was carried on, and the number of true saints multiplied, soon made a glorious alteration in the town; so that in the spring and summer following, *anno* 1735, the town seemed to be full of the presence of God: it never was so full of love, nor so full of joy; and yet so full of distress, as it was then. There were remarkable tokens of God's presence in almost every house. It was a time of joy in families on the account of salvation's being brought unto them; parents rejoicing over their children as newborn, and husbands over their wives, and wives over their husbands. The goings of God were then seen in his sanctuary [Ps 68:24], God's day was a delight, and his tabernacles were amiable [Ps 84:1]. Our public assemblies were then beautiful; the congregation was alive in God's service, everyone earnestly intent on the public worship, every hearer eager to drink in the words of the minister as they came from his mouth; the assembly in general were, from time to time, in

---

14. Heisler, *Spirit-Led Preaching*, 37.

tears while the Word was preached; some weeping with sorrow and distress, others with joy and love, others with pity and concern for the souls of their neighbors (Jonathan Edwards).[15]

In regards to Edwards view of Revival and the Holy Spirit, we read: "The church in *that great effusion of the Spirit* that was then, and the strong impressions that God's people were then under, was under the care of infallible guides, that watched over them day and night; but yet so prone were they, through the weakness and corruption of human nature, to get out of the way, that irregularity and confusion rose in some churches, where there was *an extraordinary outpouring of the Spirit*, to a very great height, even in the apostles' lifetime, and under their eye" (Jonathan Edwards) [emphasis mine].[16] For Edwards, a revival was an effusion or an extraordinary outpouring of the Spirit.

In writing his famous biography of David Brainerd, Edwards quotes what David Brainerd felt about the Holy Spirit and ministry: "When ministers feel these special gracious influences on their hearts, it wonderfully assists them to come at the consciences of men, and as it were to handle them with hands; whereas, without them, whatever reason and oratory we make use of, we do but make use of stumps instead of hands" (Jonathan Edwards).[17] Edwards here clearly demonstrates his belief that it is the grace of God's Spirit and not "reason and oratory" which enables the minister to be effective in ministry.

"From his commentary on Acts 1:8, it is clear that Edwards firmly believed that the apostles and the early church were qualified and competent to minister in general and preach for revival in particular because of the Holy Spirit's fullness and gifting and enabling and anointing." "But you will receive power when the Holy Spirit comes on you; and you will be my witnesses in Jerusalem, and in all Judea and Samaria, and to the ends of the earth" Edwards states "Christ likewise foretold what assistance the apostles should have in carrying on their work. He told 'em he would be with them in it [. . .] He told 'em that they should receive power by a Spirit that should come upon them, whereby they should be qualified to be witnesses unto him in Judea and Jerusalem and Samaria, and to the utmost parts of the earth" (Jonathan Edwards) [1740].[18]

Edwards continues, "Now 'tis most evident that they were endowed with some extraordinary spirit and uncommon influence, that endowed

---

15. Edwards, *Works*, 4: 151.
16. Edwards, *Works*, 4: 318.
17. Edwards, *Works*, 7: 467–68.
18. Edwards, *Works*, 20: 273.

them with power, strength, courage, activity, comfort and eloquence, and answered those purposes that Christ spoke of in an extraordinary manner. Nothing is more evident than [that] they were in a new and very extraordinary manner endowed with a spirit or influence that carried [them] quite above themselves and made 'em quite new men as to gifts of knowledge, courage, eloquence, zeal and activity, steadfastness and resolution, and other things to qualify 'em for that work of being witnesses for Christ, or preaching Christ in such a manner as to tend to success. Christ foretold that, by this Spirit that he promised, they should be raised to vastly higher degrees of knowledge, John 14:20, John 14:26 and John 16:13–14, John 16:23. This was most evidently fulfilled. He promised that they thereby should be endowed with eloquence and courage, readiness of mind and great force of speech, Matthew 10:19–20 and Luke 21:14–15. This also was exceeding apparent" (Jonathan Edwards) [1740][19]. What follows from these quotes is that Edwards firmly believed that the apostles and the early church were qualified and competent to minister in general and preach for revival in particular *because of the Holy Spirit's fullness and gifting and enabling and anointing.*[20]

Finally, Edwards states: "Now, therefore, except ministers are stronger than the powers of darkness, they are utterly unable to deliver the souls of men out of their hands. Ministers are set by God to pull down strongholds of Satan. But if they are *without any other help but their own strength* (i.e., a natural man having only speculative reason), alas, they are miserable, weak things to go against the power of the air and engage the god of the world . . . [Emphasis mine][21]. Hear! Hear! Only by the Spirit's enabling are we able to "engage the god of the world." As Luther puts it: "Did we in our own strength confide, our striving would be losing."

5. QUOTES BY EDWARDSEAN SCHOLARS

Referring to the role of the ministers, William Cooper, in his preface to Edwards's "Faithful Narrative," and alluding to Edwards, comments: "The manner of their preaching is not with the enticing words of man's wisdom: howbeit, they speak wisdom among them that are perfect [1 Corinthians 2:4, 1 Corinthians 2:6]. *An ardent love to Christ* and souls warms their

---

19. Edwards, *Works*, 20: 274.

20. Some may question the legitimacy of quoting Edwards's view regarding the Spirit's role during apostolic times since he believed in the cessation of the supernatural gifts. But his dependence upon the Spirit is evident (in both theory and practice).

21. Geschiere, *Taste and See*, 50.

breasts and animates their labors. *God has made these his ministers' active spirits, a flame of fire in his service: and his word in their mouths has been as a fire; and as a hammer that breaketh the rock in pieces* [Ps 104:4 and Heb 1:7; Jer 23:29]. In most places where they have labored, God has evidently wrought with them, and confirmed the Word by signs following [Mark 16:20]. Such a power and presence of God in religious assemblies, has not been known since God set up his sanctuary amongst us: he has indeed glorified the house of his glory" [Ezek 37:26; Isaiah 60:7].[22]

6. ILLUSTRATIONS FROM THE ACTUAL SERMONS OF EDWARDS

Where did Edwards preach about the need for ministers to be filled with the Spirit and empowered for life and service?

We can interpret some of the things that Edwards says with a new perspective, a kind of "second grace" prism or template. For example, Edwards preaches an entire sermon entitled "The Subjects of a First work of Grace may need a New Conversion." The reading of this sermon suggests Edwards believed in a two-tiered work of grace. Perhaps this reflects his own experience, perhaps it reflects his own theology. Edwards says:

> And so, if there be any remarkable work of God upon the soul long after its first conversion, whereby the heart is raised up to much higher degrees of grace, it goes in Scripture by the same names as the first conversion itself. Sometimes those that have long had a seed of grace in their souls, but have had that seed in a great measure as it were buried in the ground, do experience a blessed work of God in their hearts, causing a great alteration in their souls, very much delivering it from its former darkness, and also setting it much more at liberty from corruptions that before, through the weakness of grace, used much to entangle and ensnare the soul, giving the soul a new and much clearer understanding of divine things, and remarkably putting it under new advantages for the exercises and fruits of the divine life. And when it is so, such a work in Scripture is represented in like manner with the work of God in first conversion. This probably was the case of John's two disciples that followed Jesus (John 1:3335), and also of several other of Christ's disciples, who seemed to have been good men before they came to Christ in that manner that they did, when Christ saw 'em and bid them

---

22. Edwards, *Works*, 4: 218–19.

follow him, when straightway they left all and followed him—though that is represented as their coming to Christ at his effectual call (Jonathan Edwards).[23]

Edwards proceeds in the sermon to show God's similar "MO" (modus operandi) between the first work of grace, which Edwards calls "conversion" and a second work of grace, which Edwards calls "a new conversion." What he seems to be pointing to is the fact that the authentic born-again regenerate Christians can go through a second definite work of grace with remarkable parallels to their first conversion experience.[24] Edwards endeavors " . . . to show what godly persons they be that stand in need of such a work of God's Spirit, or that thus stand in great need of being converted" (Jonathan Edwards).[25] He states that "all the saints in this world do stand in need of it" (Jonathan Edwards).[26] Edwards calls this a "new conversion"[27]. In my estimation Edwards here confuses the unique work of regeneration, which happens once, with the unique inceptive work of the fullness of the Spirit, which is both a definite and distinct work of grace subsequent to conversion that introduces the born-again believer into a new spiritual dynamic. To call it a "new conversion" is to confuse the unique work of grace at regeneration. Stout comments that Edwards tends to "complicate conversion"[28]. However, it points, in my mind to the definitive and particular nature of this work. Edwards called it a second conversion, in part because of the parallel to the first entrance into saving faith. I believe that this unique second definitive work is the crisis experience of sanctification that introduces the fullness of the Spirit to the life of the beleaguered believer.

Edwards refers to this second work of grace by various terms: (All references are taken from his sermon "The Subjects of a First Work of Grace May Need a New Conversion")[29] "conversion" (185), "awakening" (199), "renewed conversion" (200), and "second work" (202).

In this same sermon Edwards made the application in which he demonstrates his convictions about the Holy Spirit and the need to pray: "*Let 'em pray that God would give them his Spirit to awaken them; this is proper for them, whether they have any true grace or not. And so let ['em] pray that God would enable to strive for salvation, and that he would help 'em to enter*

23. Edwards, *Works*, 22: 188.
24. Edwards, *Works*, 22: 192.
25. Edwards, *Works*, 22: 192.
26. Edwards, *Works*, 22: 194.
27. Edwards, *Works*, 22: 198.
28. Edwards, *Works*, 22: 181.
29. Edwards, *Works*, 22: 181–202.

in at the strait gate. Let 'em pray earnestly that God would show 'em their own hearts; {that God would} bring ['em] off from own righteousness; {that} God would convert 'em; {that God would} give a true sight of Christ, and enable 'em sincerely to close with him and trust in him alone for salvation. Let 'em pray that God would open their blind eye; {that God would} cause light to shine out of darkness; and that he [would] raise their dead souls to life. Such petitions are proper to be put up to God by a minister, as one that speaks as the mouth of a congregation; and they are proper petitions to be joined in by the whole congregation, both saints and sinners" (Jonathan Edwards).[30]

7. 70 RESOLUTIONS

I was quite disappointed to find no explicit references to the Person of the Holy Spirit in the 70 resolutions. There is, however, clear evidence that Edwards resolved to live and minister in the power of the Spirit, recognizing his own frailty and weakness. Consider, for example, the preamble to the resolutions: Being sensible that I *am unable to do anything without God's help*, I do humbly entreat him *by his grace to enable me to keep these Resolutions*, so far as they are agreeable to his will, for Christ's sake.

However, there seems to be an unusual emphasis on Edwards's own power and enabling to be able to follow through on his resolutions, rather than the power of God. Notice the references to his own power, which I have highlighted:

6. Resolved, to *live with all my might*, while I do live.

22. Resolved, to endeavor to obtain for myself as much happiness, in the other world, *as I possibly can, with all the power, might, vigor, and vehemence, yea violence, I am capable of, or can bring myself to exert*, in any way that can be thought of.

56. Resolved, never to give over, nor in the least to slacken, *my fight with my corruptions*, however unsuccessful I may be.

64. Resolved, when I find those " . . . groanings which cannot be uttered" (Rom. 8:26), of which the Apostle speaks, and those "breakings of soul for the longing it hath," of which the Psalmist speaks, (Psalm 119:20), that I will promote them *to the utmost of my power, and that I will not be weary of earnestly endeavoring* to vent my desires, nor of the repetitions of such earnestness. July 23, and August 10, 1723 [emphases mine].

Furthermore, when one reads through the tenor of the resolutions, there is a degree of ambivalence as to the real source of power in Edwards's life. While there is a recognition of his dependence upon Divine grace, there

---

30. Edwards, *Works*, 22: 201.

is no explicit reference to the need for the empowering of the Spirit or the power of Christ. Perhaps this is Edwards's way of emphasizing his responsibility in the pilgrimage of sanctification without minimizing the role of the Holy Spirit. However, it may reflect Edwards's youthful exuberance and the natural proclivity of most believers to rely upon self to live for and serve God. [The first 21 resolutions were composed in 1722, when he was 19, and the last was composed Aug. 17, 1723, when he was 20]. Many of God's choicest servants have witnessed to a "rude awakening" in their lives and ministries where they were brought to a keen realization of their complete dependence upon the Spirit to live and serve effectively. Is there any evidence of a definite encounter with the Holy Spirit in his subsequent years which introduced him, perhaps in a dramatic fashion, to that experience of the empowering or anointing of the Spirit that several choice servants (Wesley, et al) recognize and acknowledge as their experience? We know that Edwards does give abundant recognition to the Spirit of God as the sole grounds of ministerial effectiveness (see quotes below). Was there a turning point, a second work of grace, a "crisis experience, a "distinct event" in the life of Edwards subsequent to his conversion experience, where he "entered in" to the fullness of the Spirit? We will pursue this angle of questioning momentarily, but for now must conclude that the resolutions are disappointing in their minimal explicit reference to the need of the Spirit's empowering for life and service. Thankfully, we find significant evidence in the practice and writings of Edwards to cogently and convincingly illustrate a profound belief and practice in the need for the enabling of the Spirit to preach effectively. The last resolution was written in 1723, the First Phase of the Great Awakening happened in 1734. In those eleven years Edwards learned some significant lessons about the Holy Spirit.

RESOLUTIONS AND PERSONAL NARRATIVE: A TURNING POINT IN EDWARDS'S RELATIONSHIP WITH THE SPIRIT

Part of the explanation of the strong emphasis and "onus" on the self to follow through on the resolutions has to do with the colonial and semi-medieval emphasis on the role of the individual and self-flagellation in the process of sanctification. Edwards may simply be emphasizing his part of the bargain, assuming God's part. However, a case can be made for Edwards entering into a fullness of the Spirit and introducing him into a new spiritual dynamic both for life and for service. While differing authors in different times down through church history have expressed themselves in different fashions, when one examines the essence of these "deeper life" encounters, there is remarkable spiritual affinity alluding to a common type of experience. Let us explore what this looked like in the life of Edwards.

Personal Narrative

Edwards makes a very frank admission in his Personal Narrative, which he penned in 1739, just after the Great Awakening[31]. There seems to be a frank admission as to the futility and uselessness of personal resolve, as is reflected in the resolutions. Edwards writes in his narrative:

> I used to be continually examining myself, and studying and contriving for likely ways and means, how *I should live holily, with far greater diligence and earnestness*, than ever I pursued anything in my life: but *with too great a dependence on my own strength*; which afterwards proved a great damage to me. My experience had not then taught me, as it has done since, my extreme feebleness and impotence, every manner of way; and the innumerable and bottomless depths of secret corruption and deceit, that there was in my heart. However, I went on with my eager pursuit after more holiness; and sweet conformity to Christ (Jonathan Edwards).[32]

This testimony or personal narrative gives great cause for pause and reflection: Does he refer to the phase in his life when he wrote the resolutions? I think so. Certainly, the tenor of some of the resolutions, as we have noted above, places a great deal of emphasis upon personal resolve. I believe the confession *"with too great a dependence on my own strength"* is an allusion to Edwards's sense of need for something more, a supernatural empowering. Although Edwards may not express it in so many words, I believe that the spirituality of the Personal Narrative points to an auto-discovery that many saints allude to, where they come to the end of themselves and are brought to a deeper experience that is described variously: "deeper life," "filled with the Spirit" "entirely sanctified," "crisis experience" "distinct event" "victorious life," "baptism of the Spirit," etc. Our argument here is not in favor of a particular phrase or expression, but rather to point to the essential spiritual similitude between Edwards and many others who reference a unique second work of grace in their lives. The fact that Edwards testified: "My experience had not then taught me, as it has done since, my extreme feebleness

---

31. Edwards, *Works*, 6: 7.
32. Edwards, *Works*, 16: 796.

and impotence, every manner of way; and the innumerable and bottomless depths of secret corruption and deceit, that there was in my heart . . . " suggests that there came a point where he experienced a change and gave witness to a new spiritual dynamic. Particularly the phrase "My experience had not then taught me, *as it has done since*, . . . " points to a transition from a life of dependence upon the self to a life dependent upon the Spirit of God. Edwards does not necessarily state outright what that transitioning experience was, nor when. While some may wish to see Edward as moving from a state of being unregenerate to a state of regenerate grace, I believe there is sufficient evidence to suggest Edwards was in fact a believer when he wrote those resolutions, but that he entered into a different kind of spiritual dynamic at some point after, which the Personal Narrative alludes to.

Is there a particular definitive event in the life of Edwards that points to an entering into this Spirit-filled life? I cannot find it, per. se. although in his personal narrative, he does state something that comes tantalizingly close to such an experience of fullness:

> Not long after I first began to experience these things, I gave an account to my father, of some things that had passed in my mind. I was pretty much affected by the discourse we had together. And when the discourse was ended, I walked abroad alone, in a solitary place in my father's pasture, for contemplation. And as I was walking there and looked up on the sky and clouds; there came into my mind, a sweet sense of the glorious majesty and grace of God, that I know not how to express. I seemed to see them both in a sweet conjunction: majesty and meekness joined together: it was a sweet and gentle, and holy majesty; and also a majestic meekness; an awful sweetness; a high, and great, and holy gentleness (Jonathan Edwards).[33]

Conclusion: Through the narrative of Edwards, and through the writing of Edwards, there is evidence of his belief in a second definitive work of grace, with remarkable parallels to the first. I believe that what he is alluding to is not a second regeneration (which by definition is "sui generis"[34]) but rather a unique entering into a new and fresh dynamic called the fullness of the Spirit. Did Edwards call it this? I do not see that, but did he believe in it? Absolutely. And I believe his narrative and his articulation allude to it.

---

33. Edwards, *Works*, 16: 794.

34. *Sui generis* is a Latin phrase, meaning "of its own kind/genus" and hence "unique in its characteristics." What happens in "regeneration" is unique and "of its own kind" and while there may be some parallels between regeneration and a second deeper work of grace, we do well to remember the unique traits of that initial and initiating conversion experience.

His own personal experience, in both life and ministry, verifies that he lived and ministered in a dimension of the power of the Spirit that is absolutely indispensable for effective life and ministry. And here is where I wish to make the connection to my thesis: Ministers need this empowering of the Spirit in their lives and ministries if their preaching ministry is to have this revivalistic impact. Edward knew in experience what he was talking about.

8. OTHER AUTHORS

I have been affirming in this chapter the great need for a supernatural endowment of the Holy Spirit's anointing and experience of the fullness of the Spirit as an indispensable qualifier to enable God's minister to preach with effectiveness. It is heartening to find a resounding witness of God's choicest servants confirming this great need. Consider the following quotes from the Preacher's Hall of Fame.

"It is extraordinary power from God, not talent that wins the day. It is extraordinary spiritual unction not extraordinary mental power that we need. Mental power may fill a chapel but spiritual power fills the church with soul anguish. Mental power may gather a large congregation, but only spiritual power will save souls. What we need is spiritual power" (C. H. Spurgeon)[35].

Keevil, in his masterful and stimulating book *Preaching in Revival*, sums up the importance of spiritual unction this way: ". . .as critical as voice and gesture are in reflecting the affections of the preacher, behind all preaching, associated in any way with religious revival, is the unction and authority of the Spirit. This takes primary place as the antecedent of the blessing. It is undoubtedly *the central and most critical observation to make from our study of this matter* [Emphasis mine]. What is the unction of the Spirit? As Lloyd-Jones puts it, "It is the Holy Spirit falling upon the preacher in a special manner. It is an access of power. It is God giving power, and enabling, through the Spirit, to the preacher in order that he may do this work in a manner that lifts it beyond the efforts and endeavors of man to a position in which the preacher is being used by the Spirit and becomes the channel through whom the Spirit works. . .. Preaching is theology coming through a man who is on fire" (Lloyd Jones quoted in Keevil).[36]

"We who are ambassadors for God must not trifle, but we must tremble at God's Word. In addition, a preacher ought to know that he really possesses the Spirit of God, and that when he speaks there is an influence upon

---

35. Spurgeon, *Power*.
36. Keevil, *Preaching in Revival*, 168.

him that enables him to speak as God would have him, otherwise out of the pulpit he should go directly; he has no right to be there, he has not been called to preach God's truth" Spurgeon, quoted by Heisler.[37]

"Spirit-empowered preaching is the result of proclaiming the Spirit-taught word that gives a Christ-centred witness and calls for a Spirit-filled response. Consequently, the Holy Spirit not only empowers the message; he provides the source and abundance of the message in the Scripture that he has inspired"[38], (Commenting on 1 Corinthians 2:13 This is what we speak, not in words taught us by human wisdom but in words taught by the Spirit, explaining spiritual realities with Spirit-taught words).

9. CONCLUSION

I believe that Edwards had a firm conviction regarding the fundamental need for the preaching of God's Word to be done by men who were anointed and empowered by the Spirit of God. Subsequently, he encouraged people to pray for the Spirit and spoke of "our very prayers for the Spirit" (Jonathan Edwards) [1740].[39]

As Edwards affirms: "We that are ministers not only have need of some true experience of the saving influence of the Spirit of God upon our heart, but we need a double portion of the Spirit of God at such a time as this; we had need to be as full of light as a glass is, that is held out in the sun; and with respect to love and zeal, we had need at this day to be like the angels, that are a flame of fire [Psalms 104:4]. The state of the times extremely requires a fullness of the divine Spirit in ministers, and we ought to give ourselves no rest till we have obtained it" (Jonathan Edwards).[40]

APPLICATION

We as preachers need to respond. The Scriptural evidence, the testimony of Edwards and other effective preachers is compelling. We need a fresh anointing of the Spirit. We need to pray for a definite infilling of the Spirit. What did Edwards believe about praying for the Spirit?

Should believers pray for the Spirit?

---

37. Heisler, *Spirit-Led Preaching*, 25.
38. Heisler, *Spirit-Led Preaching*, 37.
39. Edwards, *Works*, 21: 263.
40. Edwards, *Works*, 4: 507.

"Let 'em pray that God would give them his Spirit to awaken them; this is proper for them, whether they have any true grace or not. Let 'em pray that God would give them his Spirit to awaken them; this is proper for them, whether they have any true grace or not. And so let ['em] pray that God would enable to strive for salvation, and that he would help 'em to enter in at the strait gate. Let 'em pray earnestly that God would show 'em their own hearts; {that God would} bring ['em] off from own righteousness; {that} God would convert 'em; {that God would} give a true sight of Christ, and enable 'em sincerely to close with him and trust in him alone for salvation. Let 'em pray that God would open their blind eye; {that God would} cause light to shine out of darkness; and that he [would] raise their dead souls to life. Such petitions are proper to be put up to God by a minister, as one that speaks as the mouth of a congregation; and they are proper petitions to be joined in by the whole congregation, both saints and sinners" (Jonathan Edwards).[41]

Praying for the Spirit

"It seems to me that the circumstances of the present work do loudly call God's people to abound in this; whether they consider the experience God has lately given 'em of the worth of his presence, and of the blessed fruits of the effusions of his Spirit, to excite them to pray for the continuance and increase, and greater extent of such blessings, or whether they consider the great encouragement God has lately given 'em, to pray for the outpourings of his Spirit and the carrying on this work, by the great manifestations he has lately made of the freeness and riches of his grace; and how much there is, in what we have seen of the glorious works of God's power and grace, to put us in mind of the yet greater things of this nature that he has spoken of in his Word, and to excite our longings for those things and hopes of their approach" (Jonathan Edwards).[42]

"Godly persons, after such a renewed work of God's Spirit upon them, are commonly not only in a much happier state themselves, but much more able to help others. Hereby their knowledge and experience and strength are greatly increased, and, having been tempted and delivered, they are the more fit to help others under temptation. And by the great access which they have received of light and strength themselves, they are abundantly the more fit to instruct and strengthen others. Hence the direction that Christ gives to Peter in the text: "When thou art converted, strengthen thy brethren." So that if you obtain such a change by a new work of the Spirit of God

41. Edwards, *Works*, 22: 201.
42. Edwards, *Works*, 4: 516.

upon your heart, you are not only likely to be a much happier man yourself, but to be a much greater blessing to all that are about you; and others are like to be the happier for it, as well as you" (Jonathan Edwards).[43]

A final encouraging word from Edwards

"The gracious, and most excellent, kind assistance of the Spirit of God in praying and preaching, is not by immediate suggesting of words to the apprehension, which may be with a cold dead heart, but by warming the heart and filling it with a great sense of those things that are to be spoken of, and with holy affections, that that sense and those affections may suggest words. Thus indeed the Spirit of God may be said, indirectly and mediately to suggest words to us, to indite[44] our petitions for us, and to teach the preacher what to say; he fills the heart, and that fills the mouth; as we know that when men are greatly affected in any matter, and their hearts are very full, it fills them with matter for speech, and makes 'em eloquent upon that subject; and much more have spiritual affections this tendency, for many reasons that might be given. When a person is in an (sic) holy and lively frame in secret prayer, it will wonderfully supply him with matter and with expressions, as every true Christian knows; and so, it will fill his mouth in Christian conversation, and it has the like tendency to enable a person in public prayer and preaching. And if he has these holy influences of the Spirit on his heart in a high degree, nothing in the world will have so great a tendency to make both the matter and manner of his public performances excellent and profitable" (Jonathan Edwards).[45]

Prayerful application

Lord, fill us as preachers with Your Holy Spirit. We confess our utter dependence upon You. Apart from Your Divine Trinitarian enabling, we can accomplish nothing of eternal value. Lord, Your Word is crystal clear. To be effective, we need to minister Your Word "in the power of the Spirit" (II Cor. 2:4) and we need to "be filled with the Spirit" (Ephesians 5:18). If Jesus was filled with the Spirit prior to His public ministry (Luke 4:14,16–21), if Peter was filled with the Spirit (Acts 2:4) and needed to be filled afresh frequently (Acts 4:8; Acts 4:31), if Paul was filled with the Spirit (Acts 9:17) and needed to be filled afresh frequently (Acts 13:9), if your servant Jonathan

---

43. Edwards, *Works*, 22: 202.
44. Indite appears to be archaic and probably means "animate" or something equivalent.
45. Edwards, *Works*, 4: 437–38.

Edwards believed in and experienced personally the fullness of Your Spirit, and taught his preaching colleagues to depend upon the Spirit, and if a multitude of effective preaching colleagues give witness to this spiritual dynamic as a significant element in their effective revival and awakening preaching, then, Lord, we as preachers need to humble ourselves and seek for that spiritual anointing without which we can do nothing. Lord, keep us on our knees until we are in fact endued with power from on high, and then enable us to so minister Your Word in Your Spirit that Your church is revitalized, and Your elect are called into the kingdom of God. May You be pleased to answer our cries for a fresh anointing and enabling of Your Spirit, so that You, Triune God, may be glorified. Amen. Amen.

Chapter 6

The Word/Spirit Blend and Preaching

"The *Spirit* gives life; the flesh counts for nothing. The *words* I have spoken to you—they are full of the *Spirit* and life" (Jesus) (*John 6:63*) (NIV).

> "*I have, many times, had a sense of the glory of the Third Person in the Trinity, and his office communications of his Holy Spirit, has appeared as an infinite fountain of divine glory and sweetness; being full, and sufficient to fill and satisfy the soul; pouring forth itself in secret communications; like the sun in its glory, sweetly and pleasantly diffusing light and life. And I have sometimes an affecting sense of the excellency of the word of God as a word of life; as the light of life; a Sweet, excellent, life-giving word; accompanied with a thirsting after that word, that it might dwell richly in my heart*" (Jonathan Edwards) [emphasis mine].[1]

INTRODUCTORY COMMENTS

We know that Edwards believed in the preaching of the Word. We have also seen his strong emphasis on the Spirit. In this chapter we want to explore

---

1. Edwards, *Works*, 16: 801.

how these two blended together in Revival Preaching. We want to explore Edwards's understanding of the relationship between the Spirit and the Word. The quote above illustrates his rich experience of the Holy Spirit and the Word. The Scriptures develop a significant theology interrelating the Spirit and the Word. Edwards was a "Word and power" person who was cultivating a "Word and power" church. We will unpack what we mean by that in this chapter.

1. DEFINE IT

In essence, by "Word and power" we mean a priority given to the Word with a corresponding recognition of the vital role of the Spirit in giving and inspiring ("ex-spiring") that Word (II Tim 3:16), illuminating the heart with the Word and illuminating the Word so that the heart understands (Eph 1:15–18) (Prov 1:23); we mean God's rich anointing upon the preacher of the Word and God's Spirit empowering the life to follow the Word (Eph 3:14–16). Therefore, we need to honor the Word of God and the Spirit of God in a balanced and complementary fashion in our personal lives and in our churches. And that needs to start with us as preachers and teachers. What exactly that balance looks like we explore below. The tendency is to be ultra-orthodox in the Word (conservative) and neglect the Person and Work of the Spirit, or to be ultra-charismatic, "charismaniac," with an unbalanced (liberal) emphasis on the Spirit, often neglecting the centrality and foundational aspect of the Word. A "Word *and* Power" Person, and a "Word *and* Power" Church, are a blend of both; they do not so much seek to find a middle ground, as they seek to be fully Word and fully Spirit. People and churches who are both Word and Spirit seek to live and minister in that dynamic correlation, refusing to compromise in either fidelity to the Word or fidelity to the Spirit. The "duo speaker" system of Edwards and the effective Revival Preacher involves two speakers with "high fidelity" to both the word and the Spirit. I believe that is the secret to Edwards's Revival Preaching and is, in my considered opinion, the secret to Revival Preaching today.

To get a better idea of what we mean by "Word and power" let me quote an important portion of Doug Banister's *The Word and Power Church*: "Both the evangelical and the charismatic traditions bring a rich legacy to the church. The evangelical legacy includes expository preaching, an emphasis on the authority and sufficiency of Scripture, a realistic affirmation that the kingdom of God is not fully here, a belief that spiritual growth is a process, and a belief that the Word must be studied in community. The charismatic legacy includes an emphasis on prayer, a hopeful affirmation that the kingdom is here in part, a belief that God speaks today, an emphasis on participatory worship, a belief that the Spirit must be experienced in community. Word and power churches seek to bring together the best of both charismatic and evangelical worlds."[2]

So, we are calling for that kind of preacher that is both "Word and power." We have seen in the two previous chapters that Edwards was a preacher of the Word, and He was also a preacher with a great deal of dependence upon the Spirit. Let us continue to explore how these two work together.

2. BIBLICAL PERSPECTIVE

There are several key biblical passages that reflect this dynamic:

- a. *Job 32:18* "For I am full of *words*, and the *spirit* within me compels me" (NIV). Elihu exemplifies this balance between the Word and the Spirit, with his words governed and directed by the Spirit within. Elihu was a kind of precursor to the Divine Discourses (Job 38—41).
- b. *Isaiah 59:21* "'As for me, this is my covenant with them,' says the Lord. 'My *Spirit*, who is on you, will not depart from you, and my *words* that I have put in your mouth will always be on your lips, on the lips of your children and on the lips of their descendants—from this time on and forever,' says the Lord" (NIV). Again, that perfect blend between the Spirit and the Word in this prophecy.
- c. *Zechariah 4:6* "So he said to me, 'This is the *word* of the Lord to Zerubbabel: "Not by might nor by power, but by my *Spirit*," says the Lord Almighty.'" The Prophetic Word of the Lord emphasizes here the power of the Spirit in contrast to mere human might or power. How critical for Revival Preaching of the Word to remember this balance and dynamic of the Word and the Spirit.
- d. *John 3:34* "For the one whom God has sent speaks the *words* of God, for God gives the *Spirit* without limit." The life of our Lord was a life of speaking the Word of God in and through and by the Spirit of God. He did not start his preaching ministry until he was filled with the Spirit of God and returned from the desert in the power of the Spirit (Luke 4:14) (NIV).

2. Banister, *Word and Power Church*, 22.

e. *John 6:63* "The *Spirit* gives life; the flesh counts for nothing. The *words* I have spoken to you—they are full of the *Spirit* and life." Jesus clearly emphasized the importance of understanding Him by the Spirit and in the Spirit, not in a fleshly legalistic manner. If Jesus spoke thus, and He commissioned as to serve in like manner (as the Father sent me, so send I you), then it is incumbent upon us in our Revival Preaching ministry to discover this Word/Spirit dynamic and live and minister within its freedom and parameters.

f. *Acts 4:31* "After they prayed, the place where they were meeting was shaken. And they were all filled with the Holy *Spirit* and spoke the *word* of God boldly." The early church followed their Master's paradigm and template by maintaining in juxtaposition the Word and the Spirit.

g. *Acts 10:44* "While Peter was still speaking these *words*, the Holy *Spirit* came on all who heard the message." The Holy Spirit honors the Word when those who expound the Word honor the Holy Spirit by giving Him the freedom to direct them (Acts 16:6), prepare them (John 16:13), illuminate them (Eph 1:18), fill them (Eph 5:18), anoint them (Ex. 29:7; Ex. 30:25; Acts 10:38; I John 2:20), guide them (John 16:13) and flow through them in the proclamation of that precious Word.

h. *1 Corinthians 2:13* "This is what we speak, not in *words* taught us by human wisdom but in *words* taught by the *Spirit*, explaining *spiritual* realities with *Spirit*-taught *words*" (NIV). The words that we choose are to be directed by the Spirit, rooted in the Word and in agreement with that Word.

i. *1 Thessalonians 1:5* "because our gospel came to you not simply with *words* but also with power, with the Holy *Spirit* and deep conviction. You know how we lived among you for your sake" (NIV). The Gospel came to the Thessalonians by the Word, but it was more than a mere learning of the information of the Gospel, it was accompanied by the power of God, the power of the Holy Spirit.

j. *1 Corinthians 4:20* "For the *kingdom* of God is not a matter of talk but of *power*" (NIV). Edwards practiced this truth in his Revival Preaching, as we shall substantiate imminently. He followed Paul. We should too.

k. *Hebrews 4:12, 13* "For the *word* of God is alive and active. Sharper than any double-edged sword, it penetrates even to dividing soul and *spirit*, joints and marrow; it judges the thoughts and attitudes of the heart. 13 Nothing in all creation is hidden from God's sight. Everything is uncovered and laid bare before the eyes of him to whom we must give account" (NIV). (See Ephesians 6 and the reference to the Sword of the Spirit). The Word of God is alive and powerful because of the instrumentality of the Spirit. By His Spirit (capital S) the spirit (small s) of the listener in the audience is penetrated, and the persons' (plural) heart is "cut to the quick" (Acts 2:37) as the sword of the Spirit penetrates; the result of this Spirit/Word "combo" is described in I Corinthians 14:25 "as the secrets of their hearts are laid bare. So they will fall down and worship God, exclaiming, 'God is really among you!'" (NIV), or as the Message portrays it: "But if some unbelieving outsiders walk in on a service where people are speaking out God's truth, the plain words will bring them up against the truth and probe their hearts. Before you know it, they're going to be on their faces before God, recognizing that God is among you."

. We can see in the book of Acts how the Holy Spirit anointed the preaching of the Word to bring about both the awakening of the sinner and the revitalization of the believer, such as the preaching of Peter on the day of Pentecost. Typical of Acts is what happened in Iconium where Paul and Barnabas "entered together into the Jewish synagogue and spoke in such a way that a great number of both Jews and Greeks believed" (Acts 14:1) (NASB). The fundamental thesis upon which this investigation is built is the premise that Spirit-anointed preaching of the Word is God's instrument for bringing revival and awakening.

3. QUOTES FROM EDWARDS

In addition to the quote at the opening of this chapter, there are numerous examples in Edwards's life and ministry that illustrate this Word/Spirit dynamic at work. For example, Edwards documents in his personal Narrative: "As I read the words, there came into my soul, and was as it were diffused through it, a sense of the glory of the divine being; a new sense, quite different from anything I ever experienced before. Never any words of Scripture seemed to me as these words did. I thought with myself, how excellent a Being that was; and how happy I should be, if I might enjoy that God, and be wrapt up to God in heaven, and be as it were swallowed up in him. I kept saying, and as it were singing over these words of Scripture to myself; and went to prayer, to pray to God that I might enjoy him; and prayed in a manner quite different from what I used to do; with a new sort of affection" (Jonathan Edwards).[3] There is clear evidence here of the Spirit working in and through the Word in Edwards's life. And that is foundational for the Spirit working through the preached Word.

Edwards alludes to John the Baptist as a burning and shining light, standing as a paradigm for the Christian minister; and as such *the truth must be ablaze in his heart*. "He must be one that is acquainted with experimental religion, and not ignorant of the inward operations of the Spirit of God, nor of Satan's devices; able to guide souls under their particular difficulties. Thus, he must be a scribe well instructed in things that pertain to the kingdom of God; one that 'brings forth out of his treasures things new and old'" [Mat 13:52] (Jonathan Edwards).[4] The truth aflame! " . . . a large measure of the Great awakening's sudden success lay in the absence of dullness in the preaching styles of its leaders."[5]

Edwards again and again alludes to the Word and the Spirit working together. The truth ablaze in the heart is the truth of God's Word made real, experientially real by the Spirit (not just notional knowledge); this combination is what produces and sustains revival and awakening in the hearts of the hearers.

Edwards's conviction regarding both the Word and the Spirit is alluded to in the following quote: "When the disciples of our glorious Lord were filled with sorrow upon the heavy tidings of his departure from them, he cheered their drooping spirits with that good word, John 16:7, 'Nevertheless, I tell you the truth; it is expedient for you that I go away; for if I go not away, the Comforter will not come unto you; but if I depart, I will send him unto you.' And after his ascension, he fulfilled this great and precious promise *by the extraordinary effusion of his Spirit, under whose conduct and influence the apostles went forth and preached everywhere, the Lord working with them*: so that when we read the Acts of the Apostles, we must say: 'Not by might, nor by power, but by the Spirit of the Lord of hosts'" (Zech 4:6) (NIV) [emphasis mine]. It was by the Spirit that the preaching of the Apostles was made impactful; Edwards believed that the same was true of his own apostolic preaching.

---

3. Edwards, *Works*, 16: 792.
4. Edwards, *Works*, 25: 93.
5. Conrad, *Importance of Preaching*, 111.

It is my conviction that "Word and power" preaching is what makes preaching passionate, and subsequently effective. I have already pointed out that Edwards believed in the importance of passionate preaching. He said: "Our people don't so much need to have their heads stored as to have their hearts touched and they stand in the greatest need of that sort of preaching that has the greatest tendency to do this" (Jonathan Edwards).[6] Revival Preaching is preaching that touches the heart and engages the mind. The way to touch both heads and hearts is by having the Spirit and the Word clearly working together in biblical juxtaposition.

Commenting on *1 Corinthians 2:13-14*, Edwards affirms: "But the wisdom of God needs not be dressed up in such gay clothing. Such ornaments are vastly too mean for divine truth, which is most amiable in her own native beauty and genuine simplicity and is as beautiful in a poor man or a babe, as in a prince, and as powerful in Paul's weakness and fear and much trembling, as it would be in all the wisdom of the philosophers and eloquence of their greatest orators. For the power of divine light don't (sic) depend on the eloquence of the speaker, but upon the demonstration of the Spirit of God. See 1 Corinthians 2:4, 'And my speech and my preaching was not with enticing words of man's wisdom, but in demonstration of the Spirit and of power.' For there is another teaching necessary in order [to facilitate] the reception of this wisdom, even the teachings of the Holy Ghost: for it is a sort of wisdom that is both out of the powers of the greatest worldly-wise men to teach, so as to make to understand, and out of the reach of men of the greatest learning and natural understanding to understand of without divine teachings. *1 Corinthians 2:13-14*, 'Which things also we speak, not in the words which man's wisdom teacheth, but which the Holy Ghost teacheth; comparing spiritual things with spiritual. But the natural man receiveth not the things of the Spirit of God: for they are foolishness unto him: neither can he know them, because they are spiritually discerned.'" (Jonathan Edwards) [1723].[7]

4. QUOTES BY EDWARDSEAN SCHOLARS

We have seen extensive references by Edwards and Edwardsean scholars informing us of his beliefs regarding the Word and his beliefs regarding the Spirit. Here we focus on his beliefs on the juxtaposition of Word and Spirit in the theology of Edwards.

---

6. Edwards, *Works*, 4: 388.
7. Edwards, *Works*, 14: 70–71.

Edwards reminds ministers for their "General Improvement" that they "ought not depend on their learning or eloquence, nor upon their diligence, or the greatness of their endeavors to promote the good of souls," nor "ought they to depend on their own experiences or the goodness of their preparations . . . ." With this statement, he is taking on those who, like Locke, placed their trust in the powers of their logic, and in the reasoning powers of their hearers. Rather, Edwards adds, "their eye should be to their master that sent them, to make their labors successful through his Spirit"[8]. In other words, preachers should not rely upon their own expository prowess, but should rely entirely upon the Lord by His Spirit.

Acknowledging that the "Word of God indeed is sharp as a two-edged sword and is quick and powerful. . . it is so only through the cooperation of that Spirit that gave the Word." Edwards also warns: "The Word alone, however managed, explained, confirmed and applied, is nothing but a dead letter without the Spirit."[9]

The Spirit and the Word worked together, creating powerful conviction. This is verified by this firsthand account of Edwards's preaching in Enfield: "We went over to Enfield—where we met dear Mr. Edwards of Northampton who preached a most awakening sermon from these words—Deut. 32:35 and before [the] sermon was done—there was a great moaning and crying out through ye [the] whole House—What shall I do to be saved?—Oh I am going to Hell—Oh what shall I do for Christ, ... So the minister was obliged to desist—the shrieks and cries were piercing and amazing—after some time of waiting for the congregation were still so then a prayer was made by Mr. W. and after that we descended from the pulpit and discoursed with the people—some in one place and some in another—and amazing and astonishing the power of God was seen—and several souls were hopefully wrought upon that night and oh the cheerfulness and pleasantness of their countenances that received comfort—oh that God would strengthen and confirm—we sung an hymn and prayed and dismissed the assembly" (Eye Witness account).[10]

Illustrations from the Actual Sermons of Edwards

Edwards himself states: "If a minister has light *without heat*, and entertains his [hearers] with learned discourses, *without a savour of the powers of goodliness, or any appearance of fervency of spirit, and zeal for God and the good of souls*, he may gratify itching ears, and fill the heads of his people with empty notions, but *it will not be very likely to teach their hearts, or save their*

---

8. Geschiere, *Taste and See*, 59.
9. Geschiere, *Taste and See*, 61.
10. Winslow, *Jonathan Edwards*, 192.

souls" (Jonathan Edwards)[11]. I believe that this light/heat combination is a reflection of Edwards's conviction that the Word and the Spirit go together.

Regarding his own personal growth in dependence upon the Spirit, it is significant that Edwards confesses to Whitefield his need for a fresh anointing, and solicits the prayers of this youth: "I desire your fervent prayers for us may yet be continued, that God would not be to us as a wayfaring man, that turns aside to tarry but a night, but that he would more and more pour out his Spirit upon us, and no more depart from us; and for me in particular, that I may be filled with HIs Spirit, and may become fervent, as a flame of fire in my work, and may be abundantly succeeded, and that it would please God, however unworthy I am, to improve me as an instrument of his glory, and advancing the kingdom of God."[12, 13] (Written December 14, 1740, just after Whitefield was there in Northampton and preached under the anointing). Was Edwards cognizant of the fact that there was a deficiency in the balance between the Word and the Spirit in his own preaching, and that he was taking steps to address that deficiency? I believe the answer is "yes."

5. 70 RESOLUTIONS

I believe that Edwards's lack of emphasis on the Spirit illustrates that later in his ministry He discovered the need to be filled and empowered by the Spirit. Perhaps in his youthful exuberance, he relied too much upon his own wisdom and insight, and God taught him through the rigors of the pastorate and his own struggles, his need for seeking Divine empowering to enable his exposition and proclamation of the Word to have the Spirit's blessing upon in.

6. OTHER AUTHORS

Wesley Duewel in his excellent treatment on Spiritual Leadership entitled *Ablaze for God* touches on the importance of the Word and Spirit blend:

"Paul knew that a faith built on words alone, i.e., the message alone, might be tempted to waver. That is why he reminded the Corinthians that both his message and his manner of preaching the message were with a "demonstration" of the Spirit's power (I Cor. 2:5) and so their faith could be based on that demonstration of power that added to the content of his

---

11. Edwards, *Works,* 25: 84–104.
12. Edwards, *Works,* 16: 87.
13. Haykin, *Jonathan Edwards,* 41.

words. The Greek word translated "demonstration" suggests evidence or proof. "It was a technical term for a compelling conclusion drawn from the premises." God's power was so evident in Paul's message that the Corinthians were compelled to conclude that his message and he as the messenger were from God. Power confirms truth. We dare not depend on truth alone; we must minister truth aflame with God's power"[14].

The blend of the Word and the Spirit is affected through the agency of prayer. Prayer is essential for both preacher and people. When both are prepared through prayer, an atmosphere is created conducive to expectations of blessing. *"The reformed synthesis of Word and Spirit means that without the Spirit, the Word is a dead letter"*[15].

Speaking about the phase of the Puritans, Keevil writes: "The pulpit was ablaze with a holy enthusiasm, born of the fires of a Pentecostal anointing. The preaching of this period also included, along with the proclamation of the truth, 'the clearing away of error'. Such preachers were described by Thomas Bacon as 'prophets'. Preaching was critical and central to our Puritan forbears, and they preached in revival"![16]

7. CONCLUSION

Ephesians 6:17 "Take the helmet of salvation and the sword of the *Spirit*, which is the *word* of God." The conclusion of the matter is that if, like Edwards, we are to be men and women of the Word/Spirit balance, with our life and ministry impregnated with both the Word and the Spirit, then we need to "take" (imperatival force) the Sword of the Spirit, which is the Word of God, and wield that sword in revival force. Our logo, our theme, will be "Yield and Wield": Yield ourselves to the Spirit's fullness, and wield the Sword of the Spirit, which is the Word of God, in spiritual warfare, taking captive the thoughts, the arguments to the obedience of Christ. The weapons of our warfare are not merely human, but they have divine power to destroy strongholds (II Cor 10:35). Effective Revival Preaching requires a blend of the Word and the Spirit. Effective Revival Preaching will mean that we aspire in our lives and preaching ministries to be "Word and Power" ministers. The prophets of the Old Testament, our Lord Jesus, the Apostles, and men and women down through church history who were effective revival preachers demonstrate this powerful blend. Will you, dear reader, become a preacher

---

14. Duewel, *Ablaze for God*, 52–53.
15. Keevil, *Preaching in Revival*, 163–64.
16. Keevil, *Preaching in Revival*, 149.

committed to both the Word and the Spirit in your preaching ministry? Do I hear a loud amen?

Perhaps the best way to conclude and appeal for a Spirit/Word blend in our ministries as preaching pastors is to heed the counsel of Edwards, as he talked about the Spirit's role in enabling ministers: "Godly persons, after such a renewed work of God's Spirit upon them, are commonly not only in a much happier state themselves, but much more able to help others. Hereby their knowledge and experience and strength are greatly increased, and, having been tempted and delivered, they are the more fit to help others under temptation. And by the great access which they have received of light and strength themselves, they are abundantly the more fit to instruct and strengthen others. Hence the direction that Christ gives to Peter in the text: "When thou art converted, strengthen thy brethren." So that if you obtain such a change by a new work of the Spirit of God upon your heart, you are not only likely to be a much happier man yourself, *but to be a much greater blessing to all that are about you; and others are like to be the happier for it, as well as you*" (Jonathan Edwards) [Emphasis mine].[17]

---

17. Edwards, *Works,* 22: 202.

*Revival Preaching—Twelve Lessons
from Jonathan Edwards*

Chapter 7

The Supremacy of God in Preaching

36 "For from Him and through Him and to Him are all things. To Him *be* the glory forever. Amen" (Rom 11:36) (NASB).

"The first objective ground of gracious affections, is *the transcendently excellent and amiable nature of divine things*, as they are *in themselves*; and not any conceived relation they bear to self, or self-interest" (Jonathan Edwards).[1]

INTRODUCTORY COMMENTS

I believe that Edwards was effective as a Revival Preacher because of His view of God, what in theology we call "theology proper." In a secular age that

---

1. Edwards, *Works*, 2: 240.

emphasizes the importance and centrality of humanity and even within the evangelical community that increasingly allows the felt needs of humanity to determine our preaching agenda, this is a significant focus shift. I believe that we as preachers would see more revival and awakening if we were to be freshly captivated in our own hearts and minds by a view of the supremacy of God and were then to reflect that head/heart knowledge in our passionate preaching. This deals with heart motivation, which is absolutely critical when it comes to revival. What motivates us to seek for and pray for and preach for revival? Is the glory of God preeminent in our motivation?

1. DEFINE IT

I have already referred to defining what I mean by the supremacy of God in the two opening quotes of this chapter. By the supremacy of God in preaching I mean that kind of preaching that is God-centered, God-focused, God-exalting, God-honoring, and faithful to the full witness of Scripture regarding the nature and essence of the Triune God. Effective Revival Preaching is preaching that emphasizes the Supremacy of God. God is passionate for His glory, and we as His people should be too. And preachers who are passionate for the glory of God are the "open secret" to developing a people of God with a similar vision. Like pastor, like people. This kind of preaching explains who God the Father, God the Son, and God the Spirit is, and their interrelationship. The Person and Work of the Father, the Son and the Spirit are central. But most of all, there is a consuming passion for the glory of God.

The term *Perichoresis*[2] captures something of this Trinitarian intimacy. As the Scriptures say, "truly our fellowship is with the Father and with his Son Jesus Christ" (I John 1:3); and in a fuller Trinitarian fashion Paul affirms "For through him we both have access to the Father by one Spirit" (Eph 2:18).

---

2. Compelling Truth, "*Perichoresis*." Perichoresis is a Greek word used to describe the binding of the Trinity, the two natures of Jesus Christ, and God's omnipresence. Nothing can divide the three members of the Trinity—the Father, Son, and Holy Spirit. People sometimes struggle to understand the combined Godhead and identity—and rightly so, as it is a mystery. However, the word *perichoresis* can help us understand. The word itself comes from the Greek *peri*, meaning "around," and *chorein*, meaning "to give way" or "to make room." Perichoresis could be translated as «rotation» or «going around.» Some scholars picture this as a sort of choreographed dance. All members of the dance move as one, precisely and fluidly, to create a meaningful work together. There is a kind of eternal "dance" in the relationship within the Trinity, and by grace we are invited into the fellowship of that intimate circle. https://www.compellingtruth.org/perichoresis.html

The Supremacy of God in preaching means that our primary motive is the glory of God. Paul instructed the Corinthian believers: *1 Corinthians 10:31* "Whether therefore ye eat, or drink, or whatsoever ye do, *do all to the glory* of God." What gives the Revival Preacher nourishment (John 4:32) and sustenance is preaching to the glory of God, with a sincere Spirit-born and Spirit-borne[3] passion that God, not self, be exalted. We say with John the Baptist, "He must increase, but I must decrease" (John 3:30) (KJV). We need that kind of a revival that glorifies God, and it will come when preachers are passionate about God's glory, to such a point that the glory of the Sun (Son) eclipses any self-glorying.

The supremacy of God in preaching meant, for Edwards, a strong emphasis on the sovereignty of God. I will deal with the theme of relating Divine sovereignty to human responsibility in a separate chapter but suffice it to say here that Edwards believed pre-eminently in the sovereignty of God.

What is the goal of preaching? The same as the goal of everything: The glory of God. What did Edwards mean by that? "The thing signified by that name, 'the glory of God,' when spoken of as the supreme and ultimate end of the work of creation, and of all God's works, is the emanation and true external expression of God's internal glory and fullness; meaning by his fullness, what has already been explained. Or in other words, God's internal glory extant, in a true and just exhibition, or external existence of it" (Jonathan Edwards).[4]

" . . . the communication of God's virtue or holiness is principally in communicating the love of himself (which appears by what has before been observed). And thus we see how, not only the creature's seeing and knowing God's excellence, but also *supremely esteeming and loving him*, belongs to the communication of God's fullness. And the communication of God's joy and happiness consists chiefly in communicating to the creature that happiness and joy, which consists in *rejoicing in God and in his glorious excellency;* for in such joy God's own happiness does principally consist. And in these things, viz. in *knowing God's excellency, loving God for it, and rejoicing in it;* and in the exercise and expression of these, *consists God's honor and praise*: so that these are clearly implied in that glory of God, which consists in *the emanation of his internal glory*" (Jonathan Edwards).[5]

---

3. Spirit born means originating with the Spirit; Spirit borne means carried along and borne up by the Spirit. The one is originating, the other is sustaining.

4. Edwards, *Works*, 8: 527.

5. Edwards, *Works*, 8: 529.

Edwards defined the glory of God in a unique way: Edwards utilizes the illustration of the Sun to explain the glory of God, or the supremacy of God:

> "Thus we see that the great and last end of God's works which is so variously expressed in Scripture, is indeed but *one*; and this *one* end is most properly and comprehensively called, "the glory of God"; by which name it is most commonly called in Scripture. And is fitly compared to an effulgence or emanation of light from a luminary, by which this glory of God is abundantly represented in Scripture. Light is the external expression, exhibition and manifestation of the excellency of the luminary, of the sun for instance: it is the abundant, extensive emanation and communication of the fullness of the sun to innumerable beings that partake of it. 'Tis by this that the sun itself is seen, and his glory beheld, and all other things are discovered: 'tis by a participation of this communication from the sun that surrounding objects receive all their luster, beauty and brightness. 'Tis by this that all nature is quickened and receives life, comfort and joy. Light is abundantly used in Scripture to represent and signify these three things, knowledge, holiness and happiness" (Jonathan Edwards).[6]

2. BIBLICAL PERSPECTIVE

OLD TESTAMENT

Our focus here is the preacher's passion for the supremacy and the glory of God as an indispensable element in revival preaching. There is a plethora of material in Scripture showing that this passion for the glory of God in the life of the preacher is a critical link in the promulgation of revival.

> a. Elijah's showdown with the prophets of Baal and the turnaround of an entire nation hinges on his motivation, which is captures for us by the biblical text: "Answer me, O lord, answer me, so that this people may know that you, o Lord, are God, and that you have turned their hearts back" (I Kgs 18:37) (NIV). The very next phrase is: "Then the fire of the Lord fell . . . " (I Kgs 18:38) (NIV). These prophets were imbibed with a passion for the supremacy of God in preaching.

---

6. Edwards, *Works*, 8: 530.

b. Isaiah's "revival preaching" was undoubtedly revitalized and energized by his vision of the glory of Christ (Is 6:18; John 12:41); certainly, Isaiah's classic sermon of the supremacy and the glory of God, which we might entitle "Behold Your God" (Isaiah 40:9) was critical in shifting the tide from judgment (chapters 1–39) to hope (chapters 40–66).

c. Ezekiel: The prophet or preacher Ezekiel was a revival preacher. He ministered in a season of exile of the people of God, and the restoration of those people from Babylon to Jerusalem, the "City of God," provides the theologian of revival with a powerful "motif" or template for revival (See Ps 137). Ezekiel's preaching, highlighted by his famous "Valley of Dry Bones" prophecy, (Ezek 37) illustrates effective revival preaching. What is significant in his ministry is the passion he had for the glory of God. His entire ministry was initiated and influenced by the theophany of the glory of God (Ezek 1:1–28), a word (glory) that occurs 24 times in his book. Ezekiel was especially passionate that God's people know who God is. The Hebrew way of expressing that passion is the phrase "they will know that I am the Lord" which occurs 25 times in the NIV of Ezekiel. Undoubtedly Ezekiel's passion for the manifest glory of the Lord contributed significantly to his success as a revival preacher, leading to the ultimate restoration from exile of God's "valley of dry bones" people.

d. The prophet Daniel, another prophet of the exile, exhibits in prayer his passion for the glory of God to be displayed and extant in the restoration and revival of God's people. In the culmination of his prayer for the restoration of God's people, (Dan 9:3–19) we hear Daniel reaching the culminating point, the apex of his prayer, in verse 19: "O Lord, hear; O Lord, forgive; O Lord, listen and act and do not delay! For your own sake, O my God, because your city and your people bear your name!" (Dan 9:19) (NASB). Daniel's passion for the glory of God and the integrity of His name becomes the culmination of his prayer. Prayer and preaching are vitally linked. There is no revival preaching without revival praying. Daniel illustrates the latter, although there is little evidence that he was a revival preacher per se.

. If we look for it, we can find this motivation documented in most if not all of the prophetic voices of the Old Testament that God used to turn the hearts of the people back to God.

NEW TESTAMENT

Jesus had a very particular view and understanding of his speaking and the glory of God. This is worth exploring. He said, "My teaching is not mine, but his who sent me" (John 7:16) (NASB). Jesus did not practice self-initiated spirituality. We commonly affirm the need to be proactive instead of reactive, and at first glance that sounds good, but Jesus turned that on its head—his spirituality was reactive, not proactive. Not reactive in the sense of reacting to his circumstances. But reactive in the sense of reacting to the initiatives of the Father, and not stepping out proactively on His own initiative. Jesus clearly affirmed: "I can do nothing on My own initiative. As I hear, I judge;" (John 5:30) (NASB).

Our ability to be proactive and not reactive (in relationship to our circumstances), that is, not be ruled by our particular circumstances but rather be proactive and rule over our life circumstances, is conditioned upon the previous commitment to be reactive and not proactive in our relationship to God. In other words, we will have the grace and power that comes from God, as we set our wills to listen to Him and do what He says, in the power and the enabling which He gives, and this directive and this enabling raises us above the fray of our circumstances, enabling and empowering us to be proactive over them, instead of reacting negatively to them. This is powerful! The initiative comes from the Father, and subsequently the glory goes to the Father. These two are intrinsically and intricately intertwined. Jesus said that the Pharisees could not believe because they were seeking the glory from one another, and they were failing to seek the glory that comes from the only God (John 5:44).

Just as Jesus took his initiatives from the Father, and exercised his will in pursuing those initiatives, so the Christian must be proactive in seeking the Father's will, listen to His directives, obtain His enabling to do what He has asked us to do (as opposed to asking God to blessing our initiatives), and then reacting to that initiative. As we face life circumstances, we can be proactive, not reactive, because previously we have been reactive to the initiatives of the Father, nor independently proactive.

Just as Jesus took his initiatives from the Father, and exercised his will in pursuing those initiatives, speaking what the Father indicated, so the preacher must listen to the Father, be reactive to His initiatives, and then proceed. The determining factor in this "paradigm" is "whose glory"? If we step out on our own, we are seeking our own glory. If we wait and react, we are seeking His glory (John 7:16–18).

3. QUOTES FROM EDWARDS

We know that Edwards struggled with "spiritual pride." It is one of the "gajes del oficio" [Spanish] or "risks of the trade" of the revivalist preacher. Edwards utilizes the phrase "spiritual pride" 145 times in his writings, and it is evident from the frequency of usage and the nature of his treatment of the matter, especially in the context of revival, that it was a significant issue in his life. In his personal Journal, Edwards yearns to be humble and not proud: *Saturday, March 2.*—O, how much pleasanter is Humility than Pride! O, that God would fill me with exceeding great Humility, and that he would evermore keep me from all Pride! The Pleasures of Humility are really the most refined, inward, and exquisite Delights in the World. How hateful is a proud Man! How hateful is a Worm that lifts up itself with Pride! What a foolish, silly, miserable, blind, deceived, poor Worm am I, when Pride works!

I believe that the way Edwards dealt with this special "thorn in the flesh" and particular weakness that he had a proclivity to, was by emphasizing the supremacy of God in all his life and ministry, but particularly in his preaching. I will develop this theme more fully when we deal with the chapter on "spiritual pride." I have dedicated an entire chapter to this ugly theme as it tends, more than any other issue, to sabotage revival in the life and ministry of the revival preacher.

To gain a fuller and more comprehensive understanding of Edwards's thinking at this point, we do well to reflect upon this quote:

> The emanation or communication of the divine fullness, consisting in the knowledge of God, love to God, and joy in God, has relation indeed both to God and the creature: but it has relation to God as its fountain, as it is an emanation from God; and as the communication itself, or thing communicated, is something divine, something of God, something of his internal fullness; as the water in the stream is something of the fountain; and as the beams are of the sun. And again, they have relation to God as they have respect to him as their object: for the knowledge communicated is the knowledge of God; and so, God is the object of the knowledge: and the love communicated, is the love of God; so God is the object of that love: and the happiness communicated, is joy in God; and so he is the object of the joy communicated. In the creature's knowing, esteeming, loving, rejoicing in, and praising God, the glory of God is both exhibited and acknowledged; his fullness is received and returned. Here is both an *emanation* and *remanation*.[7] The refulgence shines

---

7. Edwards seems to mean "reflect." God's glory in innate and essential to Himself,

upon and into the creature and is reflected back to the luminary. The beams of glory come from God, and are something of God, and are refunded back again to their original. So that the whole is *of* God, and *in* God, and *to* God; and God is the beginning, middle and end in this affair (Jonathan Edwards).[8]

What follows is my "translation" and application to preaching: The glory of God is like the water of a fountain, or like the beams of the sun. As God reveals His glory, and the light of the glory of God dawns upon the believer, something happens: In the creature's knowing, esteeming, loving, rejoicing in, and praising God, the glory of God is both exhibited and acknowledged; His fullness is received and returned. As the believer is enlightened, he now knows and so esteems, and loves and rejoices in and praises God; as a result, the glory of God shines on the believer, is received in believing, and is reflected back in praise. This Edwards calls "both an *emanation* and *remanation*. The refulgence shines upon and into the creature and is reflected back to the luminary" and the luminary is God. This is what it means, for Edwards, to live for the glory of God. This is the supremacy of God in preaching.

"Something else, entirely distinct from self-love might be the cause of this, viz. a change made in the views of his mind, and relish of his heart; whereby he apprehends a beauty, glory, and supreme good, in God's nature, as it is in itself. This may be the thing that first draws his heart to him, and causes his heart to be united to him, prior to all considerations of his own interest or happiness, although after this, and as a fruit of this, he necessarily seeks his interest and happiness in God" (Jonathan Edwards).[9]

"I think I have found that no discourses have been more remarkably blessed, than those in which the doctrine of God's absolute sovereignty with regard to the salvation of sinners, and his just liberty with regard to answering the prayers, or succeeding the pains of natural men, continuing such, have been insisted on" (Jonathan Edwards).[10]

---

and we reflect His glory as His grace transforms us. The word "remanation" is not in the English dictionary. However, we gain a better idea by reading the footnote by Ramsey as he comments on this unique word: JE's famous image of "emanation and remanation" was introduced just above by JE's assertion that the "glory of God" is "*fitly compared* to an effulgence or emanation of light from a luminary" (Ed. italics); and light (says he) is a scriptural representation. These words are followed immediately by words that plainly reflect Romans 11:36, "For of him and through him and to him are all things" Ramsey, *Works*, 8: 531, fn 8.

8. Edwards, *Works*, 8: 531.
9. Edwards, *Works*, 8: 241.
10. Edwards, *Works*, 4: 167–68.

"There is none like him, who is infinite in glory and excellency: he is the most high God, glorious in holiness, fearful in praises, doing wonders: his name is excellent in all the earth, and his glory is above the earth and the heavens: among the gods there is none like unto him; there is none in heaven to be compared to him, nor are there any among the sons of the mighty, that can be likened unto him. Their God is the fountain of all good, and an inexhaustible fountain; he is an all-sufficient God; a God that is able to protect and defend them and do all things for them: he is the King of Glory, the Lord strong and mighty, the Lord mighty in battle: a strong rock, and a high tower. There is none like the God of Jeshurun, who rideth on the heaven in their help, and in his excellency on the sky: the eternal God is their refuge, and underneath are everlasting arms: he is a God that hath all things in his hands, and does whatsoever he pleases: he killeth and maketh alive; he bringeth down to the grave, and bringeth up; he maketh poor and maketh rich: the pillars of the earth are the Lord's. Their God is an infinitely holy God: there is none holy as the Lord. And he is infinitely good and merciful. Many that others worship and serve as gods, are cruel beings, spirits that seek the ruin of souls; but this is a God that delighteth in mercy; his grace is infinite, and endures for ever: he is love itself, an infinite fountain and ocean of it" (Jonathan Edwards) (Sermon: Ruth's Resolution) (April 1735: At the height of the Great Awakening).[11]

"And there has been a wonderful alteration in my mind, with respect to the doctrine of God's sovereignty, from that day to this; so that I scarce ever have found so much as the rising of an objection against God's sovereignty, in the most absolute sense, in showing mercy on whom he will show mercy, and hardening and eternally damning whom he will. God's absolute sovereignty, and justice, with respect to salvation and damnation, is what my mind seems to rest assured of, as much as of anything that I see with my eyes; at least it is so at times. But I have oftentimes since that first conviction, had quite another kind of sense of God's sovereignty, than I had then. I have often since, not only had a conviction, but a *delightful* conviction. The doctrine of God's sovereignty has very often appeared, an exceeding pleasant, bright and sweet doctrine to me: and absolute sovereignty is what I love to ascribe to God. But my first conviction was not this" (Jonathan Edwards).[12]

---

11. Edwards, *Works*, 19: 310.
12. Edwards, *Works*, 18: 79–192.

4. QUOTES BY EDWARDSEAN SCHOLARS

"Good preaching is God-centered, not man-centered . . . Good preaching is Christ-centered not morality or behaviour centered . . . Good preaching does not make the text meaningful for us in our contemporary situation; rather, good preaching makes us and our contemporary situation meaningful in the text. In other words, good preaching does not pull the word into our world as if the word were deficient in itself and in need of our applicatory skills. Instead, good preaching testifies and declares to us that we have been pulled into the word which has its own marvelous sufficiency" (Dennison quoted in Carrick.[13])

Edwards's first sermon in Boston, preached in 1731, was "God Glorified in the Work of Redemption, by the Greatness of Man's Dependence upon Him, in the Whole of It" has a strong emphasis on the sovereignty of God. This emphasis seems to be a harbinger to the revival. Kimnach comments "God Glorified is an important sermon because it is the second installment, after the Quaestio, [thesis] of Edwards's anti-Arminian argument validating man's absolute helplessness before a sovereign God. Man was dependant "of" "by" "through" and "in" . . . to dramatize the completeness of man's dependence"[14].

Mark Noll calls this reference to the glory of God the "unifying centre"; "the glory of God . . . as an active, harmonious, ever unfolding source of absolutely perfect Being marked by supernatural beauty and love"[15].

5. ILLUSTRATIONS FROM THE ACTUAL SERMONS OF EDWARDS

The supremacy and sovereignty of God is evident in all the preaching of Edwards. We have already opened this chapter with a lengthy quote from one of his most influential sermons (Ruth's Resolution) preached during the Great Awakening . . . precisely to reinforce the relationship between this kind of God-intoxicated preaching and revival.

I will give just one more quote, although examples abound. This quote is taken from his famous sermon "The Justice of God in the Damnation of Sinners" (Rom 3:19) preached (possibly: scholars are uncertain) in May 1735.

---

13. Carrick, *Imperative of Preaching*, 132.
14. Ramsey, *Works*, 8: 111.
15. Haykin, *Jonathan Edwards*, 4.

Our obligation to love, honor, and obey any being, is in proportion to his loveliness, honorableness, and authority. For that is the very meaning of the words, when we say anyone is very lovely; it is the same as to say, that he is one very much to be loved: or if we say such an one is more honorable than another; the meaning of the words is, that he is one that we are more obliged to honor. If we say anyone has great authority over us, 'tis the same as to say that he has great right to our subjection and obedience. But *God is a being infinitely lovely* because he hath infinite excellency and beauty. To have infinite excellency and beauty, is the same thing as to have infinite loveliness. *He is a being of infinite greatness, majesty and glory; and therefore, is infinitely honorable.* He is infinitely exalted above the greatest potentates of the earth, and highest angels in heaven; and therefore, is infinitely more honorable than they. His authority over us is infinite; and the ground of his right to our obedience, is infinitely strong for he is infinitely worthy to be obeyed in himself, and we have an absolute universal and infinite dependence upon him (Jonathan Edwards).[16]

This is Edwards's way of preaching for revival. He exalts the Being of God. He places the Person of God in a position of pre-eminence in the sermon. Then he reasons with the listener and argues persuasively appealing for a commitment to this kind of a Person.

6. 70 RESOLUTIONS

Is there anything in these resolutions, even in seed form, that sheds light on His passion for the glory of God? There are 5 that very specifically refer to the place and priority of the glory of God as a primary motivation in the life of Edwards: 1, 4, 12, 23 and 27. I have presented each of these resolutions below with a brief commentary on their relevance to this point: The Supremacy of God in Preaching.

1. Resolved, that I will do whatsoever I think to be *most to God's glory*, and my own good, profit and pleasure, in the whole of my duration, without any consideration of the time, whether now, or never so many myriads of ages hence. Resolved to do whatever I think to be my duty and most for the good and advantage of mankind in general. Resolved to do this, whatever difficulties I meet with, how many soever, and how great soever.

---

16. Edwards, *Works*, 19: 342.

First, the obvious should be mentioned, and that is that pride of place goes to the mention of the glory of God as his primary motivation in this, his very first resolution. Edwards is consistent with himself in that respect. His first and foremost motivation was the glory of God.

Secondly, we can see echoes of the Shorter Catechism here: "What is the chief end of man? The chief end of man is to glorify God and enjoy Him forever." Edwards worked out that statement in his first resolution, and indeed sought to personify that in all of life and ministry.

It is curious that Edwards links God's glory with his own good, profit and pleasure, leading us to understand what Piper calls "Christian hedonism." Edwards understood that fundamentally there need not be a conflict with the ultimate glory of God and our own pleasure. If we delight ourselves in the Lord, He will give us the desires of our heart. True, in some aspects of our heart, there is a major transformation, so that our desires are synchronized with God's desires. As we seek His glory, our heart more and more buys into the things of God. We believe that Edwards's passion for preaching is subsumed under this first resolution. When he affirmed "Resolved to do whatever I think to be my duty and most for the good and advantage of mankind in general" that meant that he felt it his duty to preach well and write well, for the good and advantage of mankind in general" and by so doing he felt that this would be to the glory of God. God would be glorified when mankind would be blessed in his preaching.

4. Resolved, never to do any manner of thing, whether in soul or body, less or more, but *what tends to the glory of God;* nor be, nor suffer it, if I can avoid it.

Translation: His ultimate goal and purpose, to which he aspired that every activity, without exception, be subordinate to, was the glory of God, and all activity was to tend to or facilitate and foster that glory. Therefore, preaching and writing he believed tended to the glory of God. As Quinlan puts it: *I will also stay away from those things that do not honor God as much as I possibly can, and whenever possible, I will try to put a stop to activities that bring God dishonor*[17].

12. Resolved, if I take delight in it as a gratification of pride, or vanity, or on any such account, immediately to throw it by.

Translation: Edwards's resolutions need to be interpreted contextually. There is frequently a flow to them. This is a case in point. When he states, "if I take delight in it as a gratification of pride, or vanity, or on any such account" we are forced to ask: What is "it"? The preceding resolution provides the answer: 11. Resolved, when I think of *any theorem in divinity to*

---

17. Quinlan, *Resolutions in Plain English*.

be solved, immediately to do what I can towards solving it if circumstances do not hinder. Edwards here was determined to give himself immediately to the mental activity leading to resolution of theological difficulties unless his circumstances did not allow him to "drop everything" and think! Joining the two resolutions, once he found the solution to any theological difficulty, he was determined not to be proud of that particular theological accomplishment.

The "pulpit" or "desk" (preaching or writing) can become a platform for parading the self. This is a common malady in the ministry. Effective preachers can quickly become ineffective because they become proud of their giftedness. We need to hear the warning of Malachi 2:12: "And now this commandment is for you, O priests. If you do not listen, and if you do not take it to heart to give honor to My name," says the Lord of hosts, "then I will send the curse upon you and I will curse your blessings; and indeed, I have cursed them *already*, because you are not taking *it* to heart" (NASB).

We know that Herod had a significant issue with pride of speaking. The scriptures record the incident with compelling clarity: (Acts 12: 21–23) And upon a set day Herod, arrayed in royal apparel, sat upon his throne, and made an oration unto them. And the people gave a shout, saying, 'It is the voice of a god, and not of a man'. And immediately the angel of the Lord smote him, because he gave not God the glory: and he was eaten of worms, and gave up the ghost" (Acts 12: 21–23) (KJV).

Edwards was keenly aware of these passages and warnings. His resolution #12 speaks of "immediately to throw it by." We would say "deal with it immediately" or "cast it off."

23. Resolved, frequently to take some deliberate action, which seems most unlikely to be done, *for the glory of God*, and trace it back to the original intention, designs and ends of it; *and if I find it not to be for God's glory, to repute it as a breach of the 4th Resolution.*

Here we see the fourth reference in the Resolutions to the Glory of God. This particular resolution reflects Edwards's determination to not allow spurious or selfish motivation to creep into any of his proposed actions. When he affirms "If there be any action which seems potentially not to be 'for the glory of God,'" this particular resolution needs to be interpreted in the light of Edwards's message "The Duty of Self-Examination" (Jonathan Edwards),[18] where Edwards exhorts his hearers to "Consider your ways" (Haggai 1:5) (NASB). There is a very helpful quote in that sermon which sheds considerable light on this resolution: "Thus, all our actions ought to be strictly examined and tried, and not only barely to consider the outward

---

18. Kimnach, *Works*, 10: 482–92.

action as it is in itself: but also, from what principle our actions do arise from; what internal principle we act and live [by], for actions are either good or bad according to the principle whence they arise. We must consider whether what we do, *we do from a love to God and his commands*, or whether from *a love to ourselves*—that is, to our flesh—love to this world, and love to sin. We ought diligently to consider why it is that we pray and read and hear and sing Psalms, whether out of love of reputation and fear of disgrace; or whether only from custom, education, and fashion; or *whether we do it from love to God and godliness*. For otherwise, all these things are good for nothing: we are but emptiness and vanity, a sounding brass, and a tinkling cymbal. Thus, the nature of all our actions ought to be strictly examined and considered by us" (Jonathan Edwards).[19] This is precisely what Edwards means in resolution #23 when he speaks of the need to "trace it back to the original intention, designs and ends of it." Edwards was passionate about the glory of God, and passionate about extricating from his life any vestige of anything that would detract from the glory of God.

What does he mean to "repute it"? To "repute" has an old English sense of "consider, think, esteem, or reckon" something, to recognize it as a breach of the 4th resolution. I get the sense that he means to "repute" and then "shirk" or "abandon" any such motivation. This shows Edwards's unmitigated commitment to the glory of God. We believe that this is precisely what he did regarding preaching, which was such a large part of his calling.

27. Resolved, never willfully to omit anything, except the omission be for the glory of God; and frequently to examine my omissions.

The only caveat for failing to do something would be "for the glory of God." Again, we see the pre-eminence of this overarching motivation in Edwards's life.

7. OTHER AUTHORS

John Piper has written one of the best books in this area, "The Supremacy of God in Preaching," borrowing heavily from his life-long mentor, Jonathan Edwards. Piper establishes a connection between preaching to the glory of God and revival. There is something about Edwards's view of preaching that made it conducive to revival. His motivation is for the glory of God. Piper "calls us back to a biblical standard for preaching, a standard exemplified by many of the pulpit giants of the past, especially Jonathan Edwards and Charles Spurgeon" (Warren Wiersbe)[20]. If preachers took Piper's message

---

19. Edwards, *Works*, 10: 488.
20. Piper, *Desiring God*.

seriously and followed his instructions, we could well be on our way to the revival we so desperately need.

"The Scottish preacher James Stewart put it like this: the aims of all genuine preaching are 'to quicken the conscience by the holiness of God to feed the mind with the truth of God, to purge the imagination by the beauty of God, to open the heart to the love of God, to devote the will to the purpose of God'" (James Stewart)[21].

One of the best books I ever read was J. I. Packer's "Knowing God." He makes a passionate appeal to the Christian Community in general to know God. He them proceeds to give a magisterial treatment on the Person of God. Each Pastor would do well to start with Packer and preach through the attributes of God.

8. CONCLUSION

This work is all about that kind of preaching that tends towards revival and spiritual awakening. What we have considered in this chapter is the supremacy of God in preaching. Edwards was instrumental in sustained revival because of his particular focus on God. I wish to appeal to preachers here to rediscover the Trinity in our preaching. To Behold our God (Isaiah 40:9). *Daniel 11:32* in the King James Version, states "but *the people that do know their God* shall be strong and do exploits." We need a people who know their God, so that they will in turn be strong and do exploits for the kingdom of God. For that to happen, we need to have a contingency of preachers who know their God (notionally and emotionally) who can lead their people into that kind of a knowledge. Triune God, may You be restored to Your proper place of pre-eminence in the pulpits of the churches today.

> A Prayer[22]
> Frances Brook
>
> *My goal Is God Himself*
> My goal is God Himself, not joy, nor peace,
> Nor even blessing, but Himself, my God;
> 'Tis His to lead me there—not mine, but His—
> At any cost, dear Lord, by any road.
> <><><>
> So, faith bounds forward to its goal in God,
> And love can trust her Lord to lead her there;

---

21. Piper, *Supremacy*, 23.
22. Brook, *My Goal is God Himself*.

Upheld by Him, my soul is following hard
Till God hath full fulfilled my deepest prayer.
<><><>
No matter if the way be sometimes dark,
No matter though the cost be oft-times great,
He knoweth how I best shall reach the mark,
The way that leads to Him must needs be strait.
<><><>
One thing I know, I cannot say Him nay;
One thing I do, I press towards my Lord;
My God my glory here, from day to day,
And in the glory there my great Reward.

Chapter 8

Edwards the Man and Revival Preaching

"God sent his Son into the world to be the light of the world these two ways, viz. by revealing his mind and will, to the world, and by setting the world a perfect example. So, ministers are set to be lights, not only as teachers, but as ensamples to the flock" (1 Peter 5:3) (Jonathan Edwards).[1]

"If a man teach uprightly and walk crookedly, more will fall down in the night of his life than he built in the day of his doctrine" (John Owen)[2].

INTRODUCTORY COMMENTS

So often it is the man (person) that makes the message. Often it is the revived preacher that is the instrument of revival himself. So, we want to explore the correlation between Revival Preaching and Jonathan Edwards as a man.

---

1. Edwards, *Works*, 25: 93.
2. Owen, *Integrity*.

1. DEFINE IT

While we are clear that the absolute truth and the message we are entrusted to communicate is the Word of God, we also believe that Yale professor of preaching, Phillips Brooks, was on to something when he affirmed that preaching is truth passed through the prism of personality. The effective communication of truth involves a combination of proclamation, explanation, and demonstration. The truth is lived out before the congregation in such a way that makes it appealing. What Edwards preached; Edwards lived! Not perfectly, but authentically. This point is related to the correlation between head and heart in preaching (Chapter 1). What we are emphasizing here is the issue of integrity.

2. BIBLICAL PERSPECTIVE

Isaiah was involved in the ministry, but then he met God in a new and renovating way (Isaiah 6:18). Isaiah was re-commissioned into the ministry with a new passion, a new vision, and a new enabling. He experienced personal revival, and that qualified him to minister to God's people and to the nations with a revival and awakening edge to his ministry. The same could be said for Ezekiel (Ez. 1).

"And *the Word became flesh*, and dwelt among us, and we saw His glory, glory as of the only begotten from the Father, full of grace and truth" (John 1:14) (NASB). Jesus was a master at communication. The principle of "incarnation" involves the fleshing out of truth in the example of a Person. People were attracted to Him, and to God through Him, because of the way in which He lived the truth that He was proclaiming and explaining.

The Apostles were men who had experienced the truth of revival and awakening at Pentecost, and so they were able to transmit what they themselves had experienced. "The life appeared; we have seen it and testify to it, and we proclaim to you the eternal life, which was with the Father and has appeared to us. We proclaim to you what we have seen and heard, so that you also may have fellowship with us. And our fellowship is with the Father and with his Son, Jesus Christ" (I John 1:23) (NIV).

Paul's remarkable Damascus Road experience (Acts 9), his initial experience of the fullness of the Spirit (Acts 9:17), and his ongoing experience in the fullness of the Spirit (Acts 13:9) qualified him to minister as a revival preacher (Acts 14:1; Acts 17:1, 2; Acts 19:16). Knowing the power of example, Paul exhorted the Ephesian elders "Be on guard for yourselves and for all the flock, among which the Holy Spirit has made you overseers, to shepherd the church of God which He purchased with His own blood" (Acts 20:28) (NASB) and he exhorted Timothy to "fan into flame the gift of God" (II Tim 1:6) (NIV) knowing that a minister with a dying flame is not the best candidate for a revival and awakening ministry.

Paul wrote to Timothy: "All Scripture is inspired by God and profitable for teaching, for reproof, for correction, for training in righteousness; so that the man of God may be adequate, equipped for every good work" (II Tim 3:16, 17) (NASB). The Scriptures play a significant role in the spiritual influence of the listener, but the phrase "man of God" alludes to the character and integrity of the preacher. The influence of the man, along with the message, is difficult to underestimate.

Peter exhorted leadership: "To the elders among you, I appeal as a fellow elder and a witness of Christ's sufferings who also will share in the glory to be revealed: Be shepherds of God's flock that is under your care, watching over them—not because you must, but because you are willing, as God wants you to be; not pursuing dishonest gain, but eager to serve; not lording it over those entrusted to you, but *being examples to the flock*" (I Pet 5:13) (NIV). Pastors can be and should be examples to the flock in revival and awakening. A "revival preacher" will be a revived preacher.

The Scriptures are clear: God calls us to lead by example, and one of the foremost areas of leadership that we as pastors and preachers are called to, is in the area of revival and awakening.

3. QUOTES FROM EDWARDS

If we look to Edwards's experience of God, we discover that the word "sweetness" occurs 642 times to describe God and the nature of the spiritual life. Here is but a sampling: "The first foundation of the delight a true saint has in God, is his own perfection; and the first foundation of the delight he has in Christ, is his own beauty; he appears in himself "the chief among ten thousand," and "altogether lovely" [Canticles 5:10, 16]: the way of salvation by Christ, is a delightful way to him, for the sweet and admirable manifestations of the divine perfections in it; the holy doctrines of the gospel, by which God is exalted and man abased, holiness honored and promoted, and sin greatly disgraced and discouraged, and free and sovereign love manifested; are glorious doctrines in his eyes, and sweet to his taste, prior to any conception of his interest in these things. Indeed the saints rejoice in their interest in God, and that Christ is theirs; and so they have great reason; but this is not the first spring of their joy: they first rejoice in God as glorious and excellent in himself, and then secondarily rejoice in it, that so glorious a God is theirs: they first have their hearts filled with *sweetness*, from the view of Christ's excellency, and the excellency of his grace, and the beauty of the way of salvation by him; and then they have a secondary joy, in that so excellent a Saviour, and such excellent grace is theirs" (Jonathan Edwards)[3]. We know that this was not merely notional knowledge for Edwards—his journals demonstrate abundant evidence of experiential knowledge of the sweetness of Christ. Consider, for example, his personal narrative:

"And when the discourse was ended, I walked abroad alone, in a solitary place in my father's pasture, for contemplation. And as I was walking there, and looked up on the sky and clouds; there came into my mind, so sweet a sense of the glorious majesty and grace of God, that I know not how to express. I seemed to see them both in a sweet conjunction: majesty and meekness joined together: it was a sweet and gentle, and holy majesty; and also a majestic meekness; an awful *sweetness*; a high, and great, and holy gentleness" (Jonathan Edwards).[4]

4. QUOTES BY EDWARDSEAN SCHOLARS

"If preaching is to be effectual in revival it must never be divorced from *our experience of the presence of God*. This is critical if we wish to experience revival through our preaching"[5] [emphasis mine]. Edwards, in the aforementioned quotes, illustrates perfectly what Keevil is affirming.

According to Kimnach, "The organizing metaphor of the sermon is the conventional Christian one of light, though Edwards explores the concept with such energy and imagination that he seems to be defining a novel concept. His text's light is "burning and shining," corresponding to ardor and intelligence—or will and understanding. For Edwards, the important thing is that the two dimensions of light be *balanced equally* and united in a functional whole. Thus, the minister must be both learned in the Scripture and familiar with the *"inward operations" of the Holy Spirit*; likewise, the doctrine he preaches must be both "bright and full," or purely inspiring and rich in content. The minister must address his flock discreetly yet present true religion *authentically*"[6]. These "inward operations" refer to Edwards's experience of the truth. Edwards does not divorce the man from the message. There is minimal dissonance between the message preached and the

---

3. Edwards, *Works*, 2: 250.
4. Edwards, *Works*, 10: 274–75.
5. Keevil, *Preaching in Revival*, 166.
6. Kimnach, *Works*, 25: 82.

message lived, and this element of authenticity and integrity gives a spiritual authority to revival preaching.

In a letter written from Northampton to a Rev. Thomas Prince of Boston, and dated Dec. 12, 1743, Edwards gives careful documentation to the surprising work of God. When Whitefield preached, Edwards "wept during the whole of exercise" (Journal of Whitefield) and the congregation was "equally affected." During the afternoon, the power increased yet more. Edwards wrote (1743) that the congregation was "extraordinarily melted by every sermon" with "almost the whole assembly being in tears" during the preaching. "Whitefield's affecting preaching had rekindled the fires of revival in the Massachusetts town, as the following months would show"[7]. Edwards's response to the preaching of Whitefield is significant in that is set the tone for Edwards's parishioners. They saw in him an example of how to respond to "revival preaching." His integrity in setting the example for his parishioners is a significant factor in understanding the spiritual dynamics of revival preaching. The authenticity that Kimnach alludes to was demonstrated in his approach to revival.

Edwards had a view of preaching that was very "incarnational." According to Westra, Edwards viewed the minister as "a kind of subordinate savior" (Sermon on Acts 20:28).[8] He had a very high view of the sermon and preaching as a "means of grace" (Calvin's influence).[9] " . . . ministers stand as God's significations"[10], and "their express purpose being to prepare the hearts for the Word and to communicate with utter integrity the vital relationships and connections between words spoken and heard, and their ultimate meanings in the mind and will of God, who is both creative and redemptive Word. "In preaching the minister faithfully attempts to externalize the spiritual world of God's will and mind and at the same time to demonstrate an obedient, gracious, personal response to God's infinite perfection and glory."[11]

Endeavoring to describe Edwards's understanding of knowledge as experiential or participatory knowledge, Stout states the following: "The two parts of the doctrine embody Edwards's deeply held beliefs about conversion and its effects on the soul. In the first place he seeks to distinguish spiritual understanding from all merely "notional" knowledge, no matter how orthodox or sophisticated. It is a "taste" or "sense" of the beauty and

---

7. Haykins, *Jonathan Edwards*, 83.
8. Westra, *The Minister's Task*, ix.
9. Westra, *The Minister's Task*, ix.
10. Westra, *The Minister's Task*, x.
11. Westra, *The Minister's Task*, x.

excellency of divine things, a direct, immediate, intuitive, and self-authenticating knowledge of their truth and reality. Edwards labors hard to describe this knowledge in experiential terms: it is a "lively apprehension," "a certain seeing and feeling" that is "deep intense and affecting." It is the difference between having a notion that honey is sweet and actually tasting its *sweetness*. But precisely because it is direct and immediate it is true knowledge; hence he calls it spiritual "light."[12] This quote helps to clarify that it is Edwards's experience of truth that was the catalyst for revival.

There is some overlap here with Edwards's view of combining head and heart, or both a notional and experiential knowledge of truth. Carrick has a very helpful observation showing the correlation between moral integrity, passion and effective revival preaching: " . . . this feeling of passion, which belongs to the essence of true preaching, is inextricably related to the spirituality or piety of the preacher's heart."[13] Again, "But the most important element in the effective use of exclamation by the preacher is unquestionably the piety of his heart and the energy of his soul"[14].

Experiential preaching was more than anything else an appeal to *both the heart and minds* of men, women, and children. It aimed to change them, not just land on them. Richard Baxter carries the meaning well when he says, "As man is not so prone to live according to the truth he knows *except it do deeply affect him*, so neither doth his soul enjoy its sweetness, except *speculation do pass to affection*. The understanding is not the whole soul, and therefore cannot do the whole work. . .. The understanding must take in truths, and prepare them for the will, and it must receive them and commend them to the affections; . . .the affections are, as it were, the bottom of the soul" (Steele) [Emphasis mine].[15]

5. ILLUSTRATIONS FROM THE ACTUAL SERMONS OF EDWARDS

To appreciate the importance that Edwards gives to the role of the person in the pulpit, we turn to Edwards's Ordination Sermon entitled "The True Excellency of a Minister of the Gospel," preached in 1744. It provides his most clear and compelling vision of the preacher in a single document. It is significant that his text was "*He was a burning and a shining light*" from John 5:35.

12. Stout, *Works*, 13: 15.
13. Carrick, *The Imperative of Preaching*, 54.
14. Carrick, *The Imperative of Preaching*, 55.
15. Steele, *Classical Analysis*.

a. The preacher is to *burn with the truth, by the Spirit's enabling.* "True faith is an ardent thing, and so is true repentance; there is a holy power and ardor in true spiritual comfort and joy; yea even in true Christian humility, submission and meekness. The reason is that divine love or charity is the sum of all true grace, which is a holy flame enkindled in the soul. 'Tis by this therefore especially, that a minister of the gospel is a "burning light"; a minister that is so, has his soul enkindled with the heavenly flame; his heart burns with love to Christ, and fervent desires of the advancement of his kingdom and glory; and also with ardent love to the souls of men, and desires for their salvation" (Jonathan Edwards).[16] Again "His fervent zeal, which has its foundation and spring in that holy and powerful flame of love to God and man, that is in his heart, appears in the fervency of his prayers to God, for and with his people; and in the earnestness, and power with which he preaches the word of God, declares to sinners their misery, and warns them to fly from the wrath to come, and reproves, and testifies against all ungodliness; and the unfeigned earnestness and compassion with which he invites the weary and heavy laden to their Savior" (Jonathan Edwards).[17]

b. As a burning light, *the truth must be ablaze in his heart.* "He must be one that is acquainted with experimental religion, and not ignorant of the inward operations of the Spirit of God, nor of Satan's devices; able to guide souls under their particular difficulties. Thus he must be a scribe well instructed in things that pertain to the kingdom of God; one that 'brings forth out of his treasures things new and old'" [Matt 13:52] (Jonathan Edwards).[18]

c. Ministers are to be a source of *both light and heat,* that is, understanding and fervor. They must go together, in beautiful symmetry. Light without heat and heat without light are deficient. "'Tis the glory of the sun that such a bright and glorious light, and such a powerful, refreshing, vivifying heat, are both together diffused from that luminary" (Jonathan Edwards).[19] Edwards makes the application of these two qualities joined together in a powerfully insightful fashion: "Herein a minister of the gospel will be likely to answer the ends of his ministry: by this means

---

16. Edwards, *Works,* 25: 91–92.
17. Edwards, *Works,* 25: 91–92.
18. Edwards, *Works,* 25: 93.
19. Edwards, *Works,* 25: 95.

his ministry will not only be *amiable*, but *profitable*. If a minister has *light without heat*, and entertains his auditory with learned discourses, without a savor of the power of godliness, or any appearance of fervency of spirit, and zeal for God and the good of souls, he may gratify itching ears, and fill the heads of his people with empty notions; but will not be very likely to reach their hearts or save their souls. And if, on the other hand, he be driven on with a fierce and intemperate zeal, and *vehement heat, without light*, he will be likely to kindle the like unhallowed flame in his people, and to fire their corrupt passions and affections; but will make them never the better, nor lead them a step towards heaven, but drive them apace the other way. But if he approves himself in his ministry, as *both a burning and a shining light*, this will be the way to promote true Christianity amongst his people, and to make them both wise and good, and cause religion to flourish among them in the purity and beauty of it."[20] "But by light and heat accompanying one another, the whole face of the earth becomes fruitful, and is adorned, and all things are quickened and flourish, and mankind enjoy both life and comfort" (Jonathan Edwards).[21] The man and the message need to be intricately and inextricably intertwined.

6. 70 RESOLUTIONS

There is a sense in which the whole of the Resolutions points to this truth. Edwards is placing himself and his resolve into his relationship with God. Some of the vows bring this out more sharply. Consider the following:

6. Resolved, to *live with all my might*, while I do live.

22. Resolved, to endeavor to obtain for myself as much happiness, in the other world, *as I possibly can, with all the power, might, vigor, and vehemence, yea violence, I am capable of, or can bring myself to exert*, in any way that can be thought of.

56. Resolved, never to give over, nor in the least to slacken, *my fight with my corruptions, however unsuccessful I may be.*

64. Resolved, when I find those "groanings which cannot be uttered" (Rom. 8:26), of which the Apostle speaks, and those "breakings of soul for the longing it hath," of which the Psalmist speaks, Psalm 119:20, that I will

---

20. Edwards, *Works*, 25: 97.
21. Edwards, *Works*, 25: 97.

promote them *to the utmost of my power,* and *that I will not be weary of earnestly endeavoring* to vent my desires, nor of the repetitions of such earnestness. July 23, and August 10, 1723 [emphases mine].

All four of these resolutions show the extent to which Edwards gives himself to the pursuit of cultivating his relationship with God. In a previous chapter (Chapter 5) I highlighted these same vows to suggest that perhaps these expressions betray a fundamental self-reliance and reflect a need for the Divine empowering. However, he does preface the vows with this statement: "Being sensible that I am unable to do anything without God's help, I do humbly entreat him by his grace to enable me to keep these Resolutions . . . ." The least we can say here is that we cannot fault Edwards for the extent and degree to which he brings himself and his resolve to the table. This is especially evident in the first resolution: "Resolved to do whatever I think to be my duty and most for the good and advantage of mankind in general. Resolved to do this, whatever difficulties I meet with, how many and how great soever."

The resolutions were written primarily in a period of spiritual formation, at the outset of his ministry and career. We might say that these resolutions express the goals of Edwards and express his incipient spirituality. This is significant. He set his sails in the direction of these ideals. Edwards was a man with purpose, with vision, with aim, with resolve. In his sermon "Pressing into the Kingdom of God" (February 1735) Edwards stresses the importance of "strength of desire," "firmness of resolution," "greatness of endeavor" and "engagedness and earnestness" including a "breaking through opposition and difficulties" (Jonathan Edwards).[22] He himself exemplifies in his resolutions this same "vehemence" and "violence" that he asks of his congregants.

7. OTHER AUTHORS

What do other authors say about the role of the preacher as a person? "We are constantly on a stretch, if not on a strain, to devise new methods, new plans, and new organizations to advance the Church and secure enlargement and efficiency for the gospel. This trend of the day has a tendency to lose sight of the man or sink the man in the plan or organization. God's plan is to make much of the man, far more of him than of anything else. Men are God's method. The Church is looking for better methods; God is looking for better men."[23] How true. The issue in revival preaching has a great deal to

22. Edwards, *Works,* 19: 276–79.
23. Bounds, *Preacher and Prayer,* 6.

do with the integrity of the preacher. What are needed are men and women of God. When one listens to the accounts of revivals today, or reads from revivals from yesterday, one theme that resurfaces is the deeper work of the Holy Spirit in the life of the preacher, producing brokenness in him first, and then using him.

"He convinced me more and more that we can preach the Gospel of Christ no further than *we have experienced the power of it in our own hearts*. Being deeply convinced of sin, by God's Holy Spirit, at his first conversion, Mr. Tennent has learned experimentally to dissect the heart of the natural man" (Whitefield speaking about Tennent—could be easily applied to Edwards) [my emphasis].

As Bounds affirms, it is important that we realize that the man makes the message. That is, that the messenger is, if it were possible, more than the message; the preacher, more than the sermon, makes the sermon."[24]

"A cursory glance at the history of revivals will lead inevitably to the conclusion that those ministries that flourished during seasons of great religious awakening were characterized chiefly by unusual spiritual authority. Jonathan Edwards . . . is often referred to as an example of such preaching, read every word of his sermon, lifting his manuscript[25] up before blood-shot eyes. We know that his preaching did not just entertain the erudite and sophisticated academics of his times, but rather that some of his listeners were so affected by the Word he preached that they fell to the ground, gripped by fear in the presence of a wronged God. Undoubtedly, the effect of this man's preaching was due to the authority given him by the Spirit of God."[26]

Living within the family of the Trinity (Donald English)

---

24. Bounds, *Preacher and Prayer*, 6.

25. However, Eckhard affirms "Everything in the Yale collection indicates that Edwards preached extemporaneously, although not completely without notes. His pulpit notes even include devices to help him emphasize various points, and his outlines often clearly indicate that he intended to speak completely extemporaneously at certain points. In light of this evidence, there appears to be no reason for continuing to hold to the idea of Edwards as a manuscript preacher" *WTJ* 60:1 (Spring 1998) 84–85.

26. Keevil, *Preaching in Revival*, 167.

CONCLUSION

> Who may ascend into the hill of the Lord?
> And who may stand in His holy place?
> 4 He who has clean hands and a pure heart,
> Who has not lifted up his soul to falsehood
> And has not sworn deceitfully.
> 5 He shall receive a blessing from the Lord
> And righteousness from the God of his salvation.
> (Ps 24:3‑5) (NASB)

Lord, give us a passion for Your glory! An all-consuming passion that eclipses all self-seeking. Lord, give us a spirit of brokenness and genuine humility. Lord, give us what we need to come clean with You first, and then with others. Break our heart with what breaks Yours. Fill us with faith and courage to do a thorough job of repenting. Park our hearts in Psalm 51. Enable us to believe You for a full and free forgiveness, and a deep cleansing and fresh empowering. Direct our steps into any and all paths of reconciliation and restitution that Your Spirit and Your Word require of us. Fill and empower us to be that man, that woman of God. Then fill us with that Spirit of prayer and enable us to enter into the sphere of ministry that You have ordained for us to walk in (Eph 2:10). Enable us to be the revival that we seek, and then preach with integrity, with anointing, with brokenness, with compassion, with power, with all that You have for us. Enervate us with an all-consuming passion for Your glory. "There came a man sent from God, whose name was John (Jonathan). 7 He came as a witness, to testify about the Light, so that all might believe through him. 8 He was not the Light, but *he came* to testify about the Light" (John 1:6‑8). Amen. "He must increase, but I must decrease" (John 3:30) (KJV).

Chapter 9

Correlating Divine Sovereignty and Human Responsibility

"God is God, and He is a sovereign God" (Jonathan Edwards, Sermon #572).[1]

"God will not bestow such a great and infinite mercy as eternal life upon persons, who will not acknowledge his sovereignty in that matter. When once there has been that conviction upon the heart which casts down imaginations, and every high thing that exalts itself against God, then God is wont speedily to reveal his grace and love, and to pour the oil of comfort into the soul"[2] (Jonathan Edwards, Sermon: Natural Men in a Dreadful Condition")

"If one were to ask, given the total body of what Edwards wrote, what one idea stands out as more important than any other, the answer would have to be the utter sovereignty of God and the vehement denial of the existence of what were called 'secondary causes' or any power to operate independently of God."[3]

---

1. Edwards, *Sermon: Sovereign God*. http://edwards.yale.edu/research/sermon-index?series=1740.
2. Edwards, *Sermon: Dreadful*. https://www.biblebb.com/files/edwards/dreadful.htm.
3. Smith, *Puritan Preacher*, 142.

INTRODUCTION

We know that Edwards was Reformed, Calvinistic, and Puritan. To what degree can we trace revival to his emphasis on the sovereignty of God? Related to that is the way Edwards blends Divine sovereignty with human responsibility. To what degree can we trace revival to that particular blend?

1. DEFINE IT

We have already dealt with the centrality and supremacy of God in the preaching of Jonathan Edwards. This point is more specific. This deals with the issue of one of the attributes of God—His sovereignty. It also deals with how Edwards held together in biblical juxtaposition Divine Sovereignty and human responsibility. This is a critical matter in revival. The sovereignty of God in revival vis-à-vis[4] the role and responsibility of man in revival.

What do we mean by the sovereignty of God? With the "openness of God" and "open theism" debate in vogue with many variants on what is meant by affirming that God is sovereign, it is important to clarify concepts. Essentially, when we affirm the sovereignty of God, we affirm God has supreme power, and exercises freedom from any external control, including human influence. The dictionary gives the following synonyms for "sovereign": autonomy, independence, independency, liberty, self-determination, self-governance, self-government, freedom (Merriam-Webster)[5]. As the Scriptures affirm, "*Our God is in heaven; he does whatever pleases him*" (Ps 115:3) (NIV) [Emphasis mine]. "For from Him and through Him and to Him are all things. To Him be the glory forever. Amen" (Rom 11:36) (NASB).

The concept of the responsibility of man also needs to be clearly defined. While we affirm the concept of human responsibility, we would defer from using the term "free will." Certainly, Edwards himself would not endorse such a notion. Even the modern reduction to the title of his classic work "The Freedom of the Will" is misleading, and we would do well to retain the full title "*A Careful and Strict Inquiry into the Modern Prevailing Notions of the Freedom of Will*" [emphasis mine] to realize that Edwards was responding to then modern prevailing notions of the freedom of the will, negating such a concept and clarifying what he considered to be the more biblical representation of the truth, involving man's responsibility and accountability but certainly not his freedom and autonomy. Edwards believed

---

4. *Vis-à-vis* is a French phrase meaning "face to face," often used as "in relation to," "counterpart."

5. Merriam Webster, *Sovereignty*.

that every human being (individually) and all of humanity (collectively) are justly accountable for our actions even though we are hopelessly (apart from grace) bound in sin.

How these two concepts (Divine sovereignty and human responsibility) correlate is the challenge. And how do they relate to revival? Some theologians on revival endeavor to discuss the role of the sovereignty of God in revival and the role or responsibility of the individual Christian or the church in revival. Few theologians endeavor to correlate the two. Fewer still are as successful as Edwards.

2. BIBLICAL PERSPECTIVE

God is sovereign in all that He does. 1 Chronicles 29:11–12 affirms: "Yours, O Lord, is the greatness and the power and the glory and the victory and the majesty, for all that is in the heavens and in the earth is yours. Yours is the kingdom, O Lord, and you are exalted as head above all. Both riches and honor come from you, and you rule over all. In your hand are power and might, and in your hand it is to make great and to give strength to all." (See also: 1 Chronicles 29:11–12; Job 42:2; Ps 103:19; Lam 3:37; Is 46:9–10; Rom 9:18–21; Prov 16:4; and Job 23:13.)

God is sovereign in the election of His people. Ephesians 1:11–12: "In him we have obtained an inheritance, having been predestined according to the purpose of him who works all things according to the counsel of his will, so that we who were the first to hope in Christ might be to the praise of his glory" (NIV). Romans 9:19–21 (ESV) states "You will say to me then, "Why does he still find fault? For who can resist his will?" But who are you, O man, to answer back to God? Will what is molded say to its molder, "Why have you made me like this?" Has the potter no right over the clay, to make out of the same lump one vessel for honorable use and another for dishonorable use?" See also Ephesians 1:4; John 6:44; and Ephesians 2:10.

God is sovereign in the issue of the revival of His languishing followers. The classic vision of dry bones, with its emphasis on the Divine initiative, and Divine promise, reveals the necessity of a sovereign Divine intervention; otherwise, there is no way those dry bones can live again (Ezek 37:1–14)! Proverbs 21:1 affirms: "The king's heart is a stream of water in the hand of the Lord; he turns it wherever he will." If the king's heart, then the heart of his people, and any one of His particular people, is a stream in the Lord's hand which He may turn "wherever He will." The rhetorical questions in Job 38:37 places things in perspective (for Job and us): «Who has the wisdom to count the clouds? Who can tip over the water jars of the heavens» is an apt «liquid» metaphor for the affirmation of God's sovereignty as the source of renewal.

In the New Testament, we see the sovereignty of God in that prototype of revival recorded for us in Acts 2:14: "When the day of Pentecost arrived, they were all together in one place. And suddenly there came from heaven a sound like a mighty rushing wind, and it filled the entire house where they were sitting. And divided tongues as of fire appeared to them and rested on each one of them. And they were all filled with the Holy Spirit and began to speak in other tongues as the Spirit gave them utterance" (NIV). Also see Joel 2:23 (Revival as rain from heaven).

The Bible affirms the responsibility of the human person *in general*, in his/her salvation, and in his/her revival and spiritual awakening. From the outset, when man is made in the image of God, the commands are directed to the will. Scriptures assume humans are responsible for their actions, which is the foundation for justice and judgment. There is a broad appeal in the Scriptures to the *salvation* of all of humanity: "whosoever shall call upon the name of the Lord shall be saved" (Joel 2:32; Acts 2:21; Rom 10:13). There are numerous references of a Gospel appeal to all, as a bona fide offer (John 3:16, etc.). The Scriptures indicate that Christ died for the sins of the whole world (I John 2:2, etc.). When it comes to the matter of the *revival* of the church, there are references which appear to make the revival conditional upon the human element. Notice the "if" in the following traditional revival reference: 2 Chronicles 7:14 "If my people, which are called by my name, shall humble themselves, and pray, and seek my face, and turn from their wicked ways; then will I hear from heaven, and will forgive their sin, and will heal their land." Numerous other passages could be cited to show that revival is contingent upon the believer's appropriate activity, whether that be prayer, repentance, or some other activity. Consider James 4:810 "Come near to God and he will come near to you. Wash your hands, you sinners, and purify your hearts, you double-minded. Grieve, mourn, and wail. Change your laughter to mourning and your joy to gloom. Humble yourselves before the Lord, and he will lift you up." Numerous verses could be presented to show the emphasis on human responsibility in general, in salvation or in revival and awakening.

Their correlation

How does Divine sovereignty relate to human responsibility? We will present some intriguing Scriptures and then endeavor to sum up what we believe is the correlation of these twin truths. Acts 2:23 (ESV) states: "This Jesus, delivered up according to the definite plan and foreknowledge of God, you crucified and killed by the hands of lawless men." (This verse recognizes both God's sovereignty and human responsibility). When it comes to the sanctification of the believer, both elements work closely together: Philippians 2:12–13 "12 Therefore, my dear friends, as you have always obeyed—not only in my presence, but now much more in my absence—continue to work out your salvation with fear and trembling, 13 for it is God who works in you to will and to act in order to fulfill his good purpose." (NIV) [God takes the initiative in our salvation, its inception and its completion. But there is a vital role that the individual believer plays]. See also 2 Timothy 2:19 where both sovereignty and responsibility coexist in beautiful juxtaposition.

I believe that to be true to all of Scripture, we need to affirm the primacy of Divine Sovereignty while emphasizing human responsibility. By capturing this biblical primacy and emphasis on sovereignty without the negation of human responsibility we understand the Edwardsean approach to life, to salvation and, what is most germane to our interest, to revival.

3. QUOTES FROM EDWARDS

Edwards states "that God's moral government over mankind, his treating them as moral agents, making them the objects of his commands, counsels, calls, warnings, expostulations, promises, threatenings, rewards and punishments, is not inconsistent with a determining disposal of all events, of every kind, throughout the universe, in his providence: either by positive efficiency, or permission."[6]

God is sovereign. The evolution of his belief in the sovereignty of God is well documented in his own personal narrative. I quote here a generous portion so the reader catches how significant sovereignty was to Edwards: "From my childhood up, my mind had been wont to be full of objections against the doctrine of God's sovereignty, in choosing whom he would to eternal life, and rejecting whom he please, leaving them eternally to perish, and be everlastingly tormented in hell. It used to appear like a horrible doctrine to me. But I remember the time very well, when I seemed to be convinced, and fully satisfied, as to this sovereignty of God, and his justice in thus eternally disposing of men, according to his sovereign pleasure. But never could give an account, how, or by what means, I was thus convinced; not in the least imagining, in the time of it, nor a long time after, that there was any extraordinary influence of God's Spirit in it: but only that now I saw further, and my reason apprehended the justice and reasonableness of it. . . .

---

6. Piper, *Freedom of the Will*, 258.

I have often since, not only had a conviction, but a *delightful* conviction. The doctrine of God's sovereignty has very often appeared, an exceeding pleasant, bright and sweet doctrine to me: and absolute sovereignty is what I love to ascribe to God. But my first conviction was not this" (Jonathan Edwards).[7]

Edwards's first sermon in Boson, preached on July 8, 1731, "God Glorified in the Work of Redemption, by the Greatness of Man's Dependence upon Him, in the Whole of It" has a strong emphasis on the sovereignty of God. This emphasis seems to be a harbinger to the revival. Kimnach comments "'God Glorified' is an important sermon because it is the second installment, after the Quaestio, [Latin for Question] [thesis] of Edwards's anti-Arminian argument validating man's absolute helplessness before a sovereign God. Man was dependant "of" "by" "through" and "in" . . . to dramatize the completeness of man's dependence[8]. I have included some representative excerpts from these sermons below so that all doubt be removed as to where Edwards stands regarding the primacy of the sovereignty of God.

What about the correlation of this emphasis on sovereignty and the Great Awakening? In the series on justification by faith, so instrumental as a catalyst for the revival, the emphasis is on the mercy of God alone. God "has no regard to anything in the person justified, as godliness, or any goodness" (Jonathan Edwards).[9]

Edwards's belief in the role of God's sovereignty is not only applicable to salvation. If there is to be a revival among the people of God, it is contingent upon God's sovereignty. This is crystal clear in Edwards's account in the Faithful Narrative: I provide 4 of the 16 references to God's sovereignty to provide the reader with a sample: "Indeed God has not taken that course, nor made use of those means, to begin and carry on this great work, which men in their wisdom would have thought most advisable, if he had asked their counsel; but quite the contrary. But it appears to me that the great God has wrought like himself, in the manner of his carrying on this work; so as very much to show his own glory, and *exalt his own sovereignty*, power and all-sufficiency, and pour contempt on all that human strength, wisdom, prudence and sufficiency, that men have been wont to trust, and to glory in; and so as greatly to cross, rebuke and chastise the pride and other corruptions of men; . . . " [emphasis mine] (Jonathan Edwards).[10]

Again Edwards, reflecting on the unusual circumstances surrounding the Great Awakening, reflects theologically and states in the Faithful

---

7. Edwards, *Works*, 18: 79–192.
8. Kimnach, *Edwards as Preacher*, 111.
9. Edwards, *Works*, 19: 147.
10. Edwards, *Works*, 4: 294.

Narrative "We cannot determine how great a calamity distraction is, when considered with all its consequences, and all that might have been consequent, if the distraction had not happened; nor indeed whether (thus considered) it be any calamity at all, or whether it be not a mercy, by preventing some great sin, or some more dreadful thing, if it had not been. *'Tis a great fault in us to limit a sovereign all-wise God*, whose "judgments are a great deep" [Psalms 36:6], and "his ways past finding out" [Romans 11:33], where he has not limited himself, and in things concerning which he has not told us what his way shall be" [emphasis mine] (Jonathan Edwards).[11]

One of the traits of the revival, according to Edwards, a distinguishing mark[12] determining the authenticity of the revival, was the exaltation of God in the revival, and an increased awareness among the people of the attributes and character of God. He affirms the revival was " . . . accompanied with an admiring and exalting apprehension of the glory of the divine perfections, God's majesty, holiness, *sovereign grace*, etc.; with a sensible, strong and sweet love to God, and delight in him, far surpassing all temporal delights, or earthly pleasures; . . . " [emphasis mine];[13] and again " . . . a sweet rejoicing of soul at the thoughts of God's being infinitely and unchangeably happy, and an exulting gladness of heart that God is self-sufficient, and infinitely above all dependence, and reigns over all, and does his will with absolute *and uncontrollable power and sovereignty*" [emphasis mine] (Jonathan Edwards).[14]

Nevertheless, the genius of Edwards is not so much in his emphasis on Divine sovereignty, in my considered opinion, but rather in the way that he gives primacy to that truth while at the same time emphasizing human responsibility. It is my contention that this combination is one of the secrets to revival preaching, and it is incumbent upon us as aspiring revivalist preachers, to understand and assimilate a similar comprehension.

---

11. Edwards, *Works*, 4: 304.

12 Edwards wrote a treatise called "Distinguishing marks" in which he sets forth the criteria for ascertaining whether or not a revival is authentic and of Divine origin. After discarding several (9) false criteria for determining whether or not a revival is from God, Edwards proposes from an exposition of I John 4 five criteria for ascertaining with certainty whether or not a revival is from God: the exaltation of Jesus, the Spirit attacks Satan's interests, the promotion of an exalted view of Scripture, the elevation of Divine Doctrine and the promotion of love to God and man. Included in 'Divine Doctrine' and in 'the promotion of love to God' was an exaltation of the biblical understanding of God as sovereign. Therefore, Edwards viewed the response of the people to affirming the sovereignty of God as authenticating and establishing the legitimacy of the revival.

13. Edwards, *Works*, 4: 328.

14. Edwards, *Works*, 4: 337.

How does Edwards emphasize human responsibility while prioritizing Divine sovereignty?

Edwards makes strong and passionate appeals to the human will. His sermons exalt Divine sovereignty and then proceed to passionately and powerfully appeal to the human will. The importance that Edwards gives to the "improvement" (archaic for application) is so significant that I have dedicated one of the twelve "lessons" learned from Edwards about Revival Preaching to this. Here I simply want to emphasize that the passionate appeal, the compelling and logical force of his arguments, the persuasiveness of his rhetoric, and the sensational captivating force of his conclusions show how clearly Edwards believed in the engagement of the human mind, emotions and will. His emphasis on Divine sovereignty did not negate human responsibility, but rather informed, energized and optimized his addressing human responsibility. Some people struggle with how Calvinists can be missional, evangelistic, bona fide preachers and persuasive. Edwards would respond that it is precisely because we believe in a sovereign God that we can indeed be missional, evangelistic, bona fide preachers and persuasive. Divine sovereignty so energizes the Calvinistic preacher that he is able confidently to address the human will. Prayer to a sovereign God does not cripple evangelism, revival, and spiritual awakening—it enables and empowers it. Unless we understand this theological dynamic, our preaching, our revival preaching will be "hamstrung."[15]

Another aspect of "revival preaching" involving Divine Sovereignty and human responsibility has to do with prayer. God is sovereign, but God's sovereign means of implementing his plans and providential purposes is prayer. Edwards understood this dynamic, and that is why he took the initiative in writing the treatise (take a deep breath) "An Humble Attempt to Promote Explicit Agreement and Visible Union of God's People, in Extraordinary Prayer, for the Revival of Religion and the Advancement of Christ's Kingdom on Earth, Pursuant to Scripture Promises and Prophecies Concerning the Last Time." Divine Sovereignty and Human (Believer) Responsibility in Prayer for Revival are two truths that work together in perfect logic in Edwards biblically informed mind and heart. Rather than complaining, "Since God is sovereign, why pray?" (A question that reflects profound misunderstanding about Divine sovereignty) Edwards, biblically informed, celebrated "Since God is Sovereign, Prayer is the Key!"

---

15. For an excellent discussion, consider Piper's article on The Sovereignty and Responsibility (see Bibliography).

4. QUOTES BY EDWARDSEAN SCHOLAR PIPER

One last guideline for thinking about God's action in view of all this: Always keep in mind that everything God does toward men—His commanding, His calling, His warning, His promising, His weeping over Jerusalem,—everything is His means of creating situations which function as motives to elicit the acts of will which He has ordained to come to pass. In this way He ultimately determines all acts of volition (though not all in the same way) and yet holds man accountable only for those acts which they want most to do.

Piper offers a helpful comment clarifying what Edwards believes about the capacity of the human person to choose, and the relationship to Divine sovereignty. Using as a reference "The Freedom of the Will" Piper[16] proposes that first, Edwards argues that the thing which determines what "the will" chooses is not the will itself but rather motives which come from outside the will. More precisely, "it is that motive, which, as it stands in the view of the mind, is the strongest, that determines the will"[17]. He defines motive like this: "By motive, I mean the whole of that which moves, excites or invites the mind to volition, whether that be one thing singly, or many things conjunctly"[18]. By "strongest motive" he means "that which appears most inviting"[19]. Or as he puts it later, "the will always is as the greatest apparent good is"[20], in which case "good" means "agreeable" or "pleasing."[21]

Man's Enslaved Will

Hence the determination of our will does not lie. It is determined by the strongest motive as we perceive it, and motives are given. Therefore, all men are in a sense enslaved—as Paul says—either to righteousness or to sin (Rom. 6:16–23), or as Jesus put it, "Everyone who commits sin is the slave of sin" (John 8:34) (NASB). We are all enslaved to do what we esteem most desirable in any given moment of decision. We are enslaved to do what we want to do most. We are unable to do otherwise provided we are not physically hindered.

Edwards describes this situation with the terms *moral necessity* and *moral inability* on the one hand and *natural necessity* and *natural inability*

---

16. Piper, *Freedom of the Will*, 9.
17. Piper, *Freedom of the Will*, 9.
18. Piper, *Freedom of the Will*, 9.
19. Piper, *Freedom of the Will*, 10.
20. Piper, *Freedom of the Will*, 10.
21. Piper, *Freedom of the Will*, 11.

on the other. Moral necessity is the necessity that exists between the strongest motive and the act of volition which it elicits[22]. Thus, all choices are morally necessary since they are all determined by the strongest motive. They are necessary in that, given the existence of the motive, the existence of the choice is certain and unavoidable. Moral inability, accordingly, is the inability we all have to choose contrary to what we perceive to be the strongest motive[23]. We are morally unable to act contrary to what in any given moment we want most to do. If we lack the inclination to study, we are morally unable to study.

Natural necessity is "such necessity as men are under through the force of natural causes"[24]. Events are naturally necessary when they are constrained not by moral causes but physical ones. My sitting in this chair would be necessary with a "natural necessity" if I were chained here. Natural inability is my inability to do a thing even though I will it. If I am chained to this chair my strongest motive might be to stand up (say, if the room is on fire) but I would be unable.

Why This Clarification Matters

This distinction between moral inability and natural inability is crucial in Edwards's solution to the so-called antinomy between God's sovereign disposal of all things and man's accountability. The solution is this: Moral ability is not a prerequisite to accountability. Natural ability is. "All inability that excuses may be resolved into one thing; namely, want of natural capacity or strength; either capacity of understanding, or external strength."[25]

But moral inability to do a good thing does not excuse our failure to do it[26]. Though we love darkness rather than light and therefore cannot (because of moral inability) come to the light, nevertheless we are responsible for not coming, that is, we can be justly punished for not coming. This conforms with an almost universal human judgment, for the stronger a man's desire is to do evil the more unable he is to do good and yet the more wicked he is judged to be by men. If men really believed that moral inability excused a man from guilt, then a man's wickedness would decrease in proportion to the intensity of his love of evil. But this is contrary to the moral sensibilities of almost all men.

22. Piper, *Freedom of the Will*, 24.
23. Piper, *Freedom of the Will*, 28.
24. Piper, *Freedom of the Will*, 24.
25. Piper, *Freedom of the Will*, 150.
26. Piper, *Freedom of the Will*, 148.

Therefore, moral inability and moral necessity on the one hand and human accountability on the other are not an antinomy. Their unity is not contrary to reason or to the common moral experience of mankind. Therefore, to see how God's sovereignty and man's responsibility perfectly cohere, one need only realize that the way God works in the world is not by imposing natural necessity on men and then holding them accountable for what they cannot do even though they will to do it. But rather God so disposes all things (Eph. 1:11) so that in accordance with moral necessity all men make only those choices ordained by God from all eternity.

Here is a sampling of one of Edwards's sermons emphasizing Divine sovereignty: "But God is a being infinitely lovely, because he hath infinite excellency and beauty. To have infinite excellency and beauty, is the same thing as to have infinite loveliness. He is a being of infinite greatness, majesty and glory; and therefore is infinitely honorable. He is infinitely exalted above the greatest potentates of the earth, and highest angels in heaven; and therefore is infinitely more honorable than they. His authority over us is infinite; and the ground of his right to our obedience, is infinitely strong for he is infinitely worthy to be obeyed in himself, and we have an absolute universal and infinite dependence upon him" (Jonathan Edwards).[27]

Quotes by Other Edwardsean Scholars

John Smith, that Edwardsean scholar who wrote an excellent treatment called "Jonathan Edwards, Puritan, Preacher, Philosopher," captured an important and quintessential element in his preaching when Edwards affirms: "... the utter sovereignty of God and the vehement denial of the existence of what were called 'secondary causes' or any power to operate independently of God"[28]. The only caveat I would add to that excellent summary would be to reiterate that such a position does not negate human responsibility for, as we are seeing, Edwards believed in and addressed the will of man.

5. ILLUSTRATIONS FROM THE ACTUAL SERMONS OF EDWARDS

Edwards seems to have a proclivity to emphasizing the sovereignty of God in revival preaching. There are several references to this theme of the sovereignty of God and Divine election and predestination during both periods

---

27. Edwards. *Works*, 19: 342.
28. Smith, *Puritan Preacher*, 142.

of the Great Awakening. This can be substantiated by the sermon titles in some cases. Notice the following Sermons: #345—God is sovereign in conversion; #360—God is God, and He is a sovereign God; #572 (1741)—John 6:45: "There never was any man that once came to understand what manner of one Christ was but his heart was infallibly drawn to him"; . . . #505 Acts 9:13-15. "'Tis so with respect to God's bestowment of saving mercy on some persons, that there is no other account to be given of it but that he will show mercy." Feb. 1739; #528—Rom. 8:29-30. "The things which God doth for the salvation and blessedness of the saints are like an inviolable chain reaching from a duration without beginning to a duration without end." Dec. 7, 1739; #594—Hos. 11:3. "The affair of seeking salvation is an affair wherein persons do exceedingly need God's help." Feb. 17, 1741.[29]

But beyond the actual sermon titles is the faithfulness to the doctrine of sovereignty throughout the messages of this period. Edwards is remarkably consistent in his preaching to the great doctrines of the faith as understood by the reformed tradition. The general tenor or nature of these sermons is completely consistent with an emphasis on the sovereignty of God. As leading Edwardsean scholar Minkema affirms: "Recognition of the sovereignty of God in salvation, one of the main themes at the heart of Calvinism, is for Edwards's part and parcel of the Spirit's work in revival."[30]

Here is a sample of Edwards preaching on sovereignty; "There is an absolute and universal dependence of the redeemed on God. The nature and contrivance of our redemption is such, that the redeemed are in everything directly, immediately and entirely dependent on God: they are dependent on him for all and are dependent on him every way. The several ways wherein the dependence of one being may be upon another for its good, and wherein the redeemed of Jesus Christ depend on God for all their good, are these, viz., that they have all their good *of* him, and that they have all *through* him, and that they have all *in* him. That he is the cause and original whence all their good comes, therein it is *of* him; and that he is the medium by which it is obtained and conveyed, therein they have it *through* him; and that he is that good itself that is given and conveyed, therein it is *in* him" (Jonathan Edwards) (Sermon: God Glorified in Man's Dependence).[31]

---

29. All sermons accessible at http://edwards.yale.edu/research/sermon-index
30. Minkema, *Works*, 14: 436.
31. Edwards, *Works*, 17: 202.

6. 70 RESOLUTIONS

Edwards makes direct reference to God 11 times in his 70 resolutions, but in each and every one of them God is very present. Edwards was a "God-intoxicated" man, and there is no doubt that when He uses the word "God" it came freighted with all that the Reformed and Puritan heritage meant by God. Surprisingly, there are no explicit references to the sovereignty of God. The strong emphasis on human responsibility, together with an implicit emphasis on God as sovereign, help us to see how these two realities played out in the theology and praxis of Edwards.

7. OTHER AUTHORS

Packer, in his stimulating book "Evangelism and the Sovereignty of God," quotes a dialogue between a Calvinist, Simeon, and an Arminian, Wesley. The conversation sheds considerable light on the meaning of sovereignty in relationship to our salvation.[32]

"We should affirm the truth both of God's sovereignty and human freewill. "The Abstract of Principles" was the founding confession for The Southern Baptist Theological Seminary. It was penned by Basil Manly Jr. in 1859. Manly was a Calvinist, and yet Article IV on Providence reveals a healthy, theological balance in our Baptist forefather. Manly wrote: "God

---

32. Packer, *Evangelism*, 1314. It is instructive in this connection to ponder Charles Simeon's account of his conversation with John Wesley on December 20, 1784 (the date is given in Wesley's *Journal):* "Sir, I understand that you are called an Arminian; and I have been sometimes called a Calvinist; and therefore I suppose we are to draw daggers. But before I consent to begin the combat, with your permission I will ask you a few questions... Pray, Sir, do you feel yourself a depraved creature, so depraved that you would never have thought of turning to God, if God had not first put it into your heart?" "Yes," says the veteran, "I do indeed." "And do you utterly despair of recommending yourself to God by anything you can do; and look for salvation solely through the blood and righteousness of Christ?" "Yes, solely through Christ." "But, Sir, supposing you were at first saved by Christ, are you not somehow or other to save yourself afterwards by your own works?" "No, I must be saved by Christ from first to last." "Allowing, then, that you were first turned by the grace of God, are you not in some way or other to keep yourself by your own power?" "No." "What, then, are you to be upheld every hour and every moment by God, as much as an infant in its mother's arms?" "Yes, altogether." "And is all your hope in the grace and mercy of God to preserve you unto His heavenly kingdom?" "Yes, I have no hope but in Him." "Then, Sir, with your leave I will put up my dagger again; for this is all my Calvinism; this is my election, my justification by faith, my final perseverance: it is in substance all that I hold, and as I hold it. And therefore, if you please, instead of searching out terms and phrases to be a ground of contention between us, we will cordially unite in those things wherein we agree" (*Horae Homileticae*, Preface: I.xvii f.).

from eternity decrees or permits all things that come to pass, and perpetually upholds, directs and governs all creatures and all events; yet so as not in any wise to be author or approver of sin nor to destroy the freewill and responsibility of intelligent creatures."[33] [I would differ with Akin here on the usage of the term "freewill," as would Edwards, but we affirm the essential argument of the coexistence of Divine sovereignty and human responsibility].

Sundar Krishnan, in his fine book: *Catching the Wind of the Spirit*, uses the metaphor of sailing[34] to capture the relationship between human responsibility and Divine sovereignty. The wind blows where it wills, but we must set our sails. Whether thinking of the spiritual disciplines or revival, both elements are necessary if we are to reach our desired haven.

8. CONCLUSION

Jesus taught clearly "At that time Jesus said, 'I praise you, Father, Lord of heaven and earth, because you have hidden these things from the wise and learned and revealed them to little children. Yes, Father, for this is what you were pleased to do. All things have been committed to me by my Father. No one knows the Son except the Father, and no one knows the Father except the Son and those to whom the Son chooses to reveal him. Come to me, all you who are weary and burdened, and I will give you rest'" (Matt 11:25–28).

Clearly the prerogative to illuminate and reveal truth, and God Himself lies in the sovereign choice of the Son. " . . . no one knows he Father except the Son and those to whom the Son chooses to reveal him" (Matt 11:27). Nevertheless, Jesus continues by extending an open invitation to all who are weary and burdened and offers them unequivocally rest for their souls. Perhaps only in eternity will we fully understand how Divine sovereignty and human responsibility coexist peacefully, but we do well to maintain both in a kind of harmonious tension where the truth of God's Word on these matters is maintained with theological and evangelistic integrity.

---

33. Akin, *Debate*.
34. Krishnan, *Catching the Wind*, 11.

Chapter 10

The Importance of Application

"He took no time to describe the sensations of the doomed. Taking the eternal consequences of God's wrath for granted, *he made it seem personal and immediate* for each member of the congregation seated before him. Obliterating the world outside the meetinghouse walls, and foreshortening time until the final judgment was not eons hence but tomorrow and possibly today, he sent each unconverted Enfield citizen to his well-deserved doom. Nothing but God's own hand held him back. God was very angry. At any minute he might loose his hand"[1].

"22 Do not merely listen to the word, and so deceive yourselves. Do what it says. 23 Anyone who listens to the word but does not do what it says is like someone who looks at his face in a mirror 24 and, after looking at himself, goes away and immediately forgets what he looks like. 25 But whoever looks intently into the perfect law that gives freedom and continues in it—not forgetting what they have heard, but doing it—they will be blessed in what they do" (James 1:22–25) (NIV).

---

1. Winslow, *Edwards*, 192.

"Strength of application was, from one standpoint, the most striking feature of Puritan preaching, and it is arguable that the theory of discriminating application is the most valuable legacy that Puritan preachers have left to those who would preach the Bible and its gospel effectively today"[2].

INTRODUCTORY COMMENTS

Charles Finney said it clearly: "A revival is nothing else than a new beginning of obedience to God. Just as in the case of a converted sinner, the first step is a deep repentance, a breaking down of heart, a getting down into the dust before God, with deep humility, and forsaking of sin" (Finney, Lecture One—What a Revival of Religion is)[3]. At the point where obedience is required, that is the point where revival happens. While there is a sovereign element to revival, which is preeminent, from a human perspective the issue revolves around surrender and obedience. If that premise is true, it stands to reason that Edwards places a great deal of emphasis on the application of the Word by the Spirit addressing the will. This may in fact be the open secret to Edwards's theology of revival. Assuming a sovereign understanding of God, Edwards always brought the Word to bear upon the will. The application by the Spirit to the will addressing the matter of obedience is the heart of revival, and Edwards understood more than most the issues of the will and how God's sovereign grace related to the will of the hearer. Often it is through the application made by the preacher that the Holy Spirit applies to the heart the message; so we are co-labourers with God (I Cor 3:9). Edwards is very Calvinistic in his understanding of preaching as a Divine/human enterprise.

1. DEFINE IT

The application of the message has to do with bringing to bear the specific relevance of the Text and Doctrine to/on the listener. The Puritans also employed the term "improvement," not in the modern sense of making something better, but rather in the sense of improving our lives by assimilating the truth expounded. The dictionary does give this alternative definition of improvement: "The act of making profitable use or application of anything, or the state of being profitably employed; a turning to good

---

2. Packer, *Quest for Godliness*, 288.
3. Finney, *Lectures on Revival of Religion*.

account; practical application, as of a doctrine, principle, or theory, stated in a discourse."[4] Another term used to describe application was the term "use" or "usage," that is, what use or relevance is this truth to the listener, not in a utilitarian fashion, but rather in an edifying and helpful fashion.

There is also a need to clarify the difference between the preacher, on the one hand, appealing to the will by showing how the truth is applicable, and what steps are involved for the truth to be improved/assimilated, and, on the other hand, the Holy Spirit making the preached word efficacious and transformative through regeneration (in the unsaved) and sanctification (in the saved). It is one thing for the preacher to "apply" (appeal to the will with fervor and urgency) the text, it is another thing for the Holy Spirit to "apply" (make it real and efficacious) the text in the spirit of the listener.

2. BIBLICAL PERSPECTIVE

There are numerous Scriptural references that reinforce the importance of applying God's Word to life.

11 The words of the wise are like cattle prods—painful but helpful. Their collected sayings are like a nail-studded stick with which a shepherd drives the sheep" (Ecclesiastes 12:11) New Living Translation (NLT) or like another version reads "The wise man's words are like goads that spur to action" (TLB).

There are many exhortations in Scripture. It is easiest to see the flow in argument from indicatives to imperatives in the epistles (especially the Pauline letters), but wherever we meet a command in Scripture it is important to find the "why?" (i.e., the Gospel grounding it) as well as the "what and how" (the "reasonable service" that responds to it). Having done so, we should never shy away from pressing the claims of the imperatives. Romans 6 is an obvious example. There, Paul applies the Gospel to the question, "Should we then continue in sin so that grace may abound?" Yet what he applies there is the gospel: Being buried and raised with Christ in baptism, we are no longer under the dominion of sin. "Therefore, do not let sin reign in your mortal bodies, giving in to its every whim." The imperative itself is an application—or, better yet, implication, signified by "therefore" " (Michael Horton)[5].

The genius of Jesus' great "Sermon on the Mount" is the emphasis on application. The difference between the wise and foolish builder is the wise man " . . . hears these words of Mine and acts upon them" (Matthew 7:24)

---

4. *American Heritage Dictionary*, Fifth Edition, Improvement.
5. Horton, *Application*.

(NASB) while the foolish " . . . hears these words of mine and does not act upon them" (Matthew 7:26) (NASB). "Now that you know these things, you will be blessed if you *do* them" (Jesus) (John 13:17) [Emphasis mine]. "For whoever *does* the will of my Father in heaven is my brother and sister and mother" (Matthew 12:50) (NIV) [Emphasis mine].

Jesus said that *the Great Commission* involves " . . . teaching others to *observe* all that I commanded you . . . " (NASB) or as the NIV puts it "and teaching them to *obey* everything I have commanded you."

Paul told Titus that in his preaching there should be an emphasis on application: "You, however, must *tell everyone how to live in a way that agrees with the true teaching*" (Titus 2:1) (ERV).

In terms of describing how the Holy Spirit applies the Word, making the message effectual and fruitful in the listener, Ephesians 1:13 states "In Him, you also, after listening to the message of truth, the gospel of your salvation—having also believed, you were sealed in Him with the Holy Spirit of promise" (NASB). On the day of Pentecost, we see how the Apostle Peter made an application of the Word (Acts 2:29–36), but then we see how the Holy Spirit makes the application effectual, with the effect that: "Now when they heard *this*, they were pierced to the heart, and said to Peter and the rest of the apostles, "Brethren, what shall we do?" Again, Stephen applied the message (Acts 7:51–53) but it was the Holy Spirit who applied the preached Word by Stephen: "When they heard these things, they were *cut* to the heart, and they gnashed on him with their teeth" (Acts 7:54) (NASB) [Emphasis mine].

James exhorts us as believers to be doers of the Word. The evangelical preacher will do well to keep this central to his sermons.

3. QUOTES FROM EDWARDS

In considering the theology behind a strong application and appeal to the will, we must understand how Edwards believes in both the sovereignty of God and the responsibility of man. We have endeavored to elaborate this dynamic in Chapter 9, so here we will only give concise reference to the theology underlying the importance of addressing the will in application. Edwards states in his excellent sermon "Pressing into the Kingdom of God," preached in the apogee of the little Great Awakening (Feb. 1735), that it is incumbent upon the seeker to press hard, with "strength of desire" (Jonathan Edwards)[6], and "firmness of resolution" with a "thorough engagedness of

---

6. Edwards, *Works*, 19: 276.

the mind in this affair"[7] and an "earnestness"[8]. Edwards believed that effort and application were important: "However sinful a person is, and whatever his circumstances are, there is notwithstanding a possibility of his salvation; he himself is capable of it, and God is able to accomplish it, and have mercy sufficient for it; and there is sufficient provision made through Christ, that God may do it consistent with the honor of his majesty, justice and truth; so that there is no want either of sufficiency in God, or capacity in the sinner, in order to this: the greatest and vilest, most blind, bad, hard-hearted sinner living, is a subject capable of saving light and grace" (Jonathan Edwards)[9]. Edwards believed in addressing the will with a powerful application, because of the moral responsibility of the individual.

Edwards endeavors to differentiate between suggestive thoughts forcibly imposed upon the mind (spurious application) and authentic spiritual application: "A truly spiritual application of the Word of God is of a vastly higher nature: as much above the devil's power, as it is, so to apply the Word of God to a dead corpse, as to raise it to life; or to a stone, to turn it into an angel. A spiritual application of the Word of God consists in *applying it to the heart*, in spiritually enlightening, sanctifying influences. A spiritual application of an invitation or offer of the gospel consists in giving the soul a spiritual sense or relish of the holy and divine blessings offered, and also the sweet and wonderful grace of the offerer, in making so gracious an offer, and of his holy excellency and faithfulness to fulfill what he offers, and his glorious sufficiency for it; so leading and drawing forth the heart to embrace the offer; and thus giving the man evidence of his title to the thing offered. And so a spiritual application of the promises of Scripture, for the comfort of the saints, consists in enlightening their minds to see the holy excellency and sweetness of the blessings promised, and also the holy excellency of the promiser, and his faithfulness and sufficiency; thus drawing forth their hearts to embrace the promiser, and thing promised; and by this means, giving the sensible actings of grace, enabling them to see their grace, and so their title to the promise. An application not consisting in this divine sense and enlightening of the mind, but consisting only in the words being borne into the thoughts, as if immediately then spoken, so making persons believe, on no other foundation, that the promise is theirs, is a blind application, and belongs to the spirit of darkness, and not of light" (Jonathan Edwards)[10]. This quote is significant for it shows implicitly the relationship

---

7. Edwards, *Works*, 19: 278.
8. Edwards, *Works*, 19: 279.
9. Edwards, *Works*, 19: 281–82.
10. Edwards, *Works*, 2: 225.

between the role of the preacher making an application, and the role of the Holy Spirit, and their collaboration (I Cor 3:9).

4. QUOTES BY EDWARDSEAN AND PURITAN SCHOLARS ON THE ROLE OF APPLICATION IN PURITAN PREACHING

According to Kimnach, leading scholar on Edwards's preaching, "The first stage of the sermon is the *Text*, consisting of a passage of Scripture accompanied by a page or two of exegesis. This division introduces the theme of the sermon in the context of the Word of God, the eternal truth and reality by which all human reality is evaluated. The theme is not often so precise or explicit in its statement as human philosophy would require of a thesis; therefore, the second division of the sermon, the *Doctrine*, begins with a statement of doctrine that functions in the sermon as a thesis in a formal essay. The statement of doctrine is analyzed, explained, and confirmed in a series of numbered heads known collectively as "reasons." Finally, the third division of the sermon, the *Application* (or Improvement), offers explicit numbered directions, known collectively as "uses" for human thought and conduct that are inferred from the Doctrine. The Doctrine and Application divisions each constitute roughly 50 percent of the sermon"[11] [Emphasis mine]. This is significant: According to Kimnach, Edwards dedicated 50% of his message to the application. A quick scan of his sermons confirms what Kimnach is saying.

The Puritans stressed organization because they believed in the primacy of the intellect. They believed that grace enters the heart through the mind. According to Packer, "God does not move men to action by mere physical violence, but addresses their minds by his word, and *calls for the response of deliberate consent and intelligent obedience*. It follows that every man's first duty in relation to the word of God is to understand it; and every preacher's first duty is to explain it." It is the preacher's job to explain the Bible in a clear, organized manner so that the sheep may approach it and feed upon it[12] (Steele) (Applicatory Dialectic).

"It would grieve one to the heart to hear what excellent doctrine some ministers have in hand, while yet they let it die in their hands for want of close and lively application" (Richard Baxter, quoted by Steele)[13].

---

11. Kimnach, *Edwards as Preacher*, 105.
12. Steele, *Classical Analysis*.
13. Steele, *Classical Analysis*.

Church pews are full of people who "know" the central tenets of the Christian faith and yet sadly remain unchanged by them. There are also people in the pews that sincerely love the doctrines of the Christian faith but remain perpetually unsure of their practical relation to daily life. The Puritans were keenly aware of both of these phenomena. Consequently, the Puritans labored to bring the text of Scripture to bear upon the individual consciences of each and every listener. Puritan preachers worked hard to be practical, for they realized that "doctrine is lifeless unless a person can 'build bridges' from biblical truth to everyday living." Thus, Thomas Hooker can write, "When we read only of doctrines these may reach the understanding, but when we read or hear of examples, human affection doth as it were represent to us the case as our own." The Puritans achieved practicality in preaching predominantly through the use of application (Steele)[14].

Ryken summarizes William Perkins' seven categories of application from "The Art of Prophesying," depending on the individual conditions of the listeners: I. Unbelievers who are both ignorant and unteachable . . . . II. Some are teachable, but yet ignorant . . . . III. Some have knowledge, but are not as yet humbled . . . . IV. Some are humbled . . . . V. Some do believe . . . .VI. Some are fallen . . . . VII. There is a mingled people . . . . [21].[15]

"The main concern of Puritan preaching was to transmit God's infallible word to His people. Puritan preaching was marked by an unadulterated concern to search the Scriptures, collate their findings, and apply them to all areas of life" (Beeke quoted in Steele)[16]." . . . how could a preacher possibly endeavor to employ God's Word from the pulpit without making strident and vigorous effort to understand it not just generally, but particularly? The Puritans aimed simultaneously for telescopic knowledge of the Scriptures as well as for microscopic knowledge;" (Steele). William Perkins' suggested preaching format that appears at the end of his The Art of *Prophesying* is a cogent example of the logical progression and systematic organization that marked Puritan sermons. Perkins advocates that preachers ought to:

a. Read the text distinctly out of the canonical scriptures.

b. Give the sense and understanding of it being read, by the scripture itself.

c. Collect a few and profitable points of doctrine out of the natural sense.

---

14. Steele, *Classical Analysis*.
15. Steele, *Classical Analysis*.
16. Steele, *Classical Analysis*.

d. To apply, *if he have the gift*, the doctrines rightly collected to the life and manners of men in a simple and plain speech" (Steele quoting Ryken)[17] [Emphasis mine]. Whether or not we agree that application is optional if one does not have the gift, the point to be made here is that Edwards did indeed have the gift of applying the doctrines to the life and manners of men in a simple and plain speech, and he exercised that "gift" powerfully. I believe there is a strong correlation between this fact and the revival and awakening that happened.

"Reason follows reason, with no other transition than a period and a number; *after the last proof is stated there follow the uses or applications*, also in numbered sequence, and the sermon ends when there is nothing more to be said" [emphasis mine] (Perry Miller, quoted by Steele).[18]

"During the pre-Reformation time grace and nature were separated. This is the concept of a two-storey universe. Upstairs is spiritual and holy. Downstairs is sinful, fleshly and unholy. For example, the clergy were forbidden to marry as though marriage were earthly and therefore sinful. Luther partly reformed this and brought grace alongside nature. For example, he married an ex-nun, Katherine. John Calvin went further and taught that grace must permeate nature. The earthly must be sanctified by the heavenly. The Puritans went further still and taught in more detail than Calvin that biblical principles must be applied to every aspect of life. There are biblical principles or biblical ethics for marriage, the bringing up of children and the home, for teachers and university professors, medical doctors, lawyers, architects and artists, for farmers and gardeners, politicians and magistrates, for businessmen and shopkeepers and for men of commerce and trade, for military men and for bankers. To the Puritans the dichotomy (division) between nature and grace, the prevalent view of medieval theologians, was essentially wrong. It is not as though the heavenly things are holy but earthly things cursed or tarnished. To the Puritans grace must penetrate and permeate all earthly life and sanctify it. Even the bells on the horses are sanctified to the Lord (Zech 14:20)."[19]

Edwards was a Puritan, and in this respect, he was vintage Puritan. To appreciate Edwards's concept of the application and its importance, Smith, while discussing the conversion of "Religious Affections" from sermonic to discourse form, states: "It is interesting to note how the basically sermonic form survives within the work; in most cases a sign is first expounded and

17. Steele, *Classical Analysis*.
18. Steele, *Classical Analysis*.
19. Hulse, *Call to Extraordinary Prayer*.

defended and then there is the 'application' which consists in showing the bearing of the principle upon actual life"[20]. That is precisely the point: The application shows the bearing of the text and doctrine on actual life. To appreciate how this is true not only of his discourses, but most particularly of his sermons, we move to consider some examples of his preaching.

5. ILLUSTRATIONS FROM THE ACTUAL SERMONS OF EDWARDS

Edwards was very strong on application. Edwards switches frequently to the second person. In one message alone, (Pressing into the Kingdom)[21], preached at the height of the Great Awakening (February of 1735) he uses the word "you" and "your" 465 times in the sermon in the Application alone (pp. 282 to 304; 23 pages). Here is just a mild sampling with the words "you" and "your" highlighted to illustrate the power of a personal application: In ten lines Edwards uses "you" or "your" 22 times.

> God is now calling *you* in an extraordinary manner, and 'tis agreeable to the will and word of Christ that I should now, in his name call *you*, as one set over *you*, and sent to *you* to that end; so 'tis his will that *you* should hearken to what I say, as his voice: I therefore beseech *you* in Christ's stead now to press into the kingdom of God! Whoever *you* are, whether young or old, small, or great; whatever *you* be; if *you* are a great sinner, if *you* have been a backslider, if *you* have quenched the spirit, let *you* be who *you* will, and whatever *you* have done, don't stand making objections, but arise, apply *yourself* to *your* work! Do, what *you* have to do, with *your* might. Christ is calling *you* before, and holding forth his grace and everlasting benefits, and wrath is pursuing *you* behind; wherefore fly for *your* life, and look not behind *you*![22]

The sermons of Edwards not only illustrate personal application, but they are very pointed. Consider the following excerpt from the Application portion of the Sermon: "The Justice of God in the Damnation of Sinners," preached in May of 1735, at the height of the revival. There are 169 pointed references to "you" and "your" in this application. But notice how the preacher goes to meddling, raising personal issues.

20. Smith, *Works,* 2: 27.
21. Edwards, *Works,* 19: 272–304.
22. Edwards, *Works,* 19: 292.

"How many sorts of wickedness have you been guilty of? How manifold have been the abominations of your life? What profaneness and contempt of God has been exercised by you? How little regard have you had to the Scriptures, to the Word preached, to sabbaths, and sacraments? How profanely have you talked, many of you, about those things that are holy? After what manner have many of you kept God's holy day, not regarding the holiness of the time, nor caring what you thought of in it. Yea, *you* have not only spent the time in worldly, vain, and unprofitable thoughts, but in immoral thoughts; pleasing *yourself* with the reflection on past acts of wickedness, and in contriving new acts. Have not you spent much holy time, in gratifying *your* lusts in *your* imaginations; yea, not only holy time, but the very time of God's public worship, when *you* have appeared in God's more immediate presence? How have you not only not attended to the worship, but have in the meantime been feasting *your* lusts, and wallowing *yourself* in abominable uncleanness! How many sabbaths have *you* spent, one after another, in a most wretched manner! Some of *you* not only in worldly and wicked thoughts, but also a very wicked outward behavior! When you on sabbath days, have got along with *your* wicked companions, how has holy time been treated among *you*! What kind of conversation has there been! Yea, how have some of *you*, by a very indecent carriage, openly dishonored and cast contempt on the sacred services of God's house, and holy day! And what *you* have done some of *you* alone, what wicked practices there have been in secret, even in holy time, God and *your* own consciences know" (Jonathan Edwards).[23]

The list goes on and on! And then he concludes "Now, can you think when you have thus behaved yourself, that God is obliged to show you mercy? Are you not, after all this, ashamed to talk of its being hard with God to cast you off? Does it become one that has lived such a life to open his mouth to excuse himself, or object against God's justice in his condemnation, or to complain of it as hard in God not to give him converting and pardoning grace..." (Jonathan Edwards)[24].

For yet another extended example of Edwards's ability and emphasis on applied preaching, please see Appendix #5.

---

23. Edwards, *Works*, 19: 348–49.
24. Edwards, *Works*, 19: 352.

6. 70 RESOLUTIONS

There is a very real sense in which each of the 70 resolutions illustrates Edwards's determination to apply the Word of God to Himself. Several of the resolutions were crafted in response to a particular sermon (#43, #65). Some of them generally (#14, #6, #22, #62) reinforce the importance of diligence and determination, but all of them recognize the importance of the will in one's spiritual formation.

7. OTHER AUTHORS AND PREACHERS

"The word of God is not to teach us to prattle or be eloquent and subtle. . . it is to reform our lives, so that we desire to serve God, to give ourselves entirely to him, and to conform ourselves to his good will" (John Calvin)[25].

Robert Murray McCheyne (1814–43) spoke frequently of preaching the "action sermon." Intriguing reference, undoubtedly to the emphasis on applying and acting.

"The Bible was not given to increase our knowledge but to change our lives" (D. L. Moody)[26].

"[. . .] applicatory preaching is often costly preaching. As has often been said, when John the Baptist preached generally, Herod heard him gladly. But when John applied his preaching particularly, he lost his head. Both internally in a preacher's own conscience, as well as in the consciences of his people, a fearless application of God's truth will cost a price" (Beeke, quoted by Steele)[27].

John Stott, author of one of the best books on preaching ever written, "Between Two Worlds," affirms the importance of the application: "The conclusion should not merely recapitulate your sermon it should apply it. Obviously, you should be applying all along, but you should keep something for the end which will prevail upon your people to act. "No summons, no sermon." Preach through the head to the heart (i.e., the will). The goal of the sermon should be to "storm the citadel of the will and capture it for Jesus Christ." What do you want them to *do*? Employ a variety of methods to do this:

    a. *Argument*: anticipate objections and refute them

    b. *Admonition*: warn of the consequences of disobedience

---

25. Cole, *Calvin*.
26. Navigators, *Moody*.
27. Steele, *Critical Analysis*.

c. *Indirect Conviction*: arouse moral indignation and then turn it on them (Nathan with David)

　　d. *Pleading*: apply the gentle pressure of God's love, concern for their well-being, and the needs of others

　　e. *Vision*: paint a picture of what is possible through obedience to God in this area[28]

Finally, a very helpful quote on the place of the altar call[29] and the call to application and commitment comes from Donald English: "If we wish to give ourselves wholly to God there is something to be said for moving ourselves wholly, that is bodily, for God! For many people such action, of walking forward to a particular area in an act of worship, expresses, symbolizes, embodies, and even releases that deeper commitment that otherwise remains cerebral, internalized, and even trapped within our individualized world. For all these reasons I suggest that the altar call still has a necessary place among us."[30]

8. CONCLUSION

If there is one phrase I could use to sum up this matter, it would be "Improving the Improvement." The first word "improving" in the modern sense, the second in the 18th century sense of "profitable use or application of anything." Since there is such a close correlation between revival and the will, revival preachers need to become conversant not only with the theology sustaining the application of the message, but also the spirit and technique of making the application pointed and personal.

I like the acrostic Rick Warren[31] uses to preach with A-P-P-L-I-C-A-T-I-O-N

- A—Attitude to Adjust?
- P—Priority to Change?
- P—Plan to Implement?
- L—Lesson to Learn?

---

28. Stott, *Between Two Worlds*, 211–16.

29. Although Edwards did not have an "altar call" per. se., his emphasis on application makes him a "practical precursor" to that practice of calling people to a definitive decision.

30. English, *Evangelical Theology*, 111.

31. Akin, *Purpose-Driven Preaching*, 13.

- I—Idol to Renounce?
- C—Character to Change?
- A—Activity to Avoid?
- T—Tithe to Pay?
- I—Incident to Review?
- O—Offense to Forgive?
- N—New direction to take?

Chapter 11

Spiritual Pride and Revival Preaching

"But He gives a greater grace. Therefore *it* says,
God is opposed to the proud, but gives grace to the humble"
(I Pet 5:5) (NASB).

"Let not the foot of pride come upon me,
And let not the hand of the wicked drive me away" (Ps 36:11) (NASB).

"On the appointed day Herod, wearing his royal robes, sat on his throne and delivered a public address to the people. They shouted, 'This is the voice of a god, not of a man.' Immediately, because Herod did not give praise to God, an angel of the Lord struck him down, and he was eaten by worms and died" (Acts 12:21–23) (NIV).

"Let me particularly urge you to watch exceedingly against spiritual pride. There is great danger"[1] (Jonathan Edwards).

---

1. Edwards, *Works*, 22: 531.

"undiscerned spiritual pride... 'tis the last thing in a sinner that is overborne by conviction, in order to conversion; and here is the saint's hardest conflict: 'tis the last thing that he obtains a good degree of conquest over, and liberty from; 'tis that which most directly militates against God, and is most contrary to the Spirit of the Lamb of God; and 'tis most like the Devil its father, in a serpentine deceitfulness and secrecy; it lies deepest, and is most active, is most ready secretly to mix itself with everything" (Jonathan Edwards)[2].

"It [pride] is a sin that has, as it were, many lives; if you kill it, it will live still; if you mortify and suppress it in one shape, it rises in another; if you think it is all gone, yet it is there still. There are a great many kinds of it that lie in different forms and shapes, one under another, and encompass the heart like the coats of an onion; if you pull off one there is another underneath. We had need therefore to have the greatest watch imaginable, over our hearts, with respect to this matter, and to cry most earnestly to the great Searcher of hearts, for his help. "He that trusts his own heart is a fool" [Prov 28:26]" (Jonathan Edwards)[3].

INTRODUCTORY COMMENTS

When it comes to arriving at the heart of Edwards's view of true spirituality, we see that Edwards was enamoured with the Triune God. The chief end of man is to glorify God and enjoy him forever. As we saw in Chapter 5, "The Supremacy of God in Preaching," Edwards believed that everything revolves around God. The Copernican Revolution placed the sun, instead of the earth, at the center of the universe; it is a heliocentric, not a geocentric universe. The Scriptures in like manner propose a distinct spiritual cosmonology: Everything is to revolve around the Son, and not around humanity, or a particular human being, the self. The universe it theocentric, not egocentric. This natural self-centeredness so deeply rooted in our humanity needs a revolutionary refocus. Conversion and sanctification is, in essence, a reconfiguration of the essential center. Spiritual pride needs to be addressed if the Triune God is truly glorified. Edwards believed this. Unless you grasp what Edwards says about spiritual pride, and the need for radical conversion and deep-seated sanctification, you will not appreciate his view of revival preaching.

2. Edwards, *Works*, 4: 415–16.
3. Edwards, *Works*, 4: 416–17.

Effective Revival Preaching will see the dethroning of self and the breaking of spiritual pride. In this chapter we deal with the Preacher addressing spiritual pride in himself and then with the Preacher addressing spiritual pride in his ministry.

1. DEFINE IT

Spiritual pride may seem like an oxymoron, and theologically speaking, it is! The only thing in common between the word "s-p-i-r-i-t-u-a-l," and the word "p-r-i-d-e," like the word "s-i-n," is the central letter "i." True spirituality, from an Edwardsean perspective, involves the glorification of God and the dethroning of the self to a position of recognition of the Lordship of Jesus and the justice of the glory of the triune God. With John the Baptist, Edwards affirms "He must increase, but I must decrease" (John 3:30) (KJV).

Satan is the poster child of spiritual pride. Created in remarkable beauty, Satan became proud of his position and privilege (Isa 11:13). Paul warns Timothy of the danger of novices falling into pride, which was the reason for the fall of Satan (I Tim 3:6). Edwards warns us: "'tis most like the sin that he committed in an heaven of light and glory, where he was exalted high in divine knowledge, honor, beauty and happiness" (Jonathan Edwards).[4] Edwards states: "The deceitfulness of the heart of man appears in no one thing so much, as this of spiritual pride and self-righteousness. The subtlety of Satan appears in its height in his managing of persons with respect to this sin. And perhaps one reason may be, that here he has most experience: he knows the way of its coming in; he is acquainted with the secret springs of it" (Jonathan Edwards).[5]

Spiritual pride is the pernicious tendency among the unregenerate to endeavor to establish grounds in oneself for acceptance before God. It is an endeavor to consider one's self-righteousness based on one's own efforts, and to gloat and presume justification because of one's own merits (Eph 2:8, 9). The negative example of the Pharisee praying together with the Publican demonstrates the point:

"To some who were confident of their own righteousness and looked down on everyone else, Jesus told this parable: "Two men went up to the temple to pray, one a Pharisee and the other a tax collector. 11 The Pharisee stood by himself and prayed: 'God, I thank you that I am not like other people—robbers, evildoers, adulterers—or even like this tax collector'" (Luke 18:9–11) (NIV).

4. Edwards, *Works*, 4: 416.
5. Edwards, *Works*, 2: 319.

Edwards viewed Arminianism as a threat to the true faith because of the reinforcement of spiritual pride. He saw it as an affront to the glory of God and diametrically opposed to the theocentricity of Scriptures. "His theological arguments with both Arminians and enthusiasts found common ground in his repeated warnings against spiritual pride. The proud need a thorough humiliation, he states in No. 1009, "to bring 'em off from the opinion of their dignity and sufficiency." Whether their sufficiency is rooted in a "false and imaginary happiness" or in a "counterfeit righteousness," "the creature must be dethroned that God may be exalted"[6].

Spiritual pride is prevalent among the regenerate as well. It is that insidious and persistent tendency to assume some degree of "credit" or inordinate self-esteem *and subsequent conceit rooted in self-righteousness and a preoccupation with the self. Especially when individuals and communities are witnesses to and protagonists of revival and awakening, there is a tendency for the unsanctified self to distort such a Divine work and interpret it in such a way that elevates the religious self, reinforcing spiritual pride.*

Spiritual pride is indeed so pernicious and pervasive in Christians that it tends to infiltrate the preacher's life and ministry. In particular "Revival Preachers" must deal with pride if they are going to be effective. It is this latter aspect of "spiritual pride" in the preacher that will be the primary focus in this chapter.

2. BIBLICAL PERSPECTIVE

Baruch, a contemporary of Jeremiah, had to be confronted by Jeremiah about the issue of "spiritual pride" in his life. *"Should you then seek great things for yourself? Do not seek them"* (Jeremiah 45:5). This is a warming that every preacher needs to heed. Spiritual pride can easily find a place in the heart of a preacher, especially a preacher with a passion for revival and a great awakening! Our passion needs to be the glory of God, not our own glory!

We are warned of the precedence of spiritual pride in the life of Simon. The Scriptures say: "Now for some time a man named Simon had practiced sorcery in the city and amazed all the people of Samaria. *He boasted that he was someone great* . . . " (Acts 8:9) (NIV) [Emphasis mine]. Before his conversion, he has serious issues with pride. The next verse indicates that he had a reputation: "This man is rightly called the Great Power of God" (Acts 8:10) (NIV). When he saw the work of God, through the instrumentality of Philip, he coveted the same power that he witnessed (Acts 8:18). Peter saw through the request and recognized 'spiritual pride' and he confronted

---

6. Pauw, *Works*, 20: 27.

Simon: "thy heart is not right in the sight of God" (Acts 8:21) (KJV).[7] This is significant, for it shows that Simon was motivated by pride in his spiritual ambition to be a preacher. We as preachers need to take heed.

Of particular interest to us in the theme of "Revival Preaching and Pride" is Paul's recognized proclivity towards and struggle with spiritual pride. Paul himself said that " . . . because of these surpassingly great revelations. Therefore, *to keep me from becoming conceited*, I was given a thorn in my flesh . . . " (II Cor 12:7) (NIV) [Emphasis mine].

3. QUOTES FROM EDWARDS

Re: *Spiritual Pride among the unregenerate*

In his magnum opus,[8] a massive and profound treatment on spirituality called Religious Affections, Edwards deals extensively with the subtleties of spiritual pride *in the life of the unregenerate*. Consider this quote: "There is no man living that is lifted up with a conceit of his own experiences and discoveries, and upon the account of them glistens in his own eyes, but what trusts in his experiences, and makes a righteousness of them; however he may use humble terms, and speak of his experiences as of the great things God has done for him, and it may be calls upon others to glorify God for them; yet he that is proud of his experiences, arrogates something to himself, as though his experiences were some dignity of his" (Jonathan Edwards)[9]. This has implications for "revival preaching." Sometimes we can assume that people who profess faith possess faith, when such is often not the case. In the Gospel of John, it is reported that "many believed on Him" (John 2:23) but in the next verse we read, "But Jesus, on His part, was not entrusting himself to them, for He knew all men" (John 2:24) (NASB). With the same spiritual discernment provided by the Spirit, we should be careful not to assume that profession equals possession. Revival Preaching means, like John the Baptist, addressing the real cause and laying the axe to the root (Luke 3:9), which is spiritual pride.

Edwards affirms that "The first objective ground of gracious affections, is the transcendently excellent and amiable nature of divine things, *as they*

---

7. The sin of "simony" is named after this biblical character. Simony has been defined as "the buying or selling of a church office or ecclesiastical preferment" https://www.merriam-webster.com/dictionary/simony

8. Merriam-Webster, *Magnum opus*. (plural: *magna opera*, also *opus magnum / opera magna*), "the greatest achievement of an artist or writer."

9. Edwards, *Works*, 2: 318.

are in themselves; and not any conceived relation they bear to self, or self-interest" (Jonathan Edwards)[10]. If there is authentic conversion, according to Edwards, the prime mover of that conversion is not self-interest, but affection for God and the sweetness of Divine things, an affection inspired and generated by God and for God. " . . . For of him, and through him, and to him, are all things: to whom be glory forever. Amen" (Romans 11:36) (KJV). Spiritual pride seeks to intervene and obfuscate God, but regeneration with godly repentance always involves a fundamental shift away from the self-life, not a pious reinforcement of the religious self. Again, Edwards is radical when he affirms: "Something else, entirely distinct from self-love might be the cause of this, viz. a change made in the views of his mind, and relish of his heart; whereby he apprehends a beauty, glory, and supreme good, in God's nature, as it is in itself. This may be the thing that first draws his heart to him, and causes his heart to be united to him, *prior to all considerations of his own interest or happiness*, although after this, and as a fruit of this, he necessarily seeks his interest and happiness in God" [emphasis mine] (Jonathan Edwards).[11] Spiritual pride seeks to detract from God's pre-eminence and glory.

Re: Spiritual Pride among Mature Christians

Spiritual pride is man's chief temptation, and the true danger lies in the fact that a pride of this order is a real possibility only for the man with religious concern. Hence the man who is anxious to do his Christian duty, in contrast to the lifeless and indifferent, will be all the more prone to compare himself with others to their disadvantage and his own glory. Spiritual pride is implicit in the judgment that one is better than others or that one has a just claim before God supported by spiritual attainments. True humility is inconsistent with both judgments. In stressing this point, Edwards was confronting a great deal of the popular piety of the revivals with a decisive test; not "spiritual attainments" or "great and overwhelming experiences" which may call forth pride and self-elevation, but the fundamental acknowledgment of the divine *gloria* called forth freely and in love.[12]

"Another thing that is often mixed with the experiences of true Christians, which is the worst mixture of all, is a degree of self-righteousness or spiritual pride. This is often mixed with the joys of Christians: the joy that they have is not purely the joy of faith, or a rejoicing in Christ Jesus, but

---

10. Edwards, *Works*, 2: 240.
11. Edwards, *Works*, 2: 241.
12. Smith, *Works*, 2: 36.

is partly a rejoicing in themselves. There is oftentimes in their elevations a looking upon themselves, and a viewing their own high attainments;" (Jonathan Edwards).[13]

Re: Spiritual Pride in Promoters or "Friends" of the Revival

As Edwards analyzed the demise of the revival, he had this to say about spiritual pride operating in the lives of the "friends" of the revival: "The first, and the worst cause of errors that prevail in such a state of things, is spiritual pride. This is the main door, by which the Devil comes into the hearts of those that are zealous for the advancement of religion. 'Tis the chief inlet of smoke from the bottomless pit, to darken the mind, and mislead the judgment: this is the main handle by which the Devil has hold of religious persons, and the chief source of all the mischief that he introduces, to clog and hinder a work of God. This cause of error is the mainspring, or at least the main support of all the rest. Till this disease is cured, medicines are in vain applied to heal other diseases. 'Tis by this that the mind defends itself in other errors, and guards itself against light by which it might be corrected and reclaimed. Alas, how much pride have the best of us in our hearts! 'Tis the worst part of the body of sin and death: 'tis the first sin that ever entered into the universe, and the last that is rooted out; 'tis God's most stubborn enemy!" (Jonathan Edwards).[14]

Edwards believed that the believers in Northampton were guilty of spiritual pride and grieved the Holy Spirit, quenching His influence and dampening the revival fires. Edwards noted that spiritual pride was the primary cause of the demise of the First Great awakening. "Where are the men that have had much of the presence of [God], that have lost it and fallen into a cold dark state, unless it was by means of their forsaking God in some of those ways that have been mentioned—giving way to some lust, spiritual pride, worldliness, sloth, or some other hateful [lust]? You that have lost [it], you can't one of you say that you lost it in this way of thus taking earnest heed to keep close to God and still earnestly seeking him" (Jonathan Edwards).[15]

Writing William McCulloch, Edwards gives his explanation for the cause of demise in the Great Awakening: "'Tis probable that you have been informed by other correspondents before now what the present state of things in New England is. It is indeed on many accounts very melancholy:

13. Edwards, *Works*, 4: 461.
14. Edwards, *Works*, 4: 415.
15. Edwards, *Works*, 22: 528.

there is a vast alteration within this two years; for about so long, I think it is, since the Spirit of God began to withdraw, and this great work has been on the decline. Great numbers in the land about two years ago were raised to an exceeding great height, in joy and elevations of mind, and through want of watchfulness and sensibleness of the danger and temptation that there is in such circumstances, many were greatly exposed, and the Devil taking the advantage, multitudes were soon, and to themselves insensibly, led far away from God and their duty. God was provoked that he was not sanctified in this height of advancement, as he ought to have been; he saw our spiritual pride and self-confidence, and the polluted flames that arose of intemperate, unhallowed zeal; and he soon in a great measure withdrew from us; and the consequence has been that "the enemy has come in like a flood" [Isaiah 59:19], in various respects, until the deluge has overwhelmed the whole land" (Jonathan Edwards).[16]

Re: Spiritual Pride among Ministers

We quote Edwards as he warns the minister of the dangers of spiritual pride: "God's own people should be the more jealous of themselves, with respect to this particular, at this day, because the temptations that many have to this sin are exceeding great: the great and distinguishing privileges to which God admits many of his saints, and *the high honors that he puts on some ministers*, are great trials of persons in this respect. 'Tis true that great degrees of the spiritual presence of God tends greatly to mortify pride and all corruption; but yet, though in the experience of such favors there be much to restrain pride one way, there is much to tempt and provoke it another; and we shall be in great danger thereby without great watchfulness and prayerfulness" (Jonathan Edwards)[17]. If the Apostle Paul had to be vigilant, if the angels in heaven fell because of spiritual pride, then how vigilant must the minister of the Gospel be, especially one dedicated to Revival Preaching.

Re: Spiritual Pride in his own life and ministry

Edwards understood his own conversion to revolve around the issue of self-love versus love for God. In his own experience, he discounted any religious experience that failed to deal with the self vs God conflict, although he seems to allow for their co-existence to some degree. In his own words: "The next

---

16. Edwards, *Works*, 4: 558–59.
17. Edwards, *Works*, 4: 417.

thing I had then to do, was to inquire whether this was my religion. And here God was pleased to help me to the most easy remembrance and critical review of what had passed in course, of a religious nature, through several of the latter years of my life. And although I could discover much corruption attending my best duties, many selfish views and carnal ends, much spiritual pride, and self-exaltation, and innumerable other evils which compassed me about; I say, although I now discerned the sins of my holy things as well as other actions; yet God was pleased, as I was reviewing, quickly to put this question out of doubt, by showing me that I had, from time to time, acted above the utmost influence of mere self-love; that I had longed to please and glorify him, as my highest happiness, etc. And this review was through grace attended with a present feeling of the same divine temper of mind. I felt now pleased to think of the glory of God; and longed for heaven, as a state wherein I might glorify God perfectly, rather than a place of happiness for myself" (Jonathan Edwards).[18]

Few would disagree that Edwards showed remarkable insight and understanding into the things of God—undoubtedly, he struggled with spiritual pride in a fashion similar to the experience of the Apostle Paul mentioned above (II Cor. 12:7). And besides that, he was privileged to be the protagonist of a remarkable and surprising work of God, an unusual awakening. For evidence that Edwards struggled with pride in his own life and ministry, consider this entry in his Diary of *Saturday, March* 2, 1723: "O, how much more base and vile am I, when I feel pride working in me, than when I am in a more humble disposition of mind! How much, how exceedingly much, more lovely is an [sic] humble, than a proud, disposition! I now plainly perceive it, and am really sensible of it. How immensely more pleasant is an [sic] humble delight, than a high thought of myself! How much better do I feel, when I am truly humbling myself, than when I am pleasing myself with my own perfections. O, how much pleasanter is humility than pride! O, that God would fill me with exceeding great humility, and that he would ever more keep me from all pride! The pleasures of humility are really the most refined, inward and exquisite delights in the world. How hateful is a proud man! How hateful is a worm that lifts up itself with pride! What a foolish, silly, miserable, blind, deceived, poor worm am I, when pride works!" (Jonathan Edwards).[19]

I believe that Edwards was aware of pride in his own life because of the explanation he gives as to the cause(s) of the demise of the revival. He states: " . . . Was there too much of an appearance of a public pride, if I may

18. Edwards, *Works*, 16: 249.
19. Edwards, *Works*, 16: 768.

so call it? Were *we* not lifted up with the honor that God had put upon *us* as a people, beyond most people?" [Emphasis mine—Edwards includes himself] (Jonathan Edwards).[20]

Conclusion

As I read the following description of the subtlety of pride, I got the distinct impression that Edwards was keenly aware of the potential of pride in his own life as well as in the lives of "friends" of the revival to derail the revival and spoil its fruit because of spiritual pride:

> "Humility and self-diffidence, and an entire dependence on our Lord Jesus Christ, will be our best defense. Let us therefore maintain the strictest watch against spiritual pride, or a being lifted up with extraordinary experiences and comforts, and high favors of heaven that any of us may have received. We had need after such favors, in a special manner to keep a strict and jealous eye upon our own hearts, lest there should arise self-exalting reflections upon what we have received, and high thoughts of ourselves as being now some of the most eminent of saints and peculiar favorites of heaven, and that the secret of the Lord is especially with us, and that we above all are fit to be improved as the great instructors and censors of this evil generation: and in an high conceit of our own wisdom and discerning, should as it were naturally assume to ourselves *the airs of prophets* or *extraordinary ambassadors of heaven*. When we have great discoveries of God made to our souls, we should not shine bright in our own eyes. Moses when he had been conversing with God in the mount, though his face shone so as to dazzle the eyes of Aaron and the people, yet he did not shine in his own eyes; 'he wist not that his face shone' (Exodus 34:29). Let none think themselves out of danger of this spiritual pride, even in their best frames. God saw that the Apostle Paul (though probably the most eminent saint that ever lived) was not out of danger of it, no, not when he had just been conversing with God in the third heaven;" see 2 Corinthians 12:7.[21]

"Pride is the worst viper that is in the heart; it is the first sin that ever entered into the universe, and it lies lowest of all in the foundation of the whole building of sin, and is the most secret, deceitful and unsearchable in

---

20. Edwards, *Works*, 22: 255.
21. Edwards, *Works*, 4: 277–78.

its ways of working, of any lusts whatsoever: it is ready to mix with everything; and nothing is so hateful to God, and contrary to the spirit of the Gospel, or of so dangerous consequence; and there is no one sin that does so much let in the Devil into the hearts of the saints, and expose them to his delusions. I have seen it in many instances, and that in eminent saints. The Devil has come in at this door presently after some eminent experience and extraordinary communion with God, and has woefully deluded and led 'em astray, till God has mercifully opened their eyes and delivered them; and they themselves have afterwards been made sensible that it was pride that betrayed them" (Jonathan Edwards).[22] Perhaps the sad experience of some of his colleagues, like Davenport[23], prompted this reflection. Edwards, always endeavoring to get at the root of the matter, traced these erratic habits back to a spirit of spiritual pride.

"Pride is much more difficultly discerned than any other corruption, for that reason that the nature of it does very much consist in a person's having too high a thought of himself: but no wonder that he that has too high a thought of himself don't know it; for he necessarily thinks that the opinion he has of himself is what he has just grounds for, and therefore not too high; if he thought such an opinion of himself was without just grounds, he would therein cease to have it. But of all kinds of pride, spiritual pride is the most hidden and difficultly discovered; and that for this reason, because those that are spiritually proud, their pride consists much in an high conceit of those two things, viz. their light and their humility; both which are a strong prejudice against a discovery of their pride" (Jonathan Edwards).[24]

"An eminent saint is not apt to think himself eminent in anything; all his graces and experiences are ready to appear to him to be comparatively small; but especially his humility. There is nothing that appertains to Christian experience, and true piety, that is so much out of his sight as his

---

22. Edwards, *Works*, 4: 277–78.

23. Stamford History, *James Davenport* (1716–1757). Revivalists customarily worked in cooperation with local churches and ministers. Davenport, however, while still only 24, began to grow in prominence for his spirited words against conventional ministers and his condemnation of their leadership. He so influenced some members of First Church, New Haven that they left that congregation to form North Church. His preaching became increasingly extravagant and led to the Connecticut General Assembly's passing of an act in 1742 which in effect condemned itinerant preachers as vagrants. A newspaper report in the Boston Evening Post related statements by James which reflected the impact of the anti-itinerant legislation on him. In it he stated that most of the ministers in the country were *"unconverted, and that they were murdering of Souls by Thousands and by Millions." (Stamford, History. https://www.stamfordhistory.org/dav_james1.htm)*.

24. Edwards, *Works*, 4: 417.

humility. He is a thousand times more quick-sighted to discern his pride, than his humility: *that* he easily discerns, and is apt to take much notice of, but hardly discerns his humility. On the contrary, the deluded hypocrite that is under the power of spiritual pride is so blind to nothing as his pride; and so quick-sighted to nothing, as the shows of humility that are in him" (Jonathan Edwards).[25]

4. QUOTES BY EDWARDSEAN SCHOLARS

Bailey has researched Edwards's preaching and has noted that for Edwards, God allows difficult truths to remain obscure and unresolved by human reason to humble preachers and test whether they will be obedient in preaching God's clear word (such as sovereign election) even though they cannot resolve all the difficulties with their human understanding. Edwards would quote Proverbs 3:5, 7 (KJV) "5 Trust in the Lord with all thine heart; and lean not unto thine own understanding.7 Be not wise in thine own eyes" and apply it to preachers: "God has reasons that man's fallen reason cannot know. It is inevitable, therefore, that divine revelation—the Bible—contains mysteries and seeming inconsistencies. With our understandings being limited to lower, earthly things, it is only logical that we cannot fully understand heavenly things, which "are much more above us." It is the duty of believers, and especially of ministers, to resign themselves to the wisdom of God. Human experience has shown that things that were once mysterious are now explicable, and we have no reason not to expect that God will continue to make new discoveries known."[26]

Stoddard significantly influenced Edwards's preaching style and substance.[27] Edwards followed Stoddard in addressing spiritual pride. Stoddard expresses it, " . . . men must be brought off from their own righteousness before they are brought to Christ. Men who think they have anything to appease the wrath of God and ingratiate themselves will not accept the calls of the gospel in sincerity. While people have a foundation to build upon, they will not build upon Christ"[28]. "Men must see their malady before they see their remedy."[29]

According to Kimnach, Edwards's emphasis on "sulfurous sermons" was designed to address the matter of spiritual pride: A central goal of the

25. Edwards, *Works*, 2: 334–35.
26. Bailey, *Salvation*, 16.
27. See Appendix #3.
28. Stoddard, *Saving Conversion*, 129.
29. Stoddard, *Saving Conversion*, 128.

preaching of the terrors was to quench spiritual pride, by nurturing in sinners "a spirit to condemn themselves and justify God."[30]

Quoting Dwight: who is referring to Edwards's sermon on Rom. 3:19, Gerstner affirms: "The sermon . . . literally stops the mouth of every reader and compels him, as he stands before his Judge, to admit, if he does not feel, the justice of his sentence. I know not where to find, in any language, a discourse so adapted to strip the impenitent sinner of every excuse, to convince him of his guilt, and to bring him low before the justice and holiness of God. According to the estimate of Mr. Edwards, it was far the most powerful and effectual of his discourses, and we scarcely know of any other sermon which has been favoured with equal success"[31]. Jesus taught: "Or how can anyone enter the strong man's house and carry off his property, unless he first binds the strong *man*? And then he will plunder his house" (Matt 12:29). Once the issue of spiritual pride is addressed, then the strongman is bound, and the house can be "plundered."

5. ILLUSTRATIONS FROM THE ACTUAL SERMONS OF EDWARDS

Edwards's first published sermon was preached and published in Boston in 1731. It is probably the one single sermon that put Edwards on the map. After presenting his text: "That no flesh should glory in his presence" (I Cor 1:29) (KJV), Edwards affirms: "What God aims at in the disposition of things in the affair of redemption, viz. that man should not glory in himself, but alone in God: "That no flesh should glory in his presence; . . . that, according as it is written, He that glories, let him glory in the Lord" (Jonathan Edwards).[32] Edwards immediately proceeds to establish his central thesis: "How this end is attained in the work of redemption, viz. by that absolute and immediate dependence which men have upon God in that work, for all their good. Inasmuch as, all the good that they have is in and through Christ" (Jonathan Edwards).[33]

Again, in addressing the matter of pride in his own congregation, Edwards was merciless: "How much of a spirit of pride has appeared in you! which is in a peculiar manner the spirit and condemnation of the devil. How have some of you vaunted yourselves in your apparel! Others in their riches! Others in their knowledge and abilities! How has it galled you to see

30. Pauw, *Works*, 20: 5.
31. Gerstner, *Rational Theology*, 81–82.
32. Edwards, *Works*. 17: 200–01.
33. Edwards, *Works*, 17: 201.

others above you! How much has it gone against the grain, for you to give others their due honor! And how have you shown your pride by setting up your wills, and in opposing others, and stirring up and promoting division, and a party spirit in public affairs!" (Jonathan Edwards)[34]

Finally, Edwards explains how this danger of spiritual pride operates *in the preacher*: "Our office and work is most honorable, in that we are set by Christ to be lights or luminaries in the spiritual world. Light is the most glorious thing in the material world, and there are, it may be, no parts of the natural world that have so great an image of the goodness of God, as the lights or luminaries of heaven; and especially the sun, who is constantly communicating his benign influence to enlighten, quicken and refresh the world by his beams; which is probably the reason that the worship of the sun was (as is supposed) the first idolatry that mankind fell into. But so are ministers honored by their great Lord and Master, that they are set to be that to men's souls, that the lights of heaven are to their bodies; and that they might be the instruments and vehicles of God's greatest goodness, and the most precious fruits of his eternal love to them, and means of that life, and refreshment and joy that are spiritual and eternal, and infinitely more precious than any benefit received by the benign beams of the sun in the firmament. And we shall be likely indeed to be the instruments of those unspeakable benefits to the souls of our fellow creatures, if we have those qualifications, which have been shown to be the true and proper excellency of ministers of the gospel" (Jonathan Edwards).[35] However, that privilege carries with it an implicit danger: Ministers are to be seen as light and heat, but as "sun worship" was common among pagans, so there in an inherent tendency toward "spiritual pride" in the ministry. Many a preacher used by God has fallen into spiritual pride and disqualifies himself for further usefulness because of said pride. Especially revival preachers who, like Edwards and Whitefield, are gifted and enabled by God to be instruments of a great awakening, must keep a close vigil upon their hearts, lest they fall into "the snare of the devil" (I Tim. 3:7) which was, and continues to be, pride. Spiritual pride.

6. 70 RESOLUTIONS

There are several resolutions that reflect Edwards's passion for the glory of God. This is his positive way of expressing his aversion for spiritual pride. Such phrases as "Resolved, that I will do whatsoever I think to be most to

---

34. Edwards, *Works*, 19: 350.
35. Edwards, *Works*, 25: 97-98.

God's glory" (#1); "Resolved, never to do any manner of thing, whether in soul or body, less or more, but what tends to the glory of God" (#4).

Of course, the clearest affirmation against spiritual pride, is the 12th resolution: "Resolved, if I take delight in it as a gratification of pride, or vanity, or on any such account, immediately to throw it by" (#12). Perhaps just as adamant an expression of aversion to spiritual pride is the resolution: "Resolved, frequently to take some deliberate action, which seems most unlikely to be done, for the glory of God, and trace it back to the original intention, designs and ends of it; and if I find it not to be for God's glory, to repute it as a breach of the 4th Resolution" (#23).

7. OTHER AUTHORS

"If I appear great in their eyes, the Lord is most graciously helping me to see how absolutely nothing I am without Him, and helping me to keep little in my own eyes. He does use me. But I am so concerned that He uses me and that it is not of me the work is done. The axe cannot boast of the trees it has cut down. It could do nothing but for the woodsman. He made it, he sharpened it, and he used it. The moment he throws it aside, it becomes only old iron. O that I may never lose sight of this" (Samuel Brengle).[36]

8. CONCLUSION

I conclude with a quote from Edwards: "With such a spirit as this ought especially zealous ministers of the Gospel to be clothed, and those that God is pleased to improve as instruments in his hands of promoting his work. They ought indeed to be thorough in preaching the Word of God, without mincing the matter at all; in handling the sword of the Spirit (Eph 6:17), as the ministers of the Lord of hosts, they ought not to be mild and gentle; they are not to be gentle and moderate in searching and awakening the conscience but should be sons of thunder. The Word of God, which is in itself "sharper than any two-edged sword," ought not to be sheathed by its ministers, but so used that its sharp edges may have their full effect, even to the 'dividing asunder soul and spirit, joints and marrow' [Heb 4:12] (provided they do it without judging particular persons, leaving it to conscience and the Spirit of God to make the particular application); but all their conversation should savor of nothing but lowliness and good will, love and pity to all mankind; so that such a spirit should be like a sweet odor diffused around

---

36. Sanders, *Spiritual Leadership*, 62.

'em wherever they go, or like a light shining about 'em; their faces should as it were shine with it: they should be like lions to guilty consciences, but like lambs to men's persons" (Jonathan Edwards).[37] "Yea, the amiable Christ-like conversation of such ministers in itself would terrify consciences of men, as well as their terrible preaching; both would co-operate one with another, to subdue the hard, and bring down the proud heart" (Jonathan Edwards).[38]

CONCLUDING WARNING TO REVIVAL PREACHERS

"There ought to be the utmost watchfulness against all such appearances of spiritual pride, in all that profess to have been the subjects of this work, and especially in the promoters of it, but above all in itinerant preachers: the most eminent gifts, and highest tokens of God's favor and blessing will not excuse them. Alas! What is man at his best estate! What is the most highly favored Christian, or the most eminent and successful minister, that he should now think he is sufficient for something, and somebody to be regarded, and that he should go forth, and act among his fellow creatures, as if he were wise and strong and good!"[39] (Jonathan Edwards).

Appealing to the example of Moses, who mingled bitterness with his zeal, and was subsequently excluded from the Promised Land, Edwards warns young ministers: "Spiritual pride wrought in Moses at that time. His temptations to it were very great, for he had had great discoveries of God, and had been privileged with intimate and sweet communion with him, and God had made him the instrument of great good to his church; and though he was so humble a person, and by God's own testimony meek above all men upon the face of the whole earth, yet his temptations were too strong for him: which surely should make our young ministers, that have of late been highly favored and have had great success, exceeding careful and distrustful of themselves" (Jonathan Edwards).[40]

Spiritual pride is a great danger for successful preachers, especially revival preachers. Addressing the proclivity of preachers towards spiritual pride, Edwards warns: " . . . when a minister is greatly succeeded, from time to time, and so draws the eyes of the multitude upon him, and he sees himself flocked after, and resorted to as an oracle, and people are ready to adore him, and to offer sacrifice to him, as it was with Paul and Barnabas at Lystra (Acts 14:11–13), it is almost impossible for a man to avoid taking upon him

---

37. Edwards, *Works,* 4: 423.
38. Edwards, *Works,* 4: 423.
39. Edwards, *Works,* 4: 428.
40. Edwards, *Works,* 4: 429.

the airs of a master, or some extraordinary person; a man had need to have a great stock of humility, and much divine assistance, to resist the temptation. But the greater our dangers are, the more ought to be our watchfulness and prayerfulness, and diffidence of ourselves, lest we bring ourselves into mischief" (Jonathan Edwards).[41]

---

41. Edwards, *Works* 4: 429–30.

Chapter 12

Christocentrism

Characteristic Quotes on Christ from Edwards
" . . . if your eyes were opened to see the excellency of Christ, the work would be done. You would immediately believe in him; and you would find your heart going after him. It would be impossible to keep it back" (Edwards, Sermon "Natural Man in a Dreadful Condition")[1].

"The ingenerating of a principle of grace in the soul seems in Scripture to be compared to the conceiving of Christ in the womb. . . And the conception of Christ in the womb of the blessed virgin by the power of the Holy Ghost, seems to be a designed resemblance of the conception of Christ in the soul of a believer by the power of the same Holy Ghost" (Jonathan Edwards).[2]

---

1. Edwards, *Sermon "Natural Man."*
2. Edwards, *Works*, 2: 161.

INTRODUCTION

No work on Edwards's sermons/works/theology would be complete without addressing the concept/issue/prominence of his Christocentrism. Revival happens when Christ is honoured and exalted. Edwards was enamoured with Christ. His emphasis on Christ and his understanding of the centrality of Christ have everything to do with understanding and explaining the Great Awakening.

1. DEFINE IT:

Christocentrism, as the word suggests, is making Christ central. It is honoring and exalting Christ. More than having a pure Christology, it is having a pure and passionate Christology.

Here is a helpful quote: While the term "Christ centeredness" can refer to a variety of characteristics in a believer's life, it is a desire for the Savior that best defines Christ centeredness. A Christ-centered believer desires to grasp Christ more fully, live for him alone, and love him above all else. A Christian who is truly growing in God wants to be closer to his Savior and desires to be more like him. But Christ-centeredness can also be seen in the way a believer grows more sensitive to Christ's purposes on earth. Not only does a Christian become more attuned to Christ, his will, and his ways, but he also begins to develop a deeper tenderness toward others. Because the love of Christ his Savior is flowing into him, he begins to feel greater love for those around him. He desires to show and share Christ's love and goodness. And he seeks out ways to help and serve others so that they may also come to see, feel, and understand Christ and his love in a deeper and more real way (Taylor Wise).[3]

Sometimes a poem or a hymn can provide more precise theological definition than a complex theological treatise. A.B. Simpson[4] has provided an excellent "definition" of "Christocentrism" in his classic hymn entitled Himself:

> **HIMSELF**
> by A. B. Simpson
>
> Once it was the blessing, Now it is the Lord;
> Once it was the feeling, Now it is His Word.
> Once His gifts I wanted, Now the Giver own;
> Once I sought for healing, Now Himself alone.

---

3. Wise, *Christ-centered*.
4. Simpson, *Himself*.

Once 'twas painful trying, Now 'tis perfect trust
Once a half salvation, Now the uttermost.
Once 'twas ceaseless holding, Now He holds me fast;
Once 'twas constant drifting, Now my anchor's cast.

Once 'twas busy planning, Now 'tis trustful prayer;
Once 'twas anxious caring, Now He has the care.
Once 'twas what I wanted, Now what Jesus says;
Once 'twas constant asking, Now 'tis ceaseless praise.

Once it was my working, His it hence shall be;
Once I tried to use Him, Now He uses me.
Once the power I wanted, Now the Mighty One;
Once for self I labored, Now for Him alone.

Once I hoped in Jesus, Now I know He's mine;
Once my lamps were dying, Now they brightly shine.
Once for death I waited, Now His coming hail;
And my hopes are anchored, Safe within the veil.

This Christocentricity is clearly reflected in the Alliance's theme hymn: "Jesus Only"[5]:

JESUS ONLY
by A. B. Simpson

Jesus only is our message,
Jesus all our theme shall be;
We will lift up Jesus ever,
Jesus only will we see.

Jesus only, Jesus ever,
Jesus all in all we sing,
Savior, Sanctifier, and Healer,
Glorious Lord and coming King.

Jesus only is our Savior,
All our guilt He bore away,
He, our righteousness forever,
All our strength from day to day.

Jesus is our Sanctifier,

---

5. Simpson, *Jesus Only*.

aving us from self and sin,
And with all His Spirit's fulness,
Filling all our hearts within.

Jesus only is our Healer,
All our sicknesses He bare,
And His risen life and fulness,
All His members still may share.

Jesus only is our Power,
He the gift of Pentecost;
Jesus, breathe Thy pow'r upon us,
Fill us with the Holy Ghost.

And for Jesus we are waiting,
List'ning for the Advent Call;
But 'twill still be Jesus only,
Jesus ever, all in all.

2. BIBLICAL PERSPECTIVE

What biblical evidence is there to suggest a correlation between revival and the exaltation of Christ in preaching? Paul said, "For we do not preach ourselves but Christ Jesus as Lord, and ourselves as your bondservants for Jesus' sake" (II Cor 4:5) (NASB). Paul's primary focus was Christ. He said it again and again. He told the Corinthians: "I determined to know nothing among you, except Jesus Christ, and him crucified" (I Cor 2:2) (NASB). Paul's preaching was Christ-centered. Paul explains to the Colossians that he was called and made to be a minister according to the stewardship from God "that I might fully carry out the preaching of the word of God" (Col 1:25) (NASB). Paul proceeds to explain that the mystery "has now been manifested" (1:26) because God willed to "make known" what are the glorious riches: "Christ in you, the hope of glory" (Col. 1:27). Thus, Paul concludes "we proclaim Him" (Col 1:28) . . . "that we may present every man complete in Christ" (Col 1:29) (NASB). This is what Paul laboured and struggled for (Col 1:29). His focus clearly was "Christ Himself" (Col 2:4), "in whom are hidden all the treasures of wisdom and knowledge" (Col 2:3) (NIV). Evidently, Paul's preaching was Christocentric, par excellence. Paul, in all his epistles, is enamored with Christ. His favourite phrase "in Christ" or "in Him" is all-pervasive throughout his epistles. This teaching reflects his preaching.

Is there clear biblical evidence to connect Christ-centered preaching to revival? Indeed, there is: speaking of the ministry of the Holy Spirit, Jesus said, "But when He, the Spirit of truth, comes, He will guide you into all the truth; for He will not speak on His own initiative, but whatever He hears, He will speak; and He will disclose to you what is to come. He shall glorify Me; for He shall take of Mine, and shall disclose it to you" (John 16:14) (NASB). It is the role of the Spirit to glorify Jesus in the heart of the believer. Jesus said: "And I, if I be lifted up from the earth, will draw all men unto me" (John 12:32) (KJV).

3. QUOTES FROM EDWARDS

Next to "Religious Affections," perhaps Edwards's most significant work on spirituality and revival is his classic "Distinguishing Marks." In both these works Edwards discusses "no signs" and "yes signs," false criteria and valid criteria for determining whether or not a supposed revival is truly of Divine origin. It is most significant that one of the 5 "yes signs" providing indisputable evidence that a revival is authentic and of Divine origin is the centrality and emphasis on Christ, that is, its Christocentrism. Edwards states: "1. When that spirit that is at work amongst a people is observed to operate after such a manner, as to raise their esteem of that Jesus that was born of the Virgin, and was crucified without the gates of Jerusalem; and seems more to confirm and establish their minds in the truth of what the Gospel declares to us of his being the Son of God, and the Saviour of men; 'tis a sure sign that that spirit is the Spirit of God" (Jonathan Edwards).[6] It is most significant that Edwards reduces the "yes signs" or valid criteria for ascertaining whether or not a work is truly of God, down to five (5) signs. And the first and most important is his emphasis on Christocentrism. Developing this same point, Edwards affirms: "But the words of the Apostle are remarkable; the person that the Spirit gives testimony to, and to whom he raises their esteem and respect, must be that Jesus that appeared in the flesh, and not another Christ in his stead; not any mystical, fantastical Christ; such as the light within, which the spirit of the Quakers extols, while it diminishes their esteem of, and dependence upon an outward Christ, or Jesus as he came in the flesh, and leads them off from him; but the spirit that gives testimony for that Jesus, and leads to him, can be no other than the Spirit of God" (Jonathan Edwards).[7]

---

6. Edwards, *Works*, 4: 249.
7. Edwards, *Works*, 4: 250.

4. QUOTES BY EDWARDSEAN SCHOLARS

Lesser, undoubtedly one of the leading authorities on Edwards's sermons, states that his emphasis on Christ is critical in understanding the nature of the Great Awakening. Although Edwards is known for his sermon "Sinners in the Hands of an Angry God," it is Edwards's emphasis on the sweetness and beauty of Christ that is predominant in the corpus of Edwards's revival sermons. Lesser states that in Edwards's sermon "The Excellency of Christ" . . . "the words *friend or friendship* occur thirty times over as many manuscript leaves." " . . . the glory of Christ appears in the qualifications of his human nature . . . it appears to us in excellencies that are of our own kind, and are exercised in our own way and manner, and so, in some respects, are peculiarly fitted to invite our acquaintance, and draw our affection." In the published version he goes further, nearer the divine glory: "Christ has brought it to pass, that those that the Father has given him, should be brought into the household of God; that he, and his Father, and his people, should be as it were one society, one family; that the church should be as it were admitted into the society of the blessed Trinity" (Jonathan Edwards).[8]

We do well to remember that Edwards was Reformed and Puritan. One biblical scholar (Beeke, quoted by Steele) refers to Edwards as the last Puritan. In accordance with scriptural data such as Luke 24:44–45 and John 5:39, the Puritans read their Bibles through rose-colored lenses tinted by the blood of a crucified savior and risen Lord. It was their goal in every text to solidify that the "great theme and controlling contour of experiential preaching is Jesus Christ, for he is the supreme focus, prism, and goal of God's revelation"[9]. Hence William Perkins, the great Puritan homiletician, writes that the heart of all preaching is "to preach one Christ, by Christ, to the praise of Christ."[10]

"In five sermons Edwards preached immediately before and during the revival, and which he published under the title "Discourses on Various Important Subjects, Nearly Concerning the Great Affair of the Soul's Eternal Salvation," in 1738, the Spirit of God is but rarely mentioned, though *Christ is highly prominent*"[11] [emphasis mine].

---

8. Edwards, *Works,* 19: 21.
9. Steele, *Classical Analysis.*
10. Steele, *Classical Analysis.*
11. Haykin, *Jonathan Edwards,* 49.

5. ILLUSTRATIONS FROM THE ACTUAL SERMONS OF EDWARDS

When we review the Christological content of the revival sermons of 1734/35, we are not disappointed. Examples abound: Here is a sample from "Ruth's Resolution," preached at the height of the Great awakening in April, of 1735: "They have an excellent and glorious Savior, who is the only begotten Son of God; the brightness of his Father's glory; one in whom God from eternity had infinite delight; a Savior of infinite love; one that has shed his own blood, and made his soul an offering for their sins; and one that is able to save them to the uttermost" (Jonathan Edwards).[12]

In another fine sermon, "The Justice of God in the Damnation of Sinners," Edwards maintains a wonderful balance in appealing to two motivations, vacillating between fear and love, and emphasizing simultaneously the torments of God's justice and the sweetness of God's Saviour, the Lord Jesus Christ:

> "If you should for ever be cast off by God, it would be agreeable to your treatment of Jesus Christ. It would have been just with God if he had cast you off forever, without ever making you the offer of a Savior. But God hath not done that; but has provided a Savior for sinners, and offered him to you, even his own Son Jesus Christ; who is the only Savior of men; all that be not forever cast off, are saved by him: God offers men salvation through him, and has promised us that if we come to him we shall not be cast off. But you have treated, and still treat this Savior after such a manner, that if you should be eternally cast off by God, it would be most agreeable to your behavior towards him; which appears by this, viz., That you reject Christ, and won't have him for your Savior. If God offers you a Savior from deserved punishment, and you will not receive him, then surely 'tis just that you should go without a Savior. Or, is God obliged, because you don't like this Savior, to provide you another? If when he has given an infinitely honorable and glorious person, even his only begotten Son, to be a sacrifice for sin, in the fire of his wrath, and so provided salvation, and this Savior is offered to you, you be not suited in him, and refuse to accept him, is God therefore unjust if he don't save you? Is he obliged to save you in a way of your own choosing, because you don't like the way of his choosing? Or will you charge Christ with injustice because he don't become your Savior, when at the same time you won't have him,

---

12. Edwards, *Works*, 19: 310.

when he offers himself to you, and beseeches you to accept of him as your Savior?" (Jonathan Edwards).[13]

There are some of us today who believe in a deeper life experience for Christians, a Gospel that embraces Christ not only as Saviour from hell, but as Sanctifier delivering us from ourselves. We find in Edwards a strong ally: He criticizes the tendency of some to accommodate the Gospel: "that would be mighty pleasing to men, to be saved from the punishment of sin and yet not saved from sin, but to be allowed to enjoy it and practice it still. They would like a saviour that would save them *in* their sins much better than a savior to save them *from* their sins" [Emphasis mine][14], taken from Edwards's Sermon: "The Kind of Preaching People Want" (November 1733). It is significant that as Edwards ramped up to the Great Awakening (with the advantage of our perspective looking back on history), he prepared the ground for a revival by differentiating between cheap grace and expensive grace, calling his people to embrace the true Gospel and not a cheap imitation. The Gospel includes not only deliverance from the penalty of sin, but also from the power of sin. This was the message of A. B. Simpson, founder of the Alliance, and this was the same message of J. Edwards.

Finally, in Edwards's sermon, "Our Weakness, Christ's Strength," Edwards focuses in on the sufficiency of Christ to meet the human dilemma. "There is a sufficient mediator. And though we are without strength, yet Christ has died for us, as 'tis said in the verse wherein is the text. He is sufficient in his purchase, and he is sufficient in his power. The Captain of our salvation is able to overcome that potent adversary of our souls. He came into the world to destroy the works of the devil, as 'tis said, 1 John 3:8, "For this purpose the Son of God was manifested, that he might destroy the works of the devil." He is ready to pity, and to help the helpless. Our refuge must be in him, and in him alone we should put our trust. This is the true David who delivers the lamb out of the mouth of the lion, and out of the mouth of the bear" (Jonathan Edwards)[15].

6. 70 RESOLUTIONS

Perhaps the vow that most clearly points us to Edwards's Christocentrism is Resolution #53.

---

13. Edwards, *Works*, 19: 360.
14. Edwards, *Sermon, The Kind of Preaching People Want*.
15. Edwards, *Works*, 19: 387.

53. Resolved, to improve every opportunity, when I am in the best and happiest frame of mind, *to cast and venture my soul on the Lord Jesus Christ, to trust and confide in him, and consecrate myself wholly to him; that from this I may have assurance of my safety, knowing that I confide in my Redeemer* July 8, 1723 [Emphasis mine].

Another significant resolution that reflects this same Christocentrism is found in Resolution #63: On the supposition, that there never was to be but one individual in the world, at any one time, who was properly a complete Christian, in all respects of a right stamp, having Christianity always shining in its true luster, and appearing excellent and lovely, from whatever part and under whatever character viewed: Resolved, to act just as I would do, if I strove with all my might to be that one, who should live in my time. Jan. 14 and July 13, 1723. Edwards's passion to be "a complete Christian" and "having Christianity always shining in its true luster" can only be explained by his passion for the centrality of Christ.

7. OTHER AUTHORS

But Edwards is not alone among Christian thinkers in having a Christocentric philosophy as seen in the writing of Calvin: "As the moon and stars, though in themselves they are not merely luminous, but diffuse their light over the whole earth, do, nevertheless, disappear before the brightness of the sun; so, however glorious the law was in itself, it has, nevertheless, no glory in comparison with the excellence of the gospel. Hence it follows, that we cannot sufficiently prize, or hold in sufficient esteem the glory of Christ, which shines forth in the gospel, like the splendor of the sun when beaming forth; and that the gospel is foolishly handled, nay more, is shamefully profaned, where the power and majesty of the Spirit do not come forth to view, so as to draw up men's minds and hearts heavenward"[16] (Calvin on I Cor 3:8).

Edwards's contemporaries also reflect a strong Christocentrism. "Exhibit as much as you can of a glorious Christ. Yea, let the motto upon your whole ministry be: Christ is all. Let others develop the pulpit fads that come and go. Let us specialize in preaching our Lord Jesus Christ" (Cotton Mather).[17]

" . . . I thank God we have been taught that it is not the blessing, it is not the healing, it is not the sanctification, it is not the thing, it is not the it that you want, but it is something better. It is "the Christ"; it is Himself.

---

16. Calvin, *Calvin's Commentary: I Corinthians.*
17. Steele, *Classical Analysis.*

How often that comes out in His Word "Himself took our infirmities and bare our sicknesses," Himself "bare our sins in his own body on the tree"! It is the person of Jesus Christ we want. Plenty of people get the idea and do not get anything out of it. They get it into their head, and it into their conscience, and it into their will; but somehow, they do not get Him into their life and spirit, because they have only that which is the outward expression and symbol of the spiritual reality. I once saw a picture of the Constitution of the United States, very skillfully engraved in copper plate, so that when you looked at it closely it was nothing more than a piece of writing, but when you looked at it at a distance, it was the face of George Washington. The face shone out in the shading of the letters at a little distance, and I saw the person, not the words, nor the ideas; and I thought, "'That is the way to look at the Scriptures and understand the thoughts of God, to see in them the face of love, shining through and through; not ideas, nor doctrines, but Jesus Himself as the Life and Source and sustaining Presence of all our life" (A. B. Simpson, "Himself").[18]

8. CONCLUSION

We as preachers need to be intimately familiar with Christ. Edwards demonstrated again and again a devotional intimacy with his Saviour. We already saw that one of his resolutions reflects his determination towards intimacy with Christ: 53. Resolved, to improve every opportunity, when I am in the best and happiest frame of mind, to cast and venture my soul on the Lord Jesus Christ, to trust and confide in him, and consecrate myself wholly to him; that from this I may have assurance of my safety, knowing that I confide in my Redeemer. July 8, 1723. Here is the open secret of revival: spending time with Jesus and allowing the Spirit of Jesus to so imbibe my spirit that my life and my ministry is impregnated with the Spirit of Jesus. Then, when our hearts are filled with Christ, our mouths will be filled with a Christ-centered Gospel. And that's Good News for the world today. What the world needs, what the church needs, is Jesus.

In terms of a model for ministry, I love Edwards's Christocentrism as it relates to the minister. As you explore Edwards carefully, you discover a remarkable affinity between him and those of the deeper life emphasis like A. B Simpson with his emphasis on the life of Christ for the life of the believer, and the life of Christ for the life of the minister. Edwards strongly believed that Christ continued to minister in and through the minister. In his sermon "The minister before the judgment seat of Christ" (Luke 10:17,

18. Simpson, *Himself.*

18) preached on November 17, 1736, Edwards refers to John 4:35, 36. Jesus is the one referred to as the one that sows ... and the preacher is the one who reaps .... "Gospel ministers are only as it were sent forth to reap the fruit of his labors"[19]. "They do not save men, but are only sent forth to bring in those that he has saved"[20]. "It is Christ that has, as it were, plowed and sowed the field and by his own great labors and sufferings laid all the foundations of their salvation.... ministers have nothing to do but to reap and gather"[21]. We preachers need to rediscover afresh the spiritual dynamic of ministry. It is not about us. It is not about our ability or work. It is about Christ. As Paul has said:

"To them God has chosen to make known among the Gentiles the glorious riches of this mystery, which is Christ in you, the hope of glory. He is the one we proclaim, admonishing and teaching everyone with all wisdom, so that we may present everyone fully mature in Christ. To this end I strenuously contend with all the energy Christ so powerfully works in me" (Colossians 1:27–29). He must increase, and we must decrease. Amen.

We conclude with two precious Christological quotes from Edwards: "But that is the nature of true grace and spiritual light, that it opens to a person's view the infinite reason there is that he should be holy in a high degree. And the more grace he has, and the more this is opened to view, the greater sense he has of the infinite excellency and glory of the divine Being, and of the infinite dignity of the person of Christ, and the boundless length and breadth and depth and height of the love of Christ to sinners. And as grace increases, the field opens more and more to a distant view, until the soul is swallowed up with the vastness of the object, and the person is astonished to think how much it becomes him to love this God and this glorious Redeemer that has so loved man, and how little he does love. And so, the more he apprehends, the more the smallness of his grace and love appears strange and wonderful: and therefore he is more ready to think that others are beyond him." (Jonathan Edwards, *Religious Affections*).[22]

> How happy would you be if your hearts were but persuaded to close with Jesus Christ! Then you would be out of all danger: whatever storms and tempests were without, you might rest securely within; you might hear the rushing of the wind, and the thunder roar abroad, while you are safe in this hiding-place. O be persuaded to hide yourself in Christ Jesus! What greater

19. Bailey, *Salvation*, 83.
20. Bailey, *Salvation*, 83.
21. Bailey, *Salvation*, 83.
22. Edwards, *Works*, 2: 324.

assurance of safety can you desire? He has undertaken to defend and save you, if you will come to him: he looks upon it as his work; he engaged in it before the world was, and he has given his faithful promise which he will not break; and if you will but make your flight there, his life shall be for yours; he will answer for you, you shall have nothing to do but rest quietly in him; you may stand still and see what the Lord will do for you. If there be any thing to suffer, the suffering is Christ's, you will have nothing to suffer; if there be any thing to be done, the doing of it is Christ's, you will have nothing to do but to stand still and behold it.

But Christ Jesus has true excellency, and so great excellency, that when they come to see it they look no further, but the mind rests there. It sees a transcendent glory and an ineffable sweetness in him; it sees that till now it has been pursuing shadows, but that now it has found the substance; that before it had been seeking happiness in the stream, but that now it has found the ocean. The excellency of Christ is an object adequate to the natural cravings of the soul, and is sufficient to fill the capacity. It is an infinite excellency, such an one as the mind desires, in which it can find no bounds; and the more the mind is used to it, the more excellent it appears. Every new discovery makes this beauty appear more ravishing, and the mind sees no end; here is room enough for the mind to go deeper and deeper, and never come to the bottom. The soul is exceedingly ravished when it first looks on this beauty, and it is never weary of it. The mind never has any satiety, but Christ's excellency is always fresh and new, and tends as much to delight, after it has been seen a thousand or ten thousand years, as when it was seen the first moment. The excellency of Christ is an object suited to the superior faculties of man, it is suited to entertain the faculty of reason and understanding, and there is nothing so worthy about which the understanding can be employed as this excellency; no other object is so great, noble, and exalted.

—Jonathan Edwards: "Safety, Fullness and Sweet Refreshment in Christ[23]"

---

23. Edwards, Sermon: *"Safety"*

Chapter 13

Application to Preaching Today

Revival Preaching
Lessons from the Preaching of Jonathan Edwards

CONCLUDING REFLECTION

Extracted from his sermons preached before and during the First Great Awakening.

This book explores the relationship between preaching and revival. I wanted to understand better from history and from Scripture what kind of preaching is conducive to revival. At the outset of this book, we asked some key questions:

What kinds of sermons were preached before, during and after the Great Awakening? What themes and what texts were preached? What issues were addressed? What was Edwards's approach to preaching in general? What was his philosophy of preaching? What was Edwards's approach to preaching before, during and after the Great Awakening? What lessons are there for us as preachers today? What can we learn from the Great Awakening that would facilitate awakening in our day? What correlation exists between his preaching and revival? What made his sermons so effective? Why did God seem pleased to pour out revival through the agency of these sermons? What about the man Edwards sheds light on the correlation between preaching and revival?

As we conclude, I want to endeavor to answer precisely and punctually those questions. I run the risk of oversimplifying but have endeavored to condense the essence of Edwards and the preaching of the Great Awakening here.

1. What kinds of sermons were preached before, during and after the Great Awakening?

   Revival preaching emphasized eternity, was focused on God, Christ-centered and Spirit-empowered, and had a strong application orientated with a powerful and personal appeal to the will.

2. What themes and what texts were preached? What issues were addressed?

   a. The supremacy and sovereignty of God was preeminent.

   b. The Gospel message of the centrality of the cross and the resurrection was paramount.

   c. The messages were relevant to the listener, but always rooted in Scripture.

3. What was Edwards's approach to preaching in general? What was his philosophy of preaching?

   a. Edwards was a Reformed and Puritan Evangelical.

   b. He believed in the pre-eminence and primacy of the Word.

   c. He believed that the Spirit of God infused the Word of God with life.

   d. To preach was to be a burning and a shining light, diffusing light, and heat, beautifying the truth, expounding on the revealed truth.

   e. Edwards believed in the real presence of Christ through the sacrament of preaching.

4. What was Edwards's approach to preaching before, during and after the Great Awakening?

   a. Edwards appealed to both head and heart. He refused to compromise on either aspect. Edwards was passionate, and extremely lucid and compelling.

b. His exposure to Whitefield appeared to accentuate in his preaching more of an emphasis on the emotions and a greater dependence upon the Holy Spirit.

   c. He sought to address those issues that were particularly relevant to his congregants. He was aware of the wider issues and sought to address those matters from the pulpit.

   d. His emphasis on prayer and on the Spirit needs to be emphasized.

5. What lessons are there from Edwards for us as preachers today? What can we learn from the Great Awakening that would facilitate awakening in our day? What correlation exists between his preaching and revival? What made his sermons so effective? Why did God seem pleased to pour out revival through the agency of these sermons? We have a lot to learn from Edwards. What about the man Edwards sheds light on the correlation between preaching and revival?

   a. His passion for revival and awakening is remarkable.

   b. His passion for prayer, especially as seen in his practice of personal prayer and his appeal for united prayer revival. We can learn to join forces with similarly minded and similarly "hearted" believers who long for revival.

   c. The centrality of the pulpit, and serious thorough preparation, combined with keen awareness of the contemporary issues, and a dexterity to bring the Scriptures to bear on those issues.

   d. His remarkable humility.

   e. We can learn from the Great Awakening that there are often tares with the wheat, and we as leaders need to cultivate spiritual discernment to navigate the tempestuous rapids that often entail with revival.

   f. The correlation between preaching and revival is powerful. Anointed biblical relevant preaching is frequently the means that God uses to spark revival.

A PRAYERFUL RESPONSE TO EACH CHAPTER'S PRIMARY THEME

As a way of responding personally and prayerfully to each theme, I have expressed my own personal prayerful response to each chapter. Perhaps my response will reflect or stimulate yours. What does this work mean to me personally, and to my preaching colleagues in the ministry? Revival and Awakening are what is needed today in many latitudes. Lord, Your call is upon our lives. Equip us to preach for revival: A revival among the saved that results in an awakening among the lost…to the glory of the Triune God.

Chapter 1—The Heart, The Head and Preaching

Lord, enable me to combine head and heart in preaching. To have my heart touched deeply and my head enflamed with truth. Help me to find that perfect blend, and touch hearts but also address the issues that affect people's reasoning. Lord, forgive my pathetic preaching, and make my preaching more pathetic. Amen.

Chapter 2—Prayer and Fasting

Lord, prayer is the key to revival. I have read that so many times. And fasting is prayer on steroids. Lord, teach me the dynamics of prayer for revival. Not just about the truth in a notional way, but actually entering more fully into the life of prayer. Empower and motivate me to spend more time praying, and to take the time, the seasons, to pray with fasting. Teach me how to pray with fasting for revival. To read those inspirational books that promote prayer and fasting for revival.

Chapter 3—Hellfire

Lord, give me a fresh vision of eternity. May I see hell in a way that I have never before seen it. Put into my heart and vocal cords a solemnity and sobriety about eternity. Lord, help me to understand the issues around eternal damnation. Help me to understand the objections and respond with reasonable and compassionate responses. Most of all, give me compassion for the lost.

Chapter 4—The Word and Preaching

Lord, Your Word is life giving because You are life giving. Give me a fresh love for *Your Word*. Lord, grant a fresh hunger for *Your Word*. Lord, grant fresh insight into *Your Word*. Lord, help me to memorize, to study, to meditate on, to read, to listen to, to study and to obey *Your Word*. Lord, give me insights into *Your Word*. Give me fresh messages for the church. Give me fresh messages for the lost in Spain, for Canada, for wherever.

Chapter 5—The Holy Spirit

Lord, fill me with Your Spirit. Help me not to grieve or quench or resist your Spirit. Lord, take me into a new experience of Your fullness. Fill me and anoint me in a fresh way. May these days of reading and studying be days of renewed experience in You. So many of Your servants down through church history have sought You and found You in Your fullness, and it has meant a significant change and improvement in their lives and preaching ministries. Holy Spirit, help me to honor the Triune God, and yield my life to You, so that my lips be touched with a live coal from Your altar, and I be re-commissioned to serve You with a freshness. Holy Spirit, empower me to pay the price for seeking Your fullness and Your fresh anointing upon my preaching ministry. Purify my motives.

Chapter 6—The Word-Spirit Blend and Preaching

Lord, may I have that perfect blend of Word and Spirit in my life and in my preaching. May there be a proper balance, a proper juxta positioning of these two dynamics in my life. Lord, help me to honor the Holy Spirit. Take me into a new relationship with the Holy Spirit.

Chapter 7—Supremacy of God in Preaching

>Be Thou My Vision[1].
>Smith, Hall and Smith
>*Be Thou my Vision, O Lord of my heart;*
>*Naught be all else to me, save that Thou art.*
>Thou my best Thought, by day or by night,
>Waking or sleeping, Thy presence my light.
>
>Be Thou my Wisdom, and Thou my true Word;
>I ever with Thee and Thou with me, Lord;
>Thou my great Father, I Thy true son;
>Thou in me dwelling, and I with Thee one.
>
>Be Thou my battle Shield, Sword for the fight;
>e Thou my Dignity, Thou my Delight;
>Thou my soul's Shelter, Thou my high Tower:
>*Raise Thou me heavenward, O Power of my power.*
>
>Riches I heed not, *nor man's empty praise,*
>Thou mine Inheritance, now and always:
>Thou and Thou only, *first in my heart,*
>High King of Heaven, my Treasure Thou art.
>
>High King of Heaven, my victory won,
>May I reach Heaven's joys, O bright Heaven's Sun!
>Heart of my own heart, whatever befall,
>Still be my Vision, *O Ruler of all.*

Lord, give me a fresh vision of Your Sovereignty. Help me to truly worship You, as a sovereign God. Help me to study and get to know you better, with head and heart. Help me to declare to the Spanish community the God of the Bible. May my preaching for revival by characterized by an anointing as I present God in all His beauty and fullness. Give me a new appreciation for the Trinity. A new understanding. Help me to grow in understanding who You are. Lord, reveal *Yourself* to me, like You revealed Yourself to Moses, to Isaiah, to Ezekiel, to John, to Paul, to so many of Your choice servants. Lord, help me to know You, and preach You. Show me how to preach You, with the supremacy of God trumping everything.

---

1. Bryne, *Be Thou My Vision.*

Chapter 8—Edwards the Man as Preacher

Lord, You are looking for men. Your eyes scan the whole earth looking for those whose hearts are perfectly inclined towards You. Lord, may our eyes meet. Grant me the grace to be a man of integrity. To be a person after the heart of God. Lord, help me to be an example of revival. Lord, work so deeply, so freshly, so newly in me, that the Spanish pastors and church will perceive that there is spiritual authenticity in me. Lord, bless and renew our marriage. Enable us to serve you together.

Chapter 9—Sovereignty and Responsibility

Lord, I do not get it. Help me to move in the direction of getting it. Help me to honor all Your Word. Help me to preach a sovereign God, who extends bona fide offers of grace to the world. Enable me to understand that dynamic. Lord, unless You do not want me to understand it, and simply preach what is at this point a conundrum. Lord, Edwards honored You. He preached a sovereign God. Yet he appealed with passion and integrity to the will of his audience. Lord, enable me to more fully grasp this dynamic, so that I can preach with greater integrity, and so that I can train servants of Yours to preach with greater integrity.

Chapter 10—Application

Lord, there is something within me that shies away from calling for a commitment. I think it has a great deal to do with self. If people do not respond, that reflects back on me. Lord, I have made it about me, instead of about You. Lord, teach me, in my spiritual life and in my approach to ministry, what it means to apply Your Word to believers and unbelievers alike. Lord, whatever it takes, empower me to be a preacher who brings the Word to bear upon the will of the listener. The mind, yes, but also the will. Lord, I believe this is crucial to revival preaching. If revival is nothing more, or nothing less than a new beginning of obedience to God, then applied preaching is paramount. Lord, fill me with Your Spirit and enable me to apply Your Word to myself and to Your people.

Chapter 11—Personal Humility

Lord, humble me. Help me to tremble at Your Word. Your Word states categorically: "For thus saith the high and lofty One that inhabiteth eternity, whose name is Holy; I dwell in the high and holy place, with him also that is of a contrite and humble spirit, to *revive* the spirit of the humble, and to *revive* the heart of the contrite ones" (Is 57:15) (KJV). Lord, I humble myself, and ask that You revive me. You inhabit eternity. You are high. You are lofty. Your name is Holy. Lord, you dwell in eternity in a high and holy place. But You also dwell in the lowest place, in the spirit that is contrite and humble. Lord, deliver me from the itch for publicity (Tozer[2]). Deliver me from using the pulpit as a platform for strutting. Forgive me. Lord, give me a vision of Your glory, and may that eclipse any and every vestige of self-seeking or self-promotion.

Chapter 12—Christocentrism

Lord Jesus, You are to be the center! Your Word says (Col 1:18) "He is also head of the body, the church; and He is the beginning, the firstborn from the dead, so that He Himself will come to have first place in everything" (NASB) ... or as another respected version states "And he is the head of the body, the church: who is the beginning, the firstborn from the dead; that in all things he might have the pre-eminence" (KJV). Lord, help me to honor You. Give me a passion for Your pre-eminence. Inundate my soul with a growing hunger and thirst for Your glory. Lord, be exalted in my life, in my preaching, in my focus. May my preaching be Spirit-filled and Christ-honoring and God-glorifying. You have said that if You be lifted up, You will draw all man unto Yourself. You were lifted up on that cross, and then God exalted You through Your resurrection and gave You a name above every other. Lord, be exalted in my life and preaching. Be central. Empower me to find my text and then make a beeline for the cross and the resurrection. And may the Triune God be honored, and the church blessed with a mighty revival and awakening. *Amen.*

Additional Themes

Lord, there are indeed many aspects of revival preaching. I want to be that kind of a preacher. Lord, work in my motives. Give me clean hands and

---

2. Wax, *Prayer of a Minor Prophet.*

a pure heart. Deliver me from seeking revival for all the wrong reasons. Lord, may not even one wrong reason or one wrong motivation creep into my heart. Lord, if there is anything there that does not honor You, extract it from my heart. Lord, whether that be a purer Christology, a vision for revival, an understanding of eschatology as it relates to revival, or whatever perspective.

Conclusion

My final word to myself, and to preaching pastors: God's people need a fresh wind and a fresh fire. Whether they be in Spain, in Latin America, or in North America, or anywhere else for that matter, many of Your people languish for a fresh touch from You. Lord, forgive us for our pathetic preaching. And Lord, anoint us to preach with a fresh anointing and blessing. May Your church be revived. And may the lost who hear our preaching be saved. May the saved who hear our preaching be inspired to reach out to the lost. Lord, they are so lost. Revival and Awakening. Lord, do it again. For Your Name's sake. Do it again. You are the God of Jonathan Edwards. Do it again. Do it differently. Do it the same. Do it however and wherever and whenever and through whomever You sovereignly choose. But Lord, in Your compassion and mercy, do it powerfully, do it in Spain and in Latin America, do it everywhere, do it in these days, in these years, and Lord, be pleased to use Your servant and Your servants. That Your Name might be highly honored and esteemed among the nations. Amen.

Appendix 1

What are the Parameters for the Great Awakening?

WHAT ARE THE PARAMETERS for the Great Awakening? What criteria do we utilize for determining the bookends of the Great Awakening, both Chapter One and Chapter Two? There are several criteria that scholars utilize. Of course, different scholars differ on the exact dates of the Great Awakening, basically using various parameters to ascertain the extent of the Great Awakening. First, what did Edwards himself say? This can be traced in his work "The Faithful Narrative" and in correspondence during the period. If one focuses in on Northampton, where Edwards was a Pastor, as the primary locus of the Awakening, and if one appeals primarily to Edwards himself for determining the bookends of the awakening, one can settle on these dates: from February of 1734 to August of 1735 (The Great Awakening, Chapter One) and October of 1740 to June of 1742 (The Great Awakening, Chapter Two).

Edwards determines the parameters as follows: The beginning of an unusual work of God in Northampton seems to unfold in the winter of 1734 (Unpublished letter of May 30, 1735)[1] when "there appeared a strange flexibleness in the young people of the town, and an unusual disposition to hearken to counsel" (Jonathan Edwards)[2]. Edwards describes it as "the present

---

1. Goen, *Works,* 4: 99.
2. Goen, *Works,* 4: 99.

extraordinary circumstances of this town." "The young people also have been reforming more and more; they by degrees left off their frolicking, and have been observably more decent in their attendance on the public worship." Edwards records in his letter that he had observed a negative attitude among the youth, preferring "diversion" and "company-keeping" (Jonathan Edwards),[3] a euphemism for socializing with a negative connotation. Then Edwards writes, "I then preached a sermon on the Sabbath before the lecture, to show them the unsuitableness and inconvenience of the practice, and to persuade them to reform it; and urged it on heads of families that it should be a thing agreed among them to govern their families, and keep them in at those times" (Jonathan Edwards).[4] Edwards says in May of 1735 that "the winter before last" this stirring started with a sermon... which would place it in late 1733 or perhaps early 1734. Quite probably this sermon would be Sermon #315, Heeding the Word and Losing it, (Hebrews 2:1) preached in February of 1734. In this message he "rebukes them for practices that 'divert the mind' from the solemnity of Sabbath evenings and lecture days, diversions like company-keeping, frolicking, and drinking, practices more troubling still because found 'especially among young people'[5]. The content of this sermon fits perfectly with Edwards's own description of the beginnings of the Great Awakening in the Faithful Narrative. I believe that we are safe to conclude that the Sermon "Heeding the Word and Losing It" was the catalyst to the First Great Awakening, and proves to be a significant sermon to study. According to this research, the Great Awakening began in February of 1734. In the preface to the Faithful Narrative, Edwards writes to Colman dated November 6, 1736 that in April of 1734 "a very sudden and awful death of a young man in the bloom of life... much affected many of our young people" (Jonathan Edwards)[6]. However, Edwards, in his letter to Colman, dated May 30 of 1735, states, "then a concern about the great things of religion began, about the latter end of December and the beginning of January" of 1735. Elsewhere, in the preface to the Faithful Narrative, Edwards writes, "then it was in the latter part of December that the Spirit of God began extraordinarily to set in, and wonderfully to work among us; so that there were, very suddenly, one after another, five or six persons that were to all appearance savingly converted; and some of them wrought upon in a remarkable fashion."

3. Goen, *Works*, 4: 99.
4. Goen, *Works*, 4: 99,100.
5. Lesser, *Works*, 19: 38.
6. Goen, *Works*, 4: 216.

When did it end and why? Historian M. X. Lesser, editor of Volume 19 in the "Works of Jonathan Edwards" series, suggests that the suicide of Edwards's uncle Hawley in June of 1735 "effectively ended the Northampton awakening begun here."[7] Minkema suggests that certainly that suicide was a deterrent to the revival movement, although it might be presumptuous to define the closing "bookend" of the first segment of the Great Awakening so definitively. Edwards himself, in reflecting on the First Great Awakening in his "Faithful Narrative," describes a season of declension. He states in a May 1735 letter ". . .it began to be very sensible that the Spirit of God was gradually withdrawing" (Jonathan Edwards).[8]

Conclusion: According to this research, the actual dates of the First Chapter of the Great Awakening are from February of 1734, with an intensification coming in December of that year, through to June of 1735, a period of some 17 months. We chose to carefully explore the sermons before, during and immediately following these 17 months to ascertain significant clues correlating the relationship between revival and preaching. Thankfully, Edwards carefully documented and preserved his sermons, and most of them have been preserved for posterity.

We have been talking about two phases of the First Great Awakening, two significant chapters in that book written by God Himself. Are there any historical clues to identify the beginning and the end of the *second* chapter of the Great Awakening? We turned to the "Faithful Narrative" and adjoining correspondence to help determine the dates of the first chapter of the Great Awakening; that document was published in 1737. Thankfully, Edwards had a passion for documenting the history that he was privileged to live, and so wrote profusely in both letter and book and manuscript (sermon) form. One of the more helpful documents to assist us in defining the resurgence of the Great Awakening are "Some Thoughts Concerning the Revival" published in 1742 as well as several significant "documenting" letters analyzing the Great Awakening written during the 40's and into the 50's.

What brought about the revival of the revival or Great Awakening (Chapter Two of the Great Awakening) and when did it start? In a word, Whitefield. Whitefield was a Calvinist evangelist, (contrary to the opinion of many, not an oxymoron). He arrived in the New England states in the spring of 1740 and visited Northampton October 17–20 of that year. His ministry ignited the flickering flame of revival. That appears to mark the inception of Chapter 2 of the Great Awakening, at least so far as Northampton is concerned. It continued and grew due to the sympathetic preaching

---

7. Lesser, *Works*, 19: 38.
8. Goen, *Works*, 4: 207.

of Edwards and other invited speakers. [Samuel Buell visited Northampton in February of 1742 and was highly instrumental in kindling the flame of revival there].

When Whitefield preached, Edwards "wept during the whole of exercise" (Journal of Whitefield) and the congregation was "equally affected." During the afternoon, the power increased yet more. Edwards wrote (1743) that the congregation was extraordinarily melted by every sermon" with "almost the whole assembly being in tears" during the preaching. "Whitefield's affecting preaching had rekindled the fires of revival in the Massachusetts town, as the following months would show."[9]

Are there any indicators of the demise of the Great Awakening in Northampton? Edwards, in a letter to Prince at the end of 1743, makes reference to the "late season of revival of religion" and by the end of 1742 Edwards was writing about "in the general people's engagedness in religion and the liveliness of their affections have been on the decline: and some of the young people especially have shamefully lost their liveliness and vigor in religion, and much of the seriousness and solemnity of their spirits" (Jonathan Edwards).[10] Edwards makes reference to "the work continued more pure till we were infected from abroad." What he means by this inflection Edwards amplifies: "our people hearing, and some of them seeing the work in other places, where there was a greater visible commotion than here, and the outward appearances were more extraordinary; were ready to think that the work in those places far excelled what was amongst us; and their eyes were dazzled with the high profession and great show that some made who came hither from other places."[11]

---

9. Haykin, *Edwards*, 38.
10. Goen, *Works*, 4: 555.
11. Goen, *Works*, 4: 555.

Appendix 2

The Resolutions of Jonathan Edwards[1]

BEING SENSIBLE THAT I am unable to do anything without God's help, I do humbly entreat him by his grace to enable me to keep these Resolutions, so far as they are agreeable to his will, for Christ's sake.

Remember to read over these Resolutions once a week.

1. Resolved, that I will do whatsoever I think to be most to God's glory, and my own good, profit and pleasure, in the whole of my duration, without any consideration of the time, whether now, or never so many myriads of ages hence. Resolved to do whatever I think to be my duty and most for the good and advantage of mankind in general. Resolved to do this, whatever difficulties I meet with, how many soever, and how great soever.
2. Resolved, to be continually endeavoring to find out some new contrivance and invention to promote the aforementioned things.
3. Resolved, if ever I shall fall and grow dull, so as to neglect to keep any part of these Resolutions, to repent of all I can remember, when I come to myself again.

---

1. Edwards, *Resolutions*.

4. Resolved, never to do any manner of thing, whether in soul or body, less or more, but what tends to the glory of God; nor be, nor suffer it, if I can avoid it.

5. Resolved, never to lose one moment of time; but improve it the most profitable way I possibly can.

6. Resolved, to live with all my might, while I do live.

7. Resolved, never to do anything, which I should be afraid to do, if it were the last hour of my life.

8. Resolved, to act, in all respects, both speaking and doing, as if nobody had been so vile as I, and as if I had committed the same sins, or had the same infirmities or failings as others; and that I will let the knowledge of their failings promote nothing but shame in myself, and prove only an occasion of my confessing my own sins and misery to God. July 30.

9. Resolved, to think much on all occasions of my own dying, and of the common circumstances which attend death.

10. Resolved, when I feel pain, to think of the pains of martyrdom, and of hell.

11. Resolved, when I think of any theorem in divinity to be solved, immediately to do what I can towards solving it, if circumstances do not hinder.

12. Resolved, if I take delight in it as a gratification of pride, or vanity, or on any such account, immediately to throw it by.

13. Resolved, to be endeavoring to find out fit objects of charity and liberality.

14. Resolved, never to do anything out of revenge.

15. Resolved, never to suffer the least motions of anger towards irrational beings.

16. Resolved, never to speak evil of anyone, so that it shall tend to his dishonor, more or less, upon no account except for some real good.

17. Resolved, that I will live so, as I shall wish I had done when I come to die.

18. Resolved, to live so, at all times, as I think is best in my devout frames, and when I have clearest notions of things of the gospel, and another world.

19. Resolved, never to do anything, which I should be afraid to do, if I expected it would not be above an hour, before I should hear the last trump.

20. Resolved, to maintain the strictest temperance, in eating and drinking.

21. Resolved, never to do anything, which if I should see in another, I should count a just occasion to despise him for, or to think any way the more meanly of him.

(Resolutions 1 through 21 written in one sitting in New Haven in 1722)

22. Resolved, to endeavor to obtain for myself as much happiness, in the other world, as I possibly can, with all the power, might, vigor, and vehemence, yea violence, I am capable of, or can bring myself to exert, in any way that can be thought of.

23. Resolved, frequently to take some deliberate action, which seems most unlikely to be done, for the glory of God, and trace it back to the original intention, designs and ends of it; and if I find it not to be for God's glory, to repute it as a breach of the 4th Resolution.

24. Resolved, whenever I do any conspicuously evil action, to trace it back, till I come to the original cause; and then, both carefully endeavor to do so no more, and to fight and pray with all my might against the original of it.

25. Resolved, to examine carefully, and constantly, what that one thing in me is, which causes me in the least to doubt of the love of God; and to direct all my forces against it.

26. Resolved, to cast away such things, as I find do abate my assurance.

27. Resolved, never willfully to omit anything, except the omission be for the glory of God; and frequently to examine my omissions.

28. Resolved, to study the Scriptures so steadily, constantly and frequently, as that I may find, and plainly perceive myself to grow in the knowledge of the same.

29. Resolved, never to count that a prayer, nor to let that pass as a prayer, nor that as a petition of a prayer, which is so made, that I cannot hope that God will answer it; nor that as a confession, which I cannot hope God will accept.

30. Resolved, to strive to my utmost every week to be brought higher in religion, and to a higher exercise of grace, than I was the week before.

31. Resolved, never to say anything at all against anybody, but when it is perfectly agreeable to the highest degree of Christian honor, and of

love to mankind, agreeable to the lowest humility, and sense of my own faults and failings, and agreeable to the golden rule; often, when I have said anything against anyone, to bring it to, and try it strictly by the test of this Resolution.

32. Resolved, to be strictly and firmly faithful to my trust, that, in Prov. 20:6, "A faithful man who can find?" may not be partly fulfilled in me.

33. Resolved, to do always, what I can towards making, maintaining, and preserving peace, when it can be done without overbalancing detriment in other respects. Dec. 26, 1722.

34. Resolved, in narrations never to speak anything but the pure and simple verity.

35. Resolved, whenever I so much question whether I have done my duty, as that my quiet and calm is thereby disturbed, to set it down, and also how the question was resolved. Dec. 18, 1722.

36. Resolved, never to speak evil of any, except I have some particular good call for it. Dec. 19, 1722.

37. Resolved, to inquire every night, as I am going to bed, wherein I have been negligent,—what sin I have committed,-and wherein I have denied myself;-also at the end of every week, month, and year. Dec. 22 and 26, 1722.

38. Resolved, never to speak anything that is ridiculous, sportive, or matter of laughter on the Lord's Day. Sabbath evening, Dec. 23, 1722.

39. Resolved, never to do anything of which I so much question the lawfulness of, as that I intend, at the same time, to consider and examine afterwards, whether it be lawful or not; unless I as much question the lawfulness of the omission.

40. Resolved, to inquire every night, before I go to bed, whether I have acted in the best way I possibly could, with respect to eating and drinking. Jan. 7, 1723.

41. Resolved, to ask myself, at the end of every day, week, month and year, wherein I could possibly, in any respect, have done better. Jan. 11, 1723.

42. Resolved, frequently to renew the dedication of myself to God, which was made at my baptism; which I solemnly renewed, when I was received into the communion of the church; and which I have solemnly re-made this twelfth day of January, 1723.

43. Resolved, never, henceforward, till I die, to act as if I were any way my own, but entirely and altogether God's; agreeable to what is to be found in Saturday, January 12. Jan.12, 1723.

44. Resolved, that no other end but religion, shall have any influence at all on any of my actions; and that no action shall be, in the least circumstance, any otherwise than the religious end will carry it. Jan.12, 1723.

45. Resolved, never to allow any pleasure or grief, joy or sorrow, nor any affection at all, nor any degree of affection, nor any circumstance relating to it, but what helps religion. Jan. 12 and 13, 1723.

46. Resolved, never to allow the least measure of any fretting uneasiness at my father or mother. Resolved to suffer no effects of it, so much as in the least alteration of speech, or motion of my eye: and to be especially careful of it with respect to any of our family.

47. Resolved, to endeavor, to my utmost, to deny whatever is not most agreeable to a good, and universally sweet and benevolent, quiet, peaceable, contented and easy, compassionate and generous, humble and meek, submissive and obliging, diligent and industrious, charitable and even, patient, moderate, forgiving and sincere temper; and to do at all times, what such a temper would lead me to; and to examine strictly, at the end of every week, whether I have done so. Sabbath morning. May 5, 1723.

48. Resolved, constantly, with the utmost niceness and diligence, and the strictest scrutiny, to be looking into the state of my soul, that I may know whether I have truly an interest in Christ or not; that when I come to die, I may not have any negligence respecting this to repent of. May 26, 1723.

49. Resolved, that this never shall be, if I can help it.

50. Resolved, I will act so as I think I shall judge would have been best, and most prudent, when I come into the future world. July 5, 1723.

51. Resolved, that I will act so, in every respect, as I think I shall wish I had done, if I should at last be damned. July 8, 1723.

52. I frequently hear persons in old age, say how they would live, if they were to live their lives over again: Resolved, that I will live just so as I can think I shall wish I had done, supposing I live to old age. July 8, 1723.

53. Resolved, to improve every opportunity, when I am in the best and happiest frame of mind, to cast and venture my soul on the Lord Jesus

Christ, to trust and confide in him, and consecrate myself wholly to him; that from this I may have assurance of my safety, knowing that I confide in my Redeemer. July 8, 1723.

54. Whenever I hear anything spoken in conversation of any person, if I think it would be praiseworthy in me, Resolved to endeavor to imitate it. July 8, 1723.

55. Resolved, to endeavor to my utmost to act as I can think I should do, if, I had already seen the happiness of heaven, and hell torments. July 8, 1723.

56. Resolved, never to give over, nor in the least to slacken, my fight with my corruptions, however unsuccessful I may be.

57. Resolved, when I fear misfortunes and adversities, to examine whether I have done my duty, and resolve to do it, and let the event be just as providence orders it. I will as far as I can, be concerned about nothing but my duty, and my sin. June 9, and July 13 1723.

58. Resolved, not only to refrain from an air of dislike, fretfulness, and anger in conversation, but to exhibit an air of love, cheerfulness and benignity. May 27, and July 13, 1723.

59. Resolved, when I am most conscious of provocations to ill nature and anger, that I will strive most to feel and act good-naturedly; yea, at such times, to manifest good nature, though I think that in other respects it would be disadvantageous, and so as would be imprudent at other times. May 12, July 11, and July 13.

60. Resolved, whenever my feelings begin to appear in the least out of order, when I am conscious of the least uneasiness within, or the least irregularity without, I will then subject myself to the strictest examination. July 4, and 13, 1723.

61. Resolved, that I will not give way to that listlessness which I find unbends and relaxes my mind from being fully and fixedly set on religion, whatever excuse I may have for it-that what my listlessness inclines me to do, is best to be done, etc. May 21, and July 13, 1723.

62. Resolved, never to do anything but duty, and then according to Eph. 6:6–8, to do it willingly and cheerfully as unto the Lord, and not to man: "knowing that whatever good thing any man doth, the same shall he receive of the Lord." June 25 and July 13, 1723.

63. On the supposition, that there never was to be but one individual in the world, at any one time, who was properly a complete Christian, in

all respects of a right stamp, having Christianity always shining in its true luster, and appearing excellent and lovely, from whatever part and under whatever character viewed: Resolved, to act just as I would do, if I strove with all my might to be that one, who should live in my time. Jan. 14 and July 13, 1723.

64. Resolved, when I find those "groanings which cannot be uttered" (Rom. 8:26), of which the Apostle speaks, and those "breakings of soul for the longing it hath," of which the Psalmist speaks, Psalm 119:20, that I will promote them to the utmost of my power, and that I will not be weary of earnestly endeavoring to vent my desires, nor of the repetitions of such earnestness. July 23, and August 10, 1723.

65. Resolved, very much to exercise myself in this, all my life long, viz. with the greatest openness, of which I am capable of, to declare my ways to God, and lay open my soul to him: all my sins, temptations, difficulties, sorrows, fears, hopes, desires, and everything, and every circumstance; according to Dr. Manton's 27th Sermon on Psalm 119. July 26, and Aug. 10 1723.

66. Resolved, that I will endeavor always to keep a benign aspect, and air of acting and speaking in all places, and in all companies, except it should so happen that duty requires otherwise.

67. Resolved, after afflictions, to inquire, what I am the better for them, what good I have got by them, and what I might have got by them.

68. Resolved, to confess frankly to myself all that which I find in myself, either infirmity or sin; and, if it be what concerns religion, also to confess the whole case to God, and implore needed help. July 23, and August 10, 1723.

69. Resolved, always to do that, which I shall wish I had done when I see others do it. Aug. 11, 1723.

70. Let there be something of benevolence, in all that I speak. Aug. 17, 1723.

JONATHAN EDWARDS'S VOWS ARRANGED THEMATICALLY[2]

General Orientation

1. Resolved, that I will do whatsoever I think to be most to God's glory, and my own good, profit and pleasure, in the whole of my duration, without any consideration of the time, whether now, or never so many myriads of ages hence. Resolved to do whatever I think to be my duty and most for the good and advantage of mankind in general. Resolved to do this, whatever difficulties I meet with, how many and how great soever.

2. Resolved, to be continually endeavoring to find out some new invention and contrivance to promote the aforementioned things.

3. Resolved, if ever I shall fall and grow dull, so as to neglect to keep any part of these Resolutions, to repent of all I can remember, when I come to myself again.

4. Resolved, never to do any manner of thing, whether in soul or body, less or more, but what tends to the glory of God; nor be, nor suffer it, if I can avoid it.

6. Resolved, to live with all my might, while I do live.

22. Resolved, to endeavor to obtain for myself as much happiness, in the other world, as I possibly can, with all the power; might, vigor, and vehemence, yea violence, I am capable of, or can bring myself to exert, in any way that can be thought of.

62. Resolved, never to do anything but duty; and then according to *Eph.* 6:6–8, do it willingly and cheerfully as unto the Lord, and not to man; "knowing that whatever good thing any man doth, the same shall he receive of the Lord." *June 25* and *July 13, 1723*.

Good Works

11. Resolved, when I think of any theorem in divinity to be solved, immediately to do what I can towards solving it, if circumstances don't hinder.

13. Resolved, to be endeavoring to find out fit objects of charity and liberality.

2. Desiring God, *Resolutions*.

69. Resolved, always to do that, which I shall wish I had done when I see others do it. *Aug. 11, 1723.*

Time Management

5. Resolved, never to lose one moment of time; but improve it the most profitable way I possibly can.
7. Resolved, never to do anything, which I should be afraid to do, if it were the last hour of my life.
17. Resolved, that I will live so as I shall wish I had done when I come to die.
18. Resolved, to live so at all times, as I think is best in my devout frames, and when I have clearest notions of things of the gospel, and another world.
19. Resolved, never to do anything, which I should be afraid to do, if I expected it would not be above an hour, before I should hear the last trump.
37. Resolved, to inquire every night, as I am going to bed, wherein I have been negligent, what sin I have committed, and wherein I have denied myself: also at the end of every week, month and year. *Dec. 22 and 26, 1722.*
40. Resolved, to inquire every night, before I go to bed, whether I have acted in the best way I possibly could, with respect to eating and drinking. *Jan. 7, 1723.*
41. Resolved, to ask myself at the end of every day, week, month and year, wherein I could possibly in any respect have done better. *Jan. 11, 1723.*
50. Resolved, I will act so as I think I shall judge would have been best, and most prudent, when I come into the future world. *July 5, 1723.*
51. Resolved, that I will act so, in every respect, as I think I shall wish I had done, if I should at last be damned. *July 8, 1723.*
52. I frequently hear persons in old age say how they would live, if they were to live their lives over again: Resolved, that I will live just so as I can think I shall wish I had done, supposing I live to old age. *July 8, 1723.*
55. Resolved, to endeavor to my utmost to act as I can think I should do, if I had already seen the happiness of heaven, and hell torments. *July 8, 1723.*

61. Resolved, that I will not give way to that listlessness which I find unbends and relaxes my mind from being fully and fixedly set on religion, whatever excuse I may have for it-that what my listlessness inclines me to do, is best to be done, etc. *May 21,* and *July 13, 1723.*

Relationships

14. Resolved, never to do anything out of revenge.

15. Resolved, never to suffer the least motions of anger to irrational beings.

16. Resolved, never to speak evil of anyone, so that it shall tend to his dishonor, more or less, upon no account except for some real good.

31. Resolved, never to say anything at all against anybody, but when it is perfectly agreeable to the highest degree of Christian honor, and of love to mankind, agreeable to the lowest humility, and sense of my own faults and failings, and agreeable to the golden rule; often, when I have said anything against anyone, to bring it to, and try it strictly by the test of this Resolution.

33. Resolved, always to do what I can towards making, maintaining, establishing and preserving peace, when it can be without over-balancing detriment in other respects. *Dec. 26, 1722.*

34. Resolved, in narrations never to speak anything but the pure and simple verity.

36. Resolved, never to speak evil of any, except I have some particular good call for it. *Dec. 19, 1722.*

46. Resolved, never to allow the least measure of any fretting uneasiness at my father or mother. Resolved to suffer no effects of it, so much as in the least alteration of speech, or motion of my eye: and to be especially careful of it, with respect to any of our family.

58. Resolved, not only to refrain from an air of dislike, fretfulness, and anger in conversation, but to exhibit an air of love, cheerfulness and benignity. *May 27,* and *July 13, 1723.*

59. Resolved, when I am most conscious of provocations to ill nature and anger, that I will strive most to feel and act good-naturedly; yea, at such times, to manifest good nature, though I think that in other respects it would be disadvantageous, and so as would be imprudent at other times. *May 12, July 2,* and *July 13.*

66. Resolved, that I will endeavor always to keep a benign aspect, and air of acting and speaking in all places, and in all companies, except it should so happen that duty requires otherwise.

70. Let there be something of benevolence, in all that I speak.

Suffering

9. Resolved, to think much on all occasions of my own dying, and of the common circumstances which attend death.

10. Resolved, when I feel pain, to think of the pains of martyrdom, and of hell.

67. Resolved, after afflictions, to inquire, what I am the better for them, what good I have got by them, and what I might have got by them.

57. Resolved, when I fear misfortunes and adversities, to examine whether I have done my duty, and resolve to do it; and let it be just as providence orders it, I will as far as I can, be concerned about nothing but my duty and my sin. *June 9, and July 13, 1723.*

Character

8. Resolved, to act, in all respects, both speaking and doing, as if nobody had been so vile as I, and as if I had committed the same sins, or had the same infirmities or failings as others; and that I will let the knowledge of their failings promote nothing but shame in myself, and prove only an occasion of my confessing my own sins and misery to God.

12. Resolved, if I take delight in it as a gratification of pride, or vanity, or on any such account, immediately to throw it by.

21. Resolved, never to do anything, which if I should see in another, I should count a just occasion to despise him for, or to think any way the more meanly of him.

32. Resolved, to be strictly and firmly faithful to my trust, that that in Prov. 20:6, "A faithful man who can find?" may not be partly fulfilled in me.

47. Resolved, to endeavor to my utmost to deny whatever is not most agreeable to a good, and universally sweet and benevolent, quiet, peaceable, contented, easy, compassionate, generous, humble, meek, modest, submissive, obliging, diligent and industrious, charitable,

even, patient, moderate, forgiving, sincere temper; and to do at all times what such a temper would lead me to. Examine strictly every week, whether I have done so. *Sabbath morning. May 5, 1723.*

54. Whenever I hear anything spoken in conversation of any person, if I think it would be praiseworthy in me, Resolved to endeavor to imitate it. *July 8, 1723.*

63. On the supposition, that there never was to be but one individual in the world, at any one time, who was properly a complete Christian, in all respects of a right stamp, having Christianity always shining in its true luster, and appearing excellent and lovely, from whatever part and under whatever character viewed: Resolved, to act just as I would do, if I strove with all my might to be that one, who should live in my time. *Jan. 14 and July 3, 1723.*

27. Resolved, never willfully to omit anything, except the omission be for the glory of God; and frequently to examine my omissions.

39. Resolved, never to do anything that I so much question the lawfulness of, as that I intend, at the same time, to consider and examine afterwards, whether it be lawful or no; except I as much question the lawfulness of the omission.

20. Resolved, to maintain the strictest temperance in eating and drinking.

Spiritual Life

Assurance

25. Resolved, to examine carefully, and constantly, what that one thing in me is, which causes me in the least to doubt of the love of God; and to direct all my forces against it.

26. Resolved, to cast away such things, as I find do abate my assurance.

48. Resolved, constantly, with the utmost niceness and diligence, and the strictest scrutiny, to be looking into the state of my soul, that I may know whether I have truly an interest in Christ or no; that when I come to die, I may not have any negligence respecting this to repent of. *May 26, 1723.*

49. Resolved, that this never shall be, if I can help it.

The Scriptures

28. Resolved, to study the Scriptures so steadily, constantly and frequently, as that I may find, and plainly perceive myself to grow in the knowledge of the same.

Prayer

29. Resolved, never to count that a prayer, nor to let that pass as a prayer, nor that as a petition of a prayer, which is so made, that I cannot hope that God will answer it; nor that as a confession, which I cannot hope God will accept.

64. Resolved, when I find those "groanings which cannot be uttered" (Rom. 8:26), of which the Apostle speaks, and those "breakings of soul for the longing it hath," of which the Psalmist speaks, Psalm 119:20, that I will promote them to the utmost of my power, and that I will not be wear' [weary], of earnestly endeavoring to vent my desires, nor of the repetitions of such earnestness. *July 23, and August 10, 1723.*

The Lord's Day

38. Resolved, never to speak anything that is ridiculous, sportive, or matter of laughter on the Lord's day. *Sabbath evening, Dec. 23, 1722.*

Vivification of Righteousness

30. Resolved, to strive to my utmost every week to be brought higher in religion, and to a higher exercise of grace, than I was the week before.

42. Resolved, frequently to renew the dedication of myself to God, which was made at my baptism; which I solemnly renewed, when I was received into the communion of the church; and which I have solemnly re-made this twelfth day of January, 1722–23.

43. Resolved, never henceforward, till I die, to act as if I were any way my own, but entirely and altogether God's, agreeable to what is to be found in *Saturday, January 12, 1723.*

44. Resolved, that no other end but religion, shall have any influence at all on any of my actions; and that no action shall be, in the least circumstance, any otherwise than the religious end will carry it. *Jan.12, 1723.*

45. Resolved, never to allow any pleasure or grief, joy or sorrow, nor any affection at all, nor any degree of affection, nor any circumstance relating to it, but what helps religion. *Jan. 12–13, 1723.*

Mortification of Sin and Self Examination

23. Resolved, frequently to take some deliberate action, which seems most unlikely to be done, for the glory of God, and trace it back to the original intention, designs and ends of it; and if I find it not to be for God's glory, to repute it as a breach of the 4th Resolution.

24. Resolved, whenever I do any conspicuously evil action, to trace it back, till I come to the original cause; and then both carefully endeavor to do so no more, and to fight and pray with all my might against the original of it.

35. Resolved, whenever I so much question whether I have done my duty, as that my quiet and calm is thereby disturbed, to set it down, and also how the question was resolved. *Dec. 18, 1722.*

60. Resolved, whenever my feelings begin to appear in the least out of order, when I am conscious of the least uneasiness within, or the least irregularity without, I will then subject myself to the strictest examination. *July 4 and 13, 1723.*

68. Resolved, to confess frankly to myself all that which I find in myself, either infirmity or sin; and, if it be what concerns religion, also to confess the whole case to God, and implore needed help. *July 23 and August 10, 1723.*

56. Resolved, never to give over, nor in the least to slacken my fight with my corruptions, however unsuccessful I may be.

Communion with God

53. Resolved, to improve every opportunity, when I am in the best and happiest frame of mind, to cast and venture my soul on the Lord Jesus Christ, to trust and confide in him, and consecrate myself wholly to

him; that from this I may have assurance of my safety, knowing that I confide in my Redeemer. *July 8, 1723.*

65. Resolved, very much to exercise myself in this all my life long, viz. with the greatest openness I am capable of, to declare my ways to God, and lay open my soul to him: all my sins, temptations, difficulties, sorrows, fears, hopes, desires, and everything, and every circumstance; according to Dr. Manton's 27th Sermon on Psalm 119. *July 26* and *Aug. 10, 1723.*

Jonathan Edwards's First 10 Vows in Plain English[3]

1. Resolved, that I will do whatsoever I think to be most to God's glory, and my own good, profit and pleasure, in the whole of my duration, without any consideration of the time, whether now, or never so many myriad's of ages hence. Resolved to do whatever I think to be my duty and most for the good and advantage of mankind in general. Resolved to do this, whatever difficulties I meet with, how many and how great soever.

   Whatever I do, I will do to give the most glory to God, and also for my own good and pleasure, as long as I live, no matter how long it takes to master. I also will fulfill my calling to do good to all mankind as much as I am able, no matter how much difficulty I face.

2. Resolved, to be continually endeavoring to find out some new invention and contrivance to promote the aforementioned things.

   I will continually strive to come up with new ways to accomplish the things mentioned in #1

3. Resolved, if ever I shall fall and grow dull, so as to neglect to keep any part of these Resolutions, to repent of all I can remember, when I come to myself again.

   If I ever find myself becoming disinterested in keeping these resolutions, I vow to turn back as soon as I realize it, and do everything I can to remember and keep them.

4. Resolved, never to do any manner of thing, whether in soul or body, less or more, but what tends to the glory of God; nor be, nor suffer it, if I can avoid it.

   I vow to never do anything, in thought or deed, whether it be a big thing or a little thing, except to do that which brings honor and glory to God. I will also stay away from those things that do not honor God as

---

3. Quinlan, *Resolutions.*

much as I possibly can, and whenever possible, I will try to put a stop to activities that bring God dishonor.

5. Resolved, never to lose one moment of time; but improve it the most profitable way I possibly can.

    I realize the importance of the time I have been given by God. I vow to never lose one moment to worthless activities, but constantly think of ways to make the most of the time I have.

6. Resolved, to live with all my might, while I do live.

    I vow to live my life with all the passion I can muster up until my very last breath.

7. Resolved, never to do anything, which I should be afraid to do, if it were the last hour of my life.

    I vow to never do anything that I would be ashamed of if I knew that I was facing imminent judgment.

8. Resolved, to act, in all respects, both speaking and doing, as if nobody had been so vile as I, and as if I had committed the same sins, or had the same infirmities or failings as others; and that I will let the knowledge of their failings promote nothing but shame in myself, and prove only an occasion of my confessing my own sins and misery to God.

    I vow to live with the understanding that I am no better than the most wicked person to ever live. I vow to allow this attitude to remind me that I am constantly in need of confession and God's mercy.

9. Resolved, to think much on all occasions of my own dying, and of the common circumstances which attend death.

    I vow to always remind myself that this physical life is temporary, and that death could come at any moment . . . I will think about questions like this: "What will people think of me when I'm gone?" . . . "What will they write on my tombstone?"

10. Resolved, when I feel pain, to think of the pains of martyrdom, and of hell.

    I vow, that whenever I experience physical pain, I will remind myself of those who are suffering for the sake of Christ, and also to remind myself of the great mercies of God which saved me from the justice of eternal punishment in hell. I do this to increase my compassion for those who need Christ and motivate me to share the message of the gospel to those that do not believe.

Appendix 3

The Defects of Preachers Reproved

By Solomon Stoddard

Tracing the Influence of Stoddard in the Revival Preaching of Jonathan Edwards

ACCORDING TO STODDARD, THE cause of spiritual demise and lethargy in the country is due to poor preaching. ". . . [T]here is a great want of good preaching. Whence it comes to pass that among professors a spirit of piety runs exceedingly low" (Kistler: 127). Stoddard delineates what he considers to be the traits or characteristics of poor preaching in a message entitled "The Defects of Preachers Reproved." This is the predecessor to Edwards, the "pope" who influenced the spiritual environment and especially Northampton. Edwards was hired by him. Stoddard was Edwards's maternal grandfather. Edwards took over after Stoddard died in 1727. We would be greatly amiss if we neglected the spiritual influence of Stoddard upon Edwards. Although there are some elements in his theology and ecclesiology that Edwards jettisoned, we should not by that be deceived into thinking that Edwards was not significantly influenced by Stoddard.

One of the points that Stoddard makes is that it is possible to be a good preacher in what one does say, and yet be a bad preacher by neglecting other things that he ought to say. ". . .they were very faulty in preaching in other particulars" (Kistler: 123). It is fascinating to trace the sermon "Defects of Preachers Reproved" and trace the revivalistic preaching ministry of Edwards. This we have endeavored to do in the following reflection, comparing Stoddard's affirmation with Edwards's practice and affirmations. We have taken the characteristics of poor preaching, according to Stoddard, and considered them seriatim, in Edwards.

1. Stoddard and Edwards Compared: "If any are taught that frequently men are ignorant of the time of their conversion, that is not good preaching" (Stoddard). Stoddard believed that good preaching means reinforcing the idea of being cognizant of the time of one's conversion (Kistler: 126). To what degree did Edwards's call for a definitive type of conversion experience?

   As one reads the sermons of Edwards, especially the application section, one is struck with the appeal to a definite conversion. Here is an example taken from "Sinners in Zion." I have highlighted those words and phrases that emphasize a definitive conversion.

   > I would conclude with an earnest *Exhortation* to the sinners in Zion, *now* to fly from the devouring fire and everlasting burnings. You sinners that are here present, you are the very persons spoken of in the text; you are the sinners in Zion. How many are there of those people of God's wrath that sit here and there in the seats of this meeting house at this time. You have often been exhorted to fly from the wrath to come— this is the wrath to come. You hear today of the devouring fire and of everlasting burnings, and of that fearfulness that will seize and surprise such hereafter. And O! what reason have you of thankfulness that you only hear of it, that you don't feel it, that it has not already got hold of you! It is as it were following you, and coming nearer and nearer, every day. Those fierce flames are as it were already kindled, in that the wrath of God, yea, the fierceness and wrath of almighty God, burns against you. It is ready for you: the pit is prepared for you with fire and much wood, and the breath of the Lord, as a stream of brimstone, doth kindle it. Lot was with great urgency hastened out of Sodom, and commanded to make haste and fly for his life and escape to the mountain, lest he should be consumed in those flames that burnt up Sodom and Gomorrah. But that burning was but a flea bite to that devouring fire and those everlasting burnings that you are in danger of. Therefore, improve the recent opportunity. Now God is pleased again to be pouring out his Spirit upon us, and he is doing great things amongst [us]. God is indeed come again, the same great God that so wonderfully appeared amongst us some years ago, and that has since for our sins departed from us and left us so long in such a dull dead state, let sinners alone in their sins, so that there

has been scarce any signs to be seen of any such work as conversion. That same God is now come again. He is really come in like manner, and begins, as he did before, gloriously to manifest his mighty power and riches of his grace: he brings sinners out of darkness into marvelous light; he rescues poor captive souls out of the hands of Satan; he saves persons from that devouring fire; he plucks one and another as brands out of the burning; he is opening prison doors, and knocks off their chains, and brings out poor prisoners; he is now working salvation amongst us from this very destruction that you have now heard of. *Now, now is the time! Now is a blessed opportunity to escape those everlasting burnings!* Now God has again set open the same door, the same fountain, amongst [us], and gives one more happy opportunity for souls to escape. Now he has set open a wide door, and he stands in the doorway calling and begging with a loud voice to the sinners of Zion. "Come," says he, "to me! Come fly from the wrath to come! Here is a refuge for you! Fly hither for refuge! Lay hold on the hope set before you!" (Sermon: Sinners in Zion: pp. 280, 281).

Edwards's sermon "The Unreasonableness of Indetermination in Religion," (WJE 19: 93—105) is a very strong evangelistic appeal to conversion and provides yet another example of his strong conversion emphasis. He states, "Let me insist upon it that you now make a choice..." (p. 104).

2. Stoddard and Edwards Compared: "If any are taught that humiliation is not necessary before faith, that is not good preaching" (Stoddard). Stoddard affirms, "Men may be very moral and have no experience of a work of humiliation or being brought off from their own righteousness, or a work of faith; of the difference that is between saving and common illumination; of the working of the heart under temptation; of the way wherein godly men are wont to find relief." (Kistler: 126). As Stoddard expresses it, "... men must be brought off from their own righteousness before they are brought to Christ. Men who think they have anything to appease the wrath of God and ingratiate themselves will not accept the calls of the gospel in sincerity. While people have a foundation to build upon, they will not build upon Christ" (Kistler: 128). "Men must see their malady before they see their remedy" (Kistler: 129).

Commenting on revival preaching, Keevil observes, "The method of these preachers was to begin with the law. They would move from the condemnation it brought upon sin to the free offer of the gospel in the grace of God" (Keevil: 151, 152).

Commenting on John Wesley's style of preaching, Keevil states "HIs sermons consisted of strong appeals to conversion, beginning with the call to repent. He insisted he could not preach love and grace unless *he first preached law and wrath*. It became a paradigm for his sermons, especially those preached in the open fields. He was gripped by the conviction that like the ancient prophets of Israel he would be held accountable for the eternal destiny of those to whom he proclaimed the Word of God" (Keevil: 154) [Emphasis mine]. Undoubtedly the same could be said of Edwards, with the possible exception of the reference to preaching in the open fields. Edwards seemed to be too aristocratic for that!

Edwards was strong on creating a sense of repentance and humiliation. Even a cursory review of his sermons shows his emphasis on law preceding grace. Perhaps the best illustration is his classic sermon "Sinners in the Hands of an Angry God" where strong emphasis is made on the wrath of God for sin, inducing the hearer to repentance and then fleeing from the wrath to come. This same emphasis comes through in his treatment of justification by faith alone. For instance, his main thesis is that "we are justified only by faith in Christ, and not by any manner of virtue or goodness of our own" (Jonathan Edwards) (WJE 19: 149).

3. Stoddard and Edwards Compared: Another significant element in the preaching of Stoddard that highly influenced the preaching of Edwards was his strong emphasis on hell-fire preaching. "When men don't preach much about the danger of damnation, there is a want of good preaching" (Kistler: 129). Stoddard affirmed that "Christ knew how to deal with souls, and Paul followed His example. Men need to be terrified and have the arrows of the Almighty in them that they may be converted. Ministers should be sons of thunder. Men need to have storms in their hearts before they will betake themselves to Christ for refuge" (Kistler: 130).

Edwards was a hell-fire preacher. He inherited this emphasis from Stoddard and the Puritan tradition. This is such a significant element of Edwards's preaching that we have dedicated an entire chapter to this theme. Suffice it here to say that Edwards affirmed the following:

> If there be really a hell of such dreadful, and never-ending torments, as is generally supposed, that multitudes are in great danger of, and that the bigger part of men in Christian countries

> do actually from generation to generation fall into, for want of a sense of the terribleness of it, and their danger of it, and so for want of taking due care to avoid it; then *why is it not proper for those that have the care of souls, to take great pains to make men sensible of it?* [Emphasis mine]. Why should not they be told as much of the truth as can be? If I am in danger of going to hell, I should be glad to know as much as possibly I can of the dreadfulness of it: if I am very prone to neglect due care to avoid it, he does me the best kindness, that does most to represent to me the truth of the case, that *sets forth my misery and danger in the liveliest manner* [emphasis mine] (Jonathan Edwards) (WJE 4: 246, 247).

4. Stoddard and Edwards Compared: Stoddard also affirmed "If they [preachers] give a wrong account of the nature of justifying faith that is not good preaching" (Kistler: 131). Stoddard decries the insufficiency of a belief system that is not built upon justification by faith alone. Many believe in Jesus, but He does not believe in them (John 2:23–24). So, Stoddard warns of the dangers of reliance upon self-righteousness, and calls for a complete trust only upon the all-sufficient righteousness of Christ.

We know that Edwards gives this particular theme a major treatment first in sermon and then in print, and in his faithful narrative he attributes this emphasis as a major catalyst to the revival.

> Edwards wrote: About this time, began the great noise that was in this part of the country about Arminianism, which seemed to appear with a very threatening aspect upon the interest of religion here. The friends of vital piety trembled for fear of the issue; but it seemed, contrary to their fear, strongly to be overruled for the promoting of religion. Many who looked on themselves as in a Christless condition, seemed to be awakened by it, with fear that God was about to withdraw from the land, and that we should be given up to heterodoxy and corrupt principles; and that then their opportunity for obtaining salvation would be past; and many who were brought a little to doubt about the truth of the doctrines they had hitherto been taught, seemed to have a kind of a trembling fear with their doubts, lest they should be led into bypaths, to their eternal undoing: and they seemed with much concern and engagedness of mind, to inquire what was indeed the way in which they must come to be accepted with God. There were then some things said publicly on that occasion concerning justification by faith

alone. Although great fault was found with meddling with the controversy in the pulpit, by such a person and at that time, and though it was ridiculed by many elsewhere, yet *it proved a word spoken in season here*; [emphasis mine] and was most evidently attended with a very remarkable blessing of heaven to the souls of the people in this town. They received thence a general satisfaction with respect to the main thing in question, which they had been in trembling doubts and concern about; and their minds were engaged the more earnestly to seek that they might come to be accepted of God, and saved in the way of the Gospel, which had been made evident to them to be the true and only way. And then it was, in the latter part of December, that the Spirit of God began extraordinarily to set in, and wonderfully to work amongst us; and there were, very suddenly, one after another, five or six persons who were to all appearance savingly converted, and some of them wrought upon in a very remarkable manner (Jonathan Edwards) (Faithful Narrative: 148, 149).

5. Stoddard and Edwards Compared: "If any give false signs of godliness, that is not good preaching" (Stoddard). What Stoddard meant by this is that sometimes preachers set up false criteria for evaluating whether or not a person has genuinely experienced authentic conversion. For example, "zeal against sin" is something that both the unregenerate and the regenerate experience, and therefore is a false criterion for differentiating the sheep from the goats, the regenerate from the unregenerate. Preachers that give false signs are guilty of providing false assurance and are actually guilty of deluding people into a false hope.

Now we know that Edwards took this seriously and invested significant intellectual and emotional energy to debunk "false signs" or what he called "no signs." He did this first in his treatise on Distinguishing Marks (Kistler: 1741) where he described nine "false signs" (Stoddard) or "no signs" (Edwards) or false criteria for ascertaining the authenticity of spiritual experience. Later, in 1746, this work evolved into a major treatment on the Religious Affections, where he expounded "Shewing what are no Certain Signs that Religious Affections are Truly Gracious, or that They are not" (Jonathan Edwards) (WJE 2: 125) by elaborating twelve, and not just nine, false criteria for determining whether or not people are genuinely saved. Then Edwards proceeds to provide "true signs" of godliness. In "Distinguishing Marks" he elaborates 5 "yes signs" of authentic conversion, but he seems a little more reticent in his "Religious Affections" and elaborates 12 points "Shewing What are Distinguishing Signs of Truly gracious and Holy Affections" (WJE 2: 191). He takes 270 pages of very intricately woven arguments to prove his point. What we need to remember as we return to our focus on Edwards's Revival Preaching is that both "Distinguishing Marks" and "Religious Affections" were treatises that flowed out of sermons. Furthermore, we can trace this emphasis on "true signs" of godliness as an overarching theme of Edwards.

6. Stoddard and Edwards Compared: "If any teach men to build their faith about the divine authority of the Scripture upon probable signs, that is not good preaching." What did Stoddard mean by this? Stoddard, following Calvin, was convinced that we need to differentiate between "probable signs" that suggest and substantiate faith in God's Word, but "these things cannot be the foundation of our faith" (Kistler: 133). Stoddard allowed for the role of probable proofs but believed that conviction and certainty was a matter of Spirit-inspired faith. Stoddard, like Calvin, spoke of "self-evidencing light" (Kistler: 134). Furthermore, many of the truths revealed in Scripture are not self-evident but rely primarily upon Divine revelation in order for them to be perceived and understood by man. Good preaching does not endeavor to establish the probability of the Divine nature of Scriptures, but rather appeals to the certainty of self-authenticating revelation.

Edwards, so far as I can ascertain, never did attempt to establish the probability of the Divine origin of Scripture. Rather, he assumed their Divine authority and origin, and spoke within that framework. He would always preach from a text, expound the text, elaborate the doctrine, and then apply the teaching. In that sense, Edwards was, by Stoddard's standards, a good preacher.

7. Stoddard and Edwards Compared: "If men preach for such liberties as God does not allow, that is not good preaching." In other words, Stoddard called upon preachers to not condone licentiousness. People need to be warned of wrong behaviour. Failure to reprove sinful actions makes the preachers indictable (Jeremiah 23:22). Stoddard believed that these sins undermined the process of preparation for conversion ". . .as long as they tolerate themselves in immoralities that will be a mighty bar in the way of their conversion" (Kistler: 135).

Edwards did confront specific sins, as Stoddard recommends. He confronted some of the issues in the youth and adults of Northampton. For example, Edwards himself documents in his Faithful Narrative how issues like licentiousness, nightwalking, attending the tavern, lewd practices, mirth and jollity of both sexes, frolics, indecency in behaviour during public meetings, and a contentiousness in public affairs (Jonathan Edwards) (WJE, #4, 146). Edwards addressed and confronted some of these "liberties as God does not allow" instead of practicing a style of preaching that condoned these kinds of freedoms, and as a result, revival came.

8. Stoddard and Edwards Compared: "If men preach for such ceremonies in worship as God does not allow, that is not good preaching." By this Stoddard refers to certain liberties taken by certain preachers to endorse certain customs and ceremonies and inventions in worship that do not meet with Divine approval.

Edwards did not, to my knowledge, encourage the practice of certain ceremonies in worship that God did not allow. However, Edwards did argue strenuously for a certain latitude in allowance for those practices that were neither condemned not encouraged by Scripture. Edwards demonstrated a considerable generous latitude when it came to allowing for certain practices and procedures which accompanied the revival. Certain critics of the revival condemned the revival because of certain elements within the service which the Bible is neutral on. He called these elements "no signs."

Stoddard lamented the demise of effective and unproductive preaching because "by men's unsanctified lives and their unsavory discourses" (Kistler: 138). There can be little doubt about the sanctified nature of Edwards's spiritual life. While no man is perfect, Edwards demonstrated by his life a quality of spirituality that was pleasing to both God and men. Whitefield recorded in his journal, upon his first visit to Northampton on the 17th of October 1740, "Mr. Edwards is a solid, excellent Christian. . .I think I have not seen his fellow [equal] in all New England" (Personal Journal of Whitefield). Two days later Whitefield made another entry: "Felt great satisfaction in being at the house of Mr. Edwards. A sweeter couple I have not seen. Their children were not dressed in silks and satins, but plain, as become the children of those who, in all things, ought to be examples of Christian simplicity. Mrs. Edwards is adorned with a meek and quiet spirit; she talked solidly of the things of God, and seemed to be such a helpmeet for her husband. . ." (Personal Journal of Whitefield). Others who knew him personally, including his biographer Samuel Hopkins, gave abundant witness to the sanctity of his life.

WHERE EDWARDS DIVERGED FROM STODDARD

While we have taken considerable pains to demonstrate that Edwards was cognizant of Stoddard's counsel regarding preaching, and steered clear of those characteristics of preaching which Stoddard considered defects, nevertheless, there were several points on which Stoddard and Edwards diverged.

For example, Stoddard considered manuscript preaching as a definite defect, and the reading of sermons as "a dull way of preaching" (Kistler: 137). There is strong evidence to believe that to the end of his days, Edwards was a manuscript preacher. Although he reduced the text of his sermon to more of an outline, Edwards consistently carried into the pulpit a manuscript.

SUMMARY AND CONCLUSION

We have endeavored to trace the influence of Stoddard's treatise on the Defects of Preachers Reproved on the life and ministry of Edwards. It is remarkable the influence that Stoddard had on Edwards, and since our focus is on the revival preaching of Edwards, and since Stoddard himself was instrumental in seeing five remarkable "harvests" during his 60-year pastorate in Northampton (1679, 1683, 1696, 1712 and 1718), and since Stoddard was the Senior Pastor of the church which Edwards took over, there is a remarkable spiritual legacy that Edwards received from him. Undoubtedly the defects reproved by Stoddard proved to be a remarkable warning to Edwards and contributed significantly to his spiritual and ministerial success. Stoddard's recommendations provide a powerful template from which to interpret the revivalistic preaching ministry of Edwards, and so we include this here for the reader's consideration.

Comparing Stoddard's Indictment of Poor Preaching with Edwards's Practice (8 Points Considered)

" . . . That is Not Good Preaching" (Stoddard) Stoddard laments the demise of good preaching and characterizes poor preaching	Now That is Good Preaching (Edwards) Evidence that Edwards took Stoddard to heart in his preaching style, content, and focus.
1. If any are taught that frequently men are ignorant of the time of their conversion, which is not good preaching	Edwards gave considerable emphasis to a call for conversion, he believed in a moment of conversion

2. If any are taught that humiliation is not necessary before faith that is not good preaching.	Edwards was careful to call people to repentance before the exercise of faith. This Puritan emphasis permeates the preaching of Edwards. He calls men to repent and evangelical humiliation before He provides the "antidote." Indeed, some would say that often the antidote is missing (see Wesley's comments on "Sinners.").
3. When men do not preach much about the danger of damnation there is a want of good preaching.	We have already documented the references to "hell" in the messages prior to and during the Great Awakening (See chapter on "hell-fire preaching). Edwards did not preach only about hell, but it was certainly a significant aspect in his preaching repertoire.
4. If they give a wrong account of the nature of justifying faith, which is not good preaching.	Edwards preached carefully on the fundamental importance of justification by faith, indeed this was the essence of his Master's thesis. . . and he attributes the revival to this point.
5. If any give false signs of godliness, which is not good preaching."	Edwards wrote extensively on "false signs" and "distinguishing marks," and his opus on "Religious Affections" could be interpreted as a simple unfolding of the "false signs of godliness" that Stoddard alludes to.
6. "If any teach men to build their faith about the divine authority of the Scripture upon probable signs, which is not good preaching."	This may be one of the points that Stoddard makes that does not find much parallel or symmetry in the sermons or writings or Edwards, or that conclusion may betray my ignorance of Edwards. Certainly, he believed what Stoddard affirms, classic Calvinism, but I have not been able to trace this emphasis in his preaching.
7. "If men preach for such liberties as God does not allow, that is not good preaching."	Edwards did encourage liberties not endorsed by God, as long as they were not explicitly discouraged by God.
8. "If men preach for such ceremonies in worship as God does not allow, that is not good preaching."	Edwards did allow for those elements within traditional ceremony as long as God did not prohibit them. He demonstrated considerable latitude in his views in this regard.

Appendix 4

What Was the Great Awakening Like?

EYEWITNESS ACCOUNT OF THE SERMON

"Sinners in the Hands of an Angry God"

"We went over to Enfield—where we met dear Mr. Edwards of Northampton who preached a most awakening sermon from these words—Deut. 32:35 and before [the] sermon was done—there was a great moaning and crying out through ye [the] whole House—What shall I do to be saved?—Oh, I am going to Hell—Oh what shall I do for Christ... So the minister was obliged to desist—the shrieks and cries were piercing and amazing... after some time of waiting for the congregation were still so then a prayer was made by Mr. W. and after that we descended from the pulpit and discoursed with the people—some in one place and some in another—and amazing and astonishing the power of God was seen—and several souls were hopefully wrought upon that night and oh the cheerfulness and pleasantness of their countenances that received comfort—oh that God would strengthen and confirm—we sung an hymn and prayed and dismissed the assembly"[1] (Eye Witness account recorded by Winslow).

1. Winslow, *Jonathan Edwards*, 192.

To read the entire sermon, which we highly recommend, go to http://www.ccel.org/ccel/edwards/sermons.sinners.html.

Appendix 5

The Place of Personal Application

Another powerful illustration of the personal pronoun is found in Edwards's sermon
"The Justice of God in the Damnation of Sinners"[1]
(May 1735) (Romans 3:19).

EXCERPT FROM THE APPLICATION from "The Justice of God in the Damnation of Sinners," preached in May of 1735, at the height of the revival. Notice the 169 pointed references to "you" and "your" in this application. Edwards pulled no punches in making a personal and pointed application:

> How many sorts of wickedness have *you* been guilty of? How manifold have been the abominations of *your* life? What profaneness and contempt of God has been exercised by *you*? How little regard have *you* had to the Scriptures, to the Word preached, to sabbaths, and sacraments? How profanely have *you* talked, many of *you*, about those things that are holy? After what manner have many of *you* kept God's holy day, not regarding the holiness of the time, nor caring what *you* thought of in it. Yea, *you* have not only spent the time in worldly, vain, and unprofitable thoughts, but in immoral thoughts; pleasing *yourself* with

---

1 16. Edwards, *Sermon: Justice*.

the reflection on past acts of wickedness, and in contriving new acts. Have not you spent much holy time, in gratifying *your* lusts in *your* imaginations; yea, not only holy time, but the very time of God's public worship, when you have appeared in God's more immediate presence? How have *you* not only not attended to the worship, but have in the meantime been feasting *your* lusts, and wallowing *yourself* in abominable uncleanness! How many sabbaths have *you* spent, one after another, in a most wretched manner! Some of *you* not only in worldly and wicked thoughts, but also a very wicked outward behavior! When *you* on sabbath days, have got along with *your* wicked companions, how has holy time been treated among *you*! What kind of conversation has there been! Yea, how have some of *you*, by a very indecent carriage, openly dishonored and cast contempt on the sacred services of God's house, and holy day! And what *you* have done some of *you* alone, what wicked practices there have been in secret, even in holy time, God and *your* own consciences know.

And how have *you* behaved *yourself* in the time of family prayer! And what a trade have many of *you* made of absenting *yourselves* from the worship of the families <u>you</u> belong to, for the sake of vain company! And how have *you* continued in the neglect of secret prayer! therein willfully living in a known sin, going abreast against as plain a command as any in the Bible! Have *you* not been one that has cast off fear, and restrained prayer before God?

What wicked carriage have some of *you* been guilty of towards *your* parents! How far have *you* been from paying that honor to them, that God has required! Have *you* not even harbored ill will, and malice towards them? And when they have displeased *you*, have wished evil to them? Yea, and shown *your* vile spirit in *your* behavior? And 'tis well if *you* have not mocked them behind their backs; and like the accursed Ham and Canaan derided *your* parents' nakedness instead of covering it, and hiding *your* eyes from it. Have not some of *you* often disobeyed *your* parents, yea, and refused to be subject to them? Is it not a wonder of mercy and forbearance that that has not before now been accomplished on you, in Proverbs 30:17, "The eye that mocketh at his father, and refuseth to obey his mother, the ravens of the valley shall pick it out, and the young eagles shall eat it"?

What revenge and malice have *you* been guilty of towards *your* neighbors? How have <u>you</u> indulged this spirit of the devil, hating others, and wishing evil to them, rejoicing when evil befell them, and grieving at others' prosperity, and lived in such a way for a long time! Have not some of *you* allowed a passionate furious spirit, and behaved *yourselves* in *your* anger more like wild beasts, than like Christians?

What covetousness has been in many of *you*? Such has been *your* inordinate love of the world, and care about the things of it, that it has taken up *your* heart; *you* have allowed no room for God and religion; *you* have minded the world more than *your* eternal salvation. For the vanities of the world, *you* have neglected reading, praying, and meditation: for the things of the world, *you* have broken the sabbath: for the world *you* have spent a great deal of *your* time in quarrelling: for the world *you* have envied, and hated *your* neighbor: for the world *you* have cast God, and Christ, and heaven behind your back: for the world *you* have sold *your* own soul: *you* have as it were drowned your soul in worldly cares and desires: *you* have been a mere earthworm, that is never in its element but when grovelling and buried in the earth.

How much of a spirit of pride has appeared in *you*! which is in a peculiar manner the spirit and condemnation of the devil. How have some of *you* vaunted *yourselves* in *your* apparel! Others in their riches! Others in their knowledge and abilities! How has it galled *you* to see others above *you*! How much has it gone against the grain, for *you* to give others their due honor! And how have *you* shown *your* pride by setting up *your* wills, and in opposing others, and stirring up and promoting division, and a party spirit in public affairs!

How sensual have *you* been! Are there not some here, that have debased themselves below the dignity of human nature, by wallowing in sensual filthiness, as swine in the mire, or as filthy vermin feeding with delight on rotten carrion? What intemperance have some of *you* been guilty of! How much of *your* precious time have *you* spent away at the tavern, and in drinking companies, when *you* ought to have been at home seeking God, and *your* salvation in *your* families and closets!

And what abominable lasciviousness have some of *you* been guilty of! How have *you* indulged *yourself*, from day to day, and from night to night, in all manner of unclean imaginations! Has not *your* soul been filled with them, till it has become an hold of foul spirits, and a cage of every unclean and hateful bird? What foul-mouthed persons have some of *you* been, often in lewd and lascivious talk, and unclean songs, wherein were things not fit to be spoken! And such company, where such conversation has been carried on has been *your* delight. And what unclean acts and practices have *you* defiled *yourself* with!

God and *your* own consciences know what abominable lasciviousness *you* have practiced in things not fit to be named, when *you* have been alone; when *you* ought to have been reading, or meditating, or on *your* knees before God in secret prayer. And how have *you* corrupted others, as well as polluted *yourselves*! What vile uncleanness have *you* practiced in company! What abominations have *you* been guilty of in the dark! Such as the Apostle doubtless had respect to, in Ephesians 5:12, "For 'tis a shame even to speak of those things, that are done of them in secret." Some of *you* have corrupted others, and done what in *you* lay to undo their souls (if *you* have not actually done it), and by *your* vile practices and examples, have made room for Satan, and invited his presence, and established his interest, in the town where *you* have lived.

What lying have some of *you* been guilty of, especially in *your* childhood! And have not *your* heart and lips often disagreed, since *you* came to riper years? What fraud, and deceit, and unfaithfulness, have many of *you* practiced in *your* dealings with *your* neighbors that *your* own heart is conscious to, if *you* have not been noted for it by others.

And how have some of *you* behaved *yourselves* in *your* family relations! How have *you* neglected *your* children's souls! And not only so, but have corrupted their minds by *your* bad examples; and instead of training them up in the nurture and admonition of the Lord, have rather brought them up in the devil's service!

How have some of *you* attended that sacred ordinance of the Lord's Supper, without any manner of serious preparation, and in a careless slighty frame of spirit, and chiefly to comply with custom! Have *you* not ventured to put the sacred symbols of the body and blood of Christ into *your* mouth, while at the same time *you* lived in ways of known sins and intended no other than still to go on in the same wicked practices? And it may be have sat at the Lord's table, with rancor in *your* heart against some of *your* brethren, that *you* have sat there with. *You* have come even to that holy feast of love among God's children, with the leaven of malice and envy in *your* heart; and so have eat and drank judgment to *yourself*.

What stupidity and sottishness has attended *your* course of wickedness! which has appeared in *your* obstinacy under awakening dispensations of God's word and providence. And how have some of *you* backslidden, after *you* have set out in religion, and quenched God's Spirit after he had been striving with *you*! And what unsteadiness, and slothfulness, and great misimprovement of God's strivings with *you*, have *you* been chargeable with, that having long been subjects of them!

Now, can *you* think when *you* have thus behaved *yourself*, that God is obliged to show *you* mercy? Are *you* not, after all this, ashamed to talk of its being hard with God to cast *you* off? Does it become one that has lived such a life, to open his mouth to excuse himself, or object against God's justice in his condemnation, or to complain of it as hard in God not to give him converting and pardoning grace, and make him his child, and bestow on him eternal life! Or to talk of his duties and great pains in religion, and such like things, as if such performances were worthy to be accepted, and to draw God's heart to such a creature! If this has been *your* manner, does it not show how little *you* have considered *yourself*, and how little a sense *you* have had of *your* own sinfulness?

Second. Be directed to consider, if God should eternally reject and destroy *you*, what an agreeableness, and exact mutual answerableness, there would be between God's so dealing with *you*, and *your* spirit and behavior. There would not only be an equality but a similitude. God declares that his dealings with men, shall be suitable to their disposition and practice. Psalms 18:25–26, "With the merciful man, thou wilt show thyself merciful: with an upright man, thou wilt show thyself upright: with the pure, thou wilt show thyself pure: and with the froward, thou wilt show thyself froward." How much soever *you* dread damnation, and are affrighted and concerned at the thoughts of it; yet if God should indeed eternally damn *you*, *you* would but be met with in *your* own way: *you* would be dealt with exactly according to *your* own dealing; God would but measure to *you*, in the same measure in which *you* mete. Surely 'tis but fair that *you* should be made to buy in the same measure in which *you* sell.

A FINAL WORD FROM THE AUTHOR

Thank you for reading and reflecting on this work of "Revival Preaching." I sincerely hope that your preaching and God's people will be enriched as a result of reading and acting upon aspects of this material. Thank you to WIPF and STOCK for investing in the publication of this work. If you would like to communicate with me regarding any aspect of this book, I would welcome your email. You can reach me at Ernie Klassen (revernieklassen@gmail.com). This book has been translated and published in Spanish by CLIE. https://www.clie.es/la-predicacion-que-aviva-lecciones-de-jonathan-edwards

For Further Reading

THERE ARE MANY EXCELLENT *biographies and studies on the life and times of Jonathan Edwards. Here are some of the author's recommendations.*

Allen, Alexander V. G. *Jonathan Edwards.* Eugene, OR: Wipf & Stock, 2007.
Dodds, Elizabeth D. *Marriage to a difficult man: the "uncommon union" of Jonathan and Sarah Edwards.* Philadelphia: Westminster, 1971.
Dwight, S. E. *The Life of President Edwards.* New York: G. & C. & H. Carvill, 1830.
Gerstner, Edna. *Jonathan and Sarah-an uncommon union: a novel based on the family of Jonathan and Sarah Edwards (the Stockbridge years, 1750-1758).* Morgan, PA: Soli DeoGloria, 1995.
Gerstner, John. *A Theology of Jonathan Edwards.* (Video). Ligonier Ministries.
Gura, Philip F. *Jonathan Edwards: America's Evangelical.* New York: Hill and Wang, 2005.
Hopkins, Samuel. *Life of the Rev. Jonathan Edwards, President of Princeton College, New Jersey.* London: Religious Tract Society, 1834.
Marsden, George M. *Jonathan Edwards, A Life.* New Haven: Yale University Press, 2003.
McDermott, Gerald R. *Understanding Jonathan Edwards: An Introduction to America's Theologian.* Oxford: New York: Oxford University Press, 2009.
Miller, Perry. *Jonathan Edwards.* New York: W. Sloane Associates, 1949.
Murray, Iain H. *Jonathan Edwards, a New Biography.* Banner of Truth Trust: 1987.
Parkes, Henry Bamford. *Jonathan Edwards, the Fiery Puritan.* New York: AMS, 1979, 1930.
Simonson, Harold Peter. *Jonathan Edwards: Theologian of the Heart.* Grand Rapids: W.B. Eerdmans, 1974.
Smith, John E. *Jonathan Edwards: Puritan, Preacher, Philosopher.* Notre Dame:University of Notre Dame Press, 1992.
Winslow, Ola Elizabeth. *Jonathan Edwards, 1703-1758.* New York, N.Y.: Collier, 1961.

Bibliography

REVIVAL PREACHING—TWELVE LESSONS FROM JONATHAN EDWARDS

Akin, Daniel. *Debate,* http://www.bpnews.net/bpnews.asp?ID=22970
———. *Purpose-Driven Preaching,* https://www.danielakin.com/
Alliance Canada, *Statement of Faith,* https://www.cmacanorg/beliefs/.
American Heritage Dictionary, 4th ed. Houghton Mifflin, 2000.
American Heritage Dictionary, 5th ed. https://www.wordnik.com/words/improvement,
Autrey, C. E. *Revivals of the Old Testament.* Grand Rapids: Zondervan, 1960.
Bailey, Richard A. & Gregory A. Wills. *The Salvation of Souls.* Wheaton: Crossway Books, 2002.
———. *Driven by Passion: Jonathan Edwards and the Art of Preaching.* Hart, et. al. "Legacy" Grand Rapids, Baker: 6478.
Ballard, Larry. *Multigenerational Legacies: The Story of Jonathan Edwards.* https://www.ywam-fmi.org/news/multigenerational-legacies-the-story-of-jonathan-edwards/.
Banister, Doug. *The Word and Power Church.* Grand Rapids: Zondervan, 1999.
Baxter, Sidlow. *The Reformed Pastor.* https://ccel.org/ccel/baxter/pastor/pastor.iii.ii.html
Beach, J. Mark. *The real presence of Christ in the preaching of the gospel: Luther and Calvin on the Nature of Preaching.* Mid-America Journal of Theology 10 (1999) 77–134.
Beeke, Joel et. al. *Meet the Puritans.* Grand Rapids, Mi.: Reformation Books, 2006.
Bounds, E. M. *The Preacher and Prayer.* Chicago: Bible Institute Colportage, 1907.
Boyer, Orlando. *Biografías de Grandes Cristianos.* 43–49, (Jonatán Edwards, El Gran Avi-vador). Miami: Editorial Vida, 2001.
Brook, Frances. *My Goal is God Himself.* https://library.timelesstruths.org/music/My_Goal_Is_God_Himself/.
Brown, Robert E. *Jonathan Edwards and the Bible.* Bloomington: Indiana University Press, 2002.
Bryne, Mary. *Be Thou My Vision.* https://hymnary.org/text/be_thou_my_vision_o_lord_of_my_heart.

Burns, James. *Revivals, Their Law and Leaders*. Grand Rapids: Baker, 1960.
Bushman, Richard L. *The Great Awakening—Documents of the Revival of Religion, 1740–1745*.
Chapel Hill: University of North Carolina Press, 1969.
Cairns, Earle E. *An Endless Line of Splendor—Revival and Their Leaders from the Great Awakening to the Present*. Wheaton: Tyndale House, 1986.
Carrick, John. *The Imperative of Preaching—A Theology of Sacred Rhetoric*. Edinburgh: The Banner of Truth Trust, 2002.
Calvin, John. *Calvin's Commentaries: I Corinthians*. https://www.ccel.org/ccel/calvin/commentaries.i.html
———. *Calvin's Commentaries: Galatians and Ephesians*. Grand Rapids: Eerdmans, 1955.
———. *Calvin's Commentaries: Isaiah*. https://www.bibliaplus.org/en/commentaries/3/john-calvins-bible-commentary/isaiah/55/11
Carrick, John. *The Preaching of Jonathan Edwards*. Edinburgh: The Banner of Truth Trust, 2008.
Cauchi, Tony. *Let's put fasting back on the menu!* http://www.thegloryofgodoncapecod.com/articles/_bloq_news_articles/let-us-put-fasting-back-on-the-menu/420?news_article=true
Chamberlain, Ava, ed. *The Miscellanies*. Works of Jonathan Edwards 18. New Haven: Yale University Press, 2000.
Chan, Francis and Preston Sprinkle, *Erasing Hell*, Colorado Springs: David Cook, 2011.
Christianpost. *Powerful Message*. http://gnli.christianpost.com/video/christians-preaching-a-powerfull-message-14780
Claghorn, George S. *Letters and Personal Writings*. Works of Jonathan Edwards 16. New Haven: Yale University Press, 1999.
Cole, Steven. *John Calvin: The Man and His Preaching*. https://bible.org/seriespage/2-john-calvin-man-and-his-preaching.
Compelling Truth, *Perichoresis*, https://www.compellingtruth.org/perichoresis.html
Conrad, Leslie, Jr. "The Importance of Preaching in the Great Awakening." *The Lutheran Quar-terly*, XII: 2, May 1960.
———. "Jonathan Edwards' Pattern of Preaching" Church Management 33 (September) 45–47.
DeArteaga, William L. *Quenching the Spirit: Discover the Real Spirit behind the Charismatic Controversy*. Lake Mary: Strang, 1996.
Desiring God, *Resolutions*. http://www.desiringgod.org/articles/the-resolutions-of-jonathan-edwards.
Duewel, Wesley. *Ablaze for God*. Grand Rapids: Zondervan, 1989.
———. *Revival Fire*. Grand Rapids: Zondervan, 1995.
Edwards, Jonathan. *Jonathan Edwards on Revival*. Edinburgh: Banner of Truth Trust, 1965.
———. *Religious Affections*. Uhrichsville, Ohio: Barbour, 1999.
———. *Resolutions* https://www.ccel.org/ccel/edwards/works1.i.iii.html
———. Sermon: "Dreadful." https://www.biblebb.com/files/edwards/dreadful.htm
———. Sermon: "Justice." http://edwards.yale.edu/research/sermon-index?series=1735
———. Sermon: "Kind of Preaching People Want." http://edwards.yale.edu/research/sermon-index?series=1733.
———. Sermon: "Natural Man." https://www.biblebb.com/files/edwards/dreadful.htm
———. Sermon: "Safety." https://www.biblebb.com/files/edwards/je-safety.htm

———. *Sermon: "Sovereign God."* http://edwards.yale.edu/research/sermon-index?series=1740.

———. *Works of Jonathan Edwards*, 73 Volumes, Edited by Stout, New Haven, Yale University Press, 1985.

English, Donald. *An Evangelical Theology of Preaching*. Nashville: Abington, 1996.

Evans, W. Glyn. *Jonathan Edwards—Puritan Paradox*. Bibliotheca Sacra 124 (January) 51–65.

Ehrhard, Jim. "A Critical Analysis of the Tradition of Jonathan Edwards as a Manuscript Preacher." *Westminster Theological Journal* 60 (Spring) 71–84.

Fant, Clyde E., Jr. *20 Centuries of Great Preaching*. Waco, Texas: Word, 3: 41–55.

Finney, Charles. *Lectures on Revival*. https://wwnorton.com/college/history/archive/resources/documents/ch13_02.htm

Foord, Marty. *Sola Scriptura*. https://au.thegospelcoalition.org/article/the-real-meaning-of-sola-scriptura/

Flynt, William T. *Jonathan Edwards and His Preaching*. Th.D. dissertation, Southern Baptist Theological Seminary, 1954.

Galloway, Bryan. *Pray for Revival*. https://prayforrevival.wordpress.com/category/j-i-packer/

———. *Pray for Revival*. https://prayforrevival.wordpress.com/category/richard-owen-roberts/

———. *Pray for Revival*. https://prayforrevival.wordpress.com/category/stephen-f-olford/

Gardiner, H. Norman. *"Introduction." Selected Sermons of Jonathan Edwards*. New York: MacMillan, 1904.

Garvie, A. E. *Jonathan Edwards The Christian Preacher*. New York: Charles Scribner's Sons, 1921.

Gaustad, E.S. *The Great Awakening in New England*. Gloucester, Mass: 1965.

Gerstner, John H. *Jonathan Edwards on Heaven and Hell*. Morgan, Pa: Soli Deo Gloria, 1998.

———. *The Rational Biblical Theology of Jonathan Edwards*. 1 3. Orlando: Ligonier Ministries, 1991.

Geschiere, Charles L. *"Taste and see that the Lord is good: The Aesthetic-Affectional Preaching of Jonathan Edwards."* Grand Rapids, Mi.: Calvin Theological Seminary, 2008.

Gillies, John. *Historical Collections of Accounts of Revivals*. Fairfield: Fairfield Graphics, 1845.

———. *Memoirs of Reverend George Whitefield*. New Ipswich, N.H.: Pietan, 1993.

Goen, C.C., ed. *The Great Awakening*. Works of Jonathan Edwards 4. New Haven: Yale University Press, 1972.

Grazier, James Lewis. *"The Preaching of Jonathan Edwards: A Study of His Published Sermons with Special Reference to the Great Awakening."* Ph. D. dissertation, Temple University, 1958.

Hannah, John D. "Jonathan Edwards and the Art of Effective Communication." *Reformation & Revival Journal* 11 (Fall) 109–31.

Hardman, Keith J. *Seasons of Refreshing*. Grand Rapids: Baker, 1994.

Hart, D. G. *The Legacy of Jonathan Edwards: American Religion and the Evangelical Tradition*. Grand Rapids, Mich.: Baker Academic, 2003.

Hart, Richard. *Preaching, the Secret to Parish Revival*. Mystic: Twenty-Third, 2000.

Haykin, Michael A. G. *Jonathan Edwards: The Holy Spirit in Revival*. Webster: Evangelical, 2005.

Hedberg, Alan. *Jonathan Edwards: A Life Will Lived*. Bloomington, IN, Westbow, 2016.

Heisler, Greg. *Spirit-Led Preaching: The Holy Spirit's Role in Sermon Preparation and Delivery*. Nashville: B & H Academic, 2007.

Hickman, Edward. *The Works of Jonathan Edwards*, 1 and 2. Edinburgh, Scotland: The Banner of Truth Trust, 1992.

Horton, Michael. *Application*. https://whitehorseinn.org/resource-library/articles/application-in-sermons/.

Houdmann S. Michael. "*Hell-Fire Preaching.*" GotQuestions.org

Hoyt, Arthur S. "*Jonathan Edwards*" *The Pulpit and American Life*. New York: MacMillan, 1921.

Hulse, Erroll. *A Call to Extraordinary Prayer for Revival*. www.evanwiggs.com/revival/prinpray/callpray.html

Istafanous, Abd-el-Masih, *Calvin's Doctrine of Biblical Authority*. Eugene, OR: Wipf & Stock, 2010.

Johnson, Darrell W. *The Glory of Preaching*. Downers Grove, IL: IVP Academic, 2009.

Kaiser, Walter C. *Quest for Renewal: Personal Revival in the Old Testament*. Chicago: Moody, 1986.

———. *Revive Us Again*. Nashville: Broadman and Holman, 1999.

Keevil, Philip W. *Preaching in Revival: Preaching and a Theology of Awakening*. New York: University Press, 1999.

Kidd, Thomas S. *The Great Awakening—The Roots of Evangelical Christianity in ColonialAmerica*. New Haven: Yale University Press, 2007.

Kimnach, Wilson H. "The Brazen Trumpet: Jonathan Edwards's Conception of the Sermon." In *Jonathan Edwards, His Life and Influence*, edited by Charles Angoff, 29–44. Cranbury, New Jersey: Associated University Presses, 1975.

———. "Edwards as Preacher" *The Cambridge Companion to Jonathan Edwards*. edited by Stein, 103–24; Cambridge: Cambridge University Press, 2007.

Kimnach, Wilson H., ed. *Sermons of Jonathan Edwards*. Works of Jonathan Edwards 10. New Haven: Yale University Press, 1999.

———. *Sermons and Discourses, 1743–1758*. Works of Jonathan Edwards 25. New Haven: Yale University Press, 2006.

Kimnach, Wilson H., Caleb J.D. Maskell and Kenneth P. Minkema, eds. *Jonathan Edwards's Sinners in the Hands of an Angry God: A Casebook*. New Haven: Yale University Press, 2010.

Kimnach, Wilson H., Kenneth P. Minkema and Douglas Sweeney, eds. *The Sermons of Jona-than: A Reader*. New Haven: Yale University Press, 1999.

Krishnan, Sunder. *Catching the Wind of the Spirit*. Camp Hill: Wingspread, 2010.

LaHaye, Tim. *The Family Subject to the Spirit*. Minneapolis: Bethany, 1980.

Larson, Steven. *Divine Wrath*. http://www.sermoncentral.com/pastors-preaching-articles/steven-lawson-is-it-necessary-to-preach-divine-wrath-2194.asp?utm_

Lawson, Steven. *The Biblical Preaching of John Calvin*. https://sbts-wordpress-uploads.s3.amazonaws.com/equip/uploads/2015/10/9037-SBJT-V13-N.4-Lawson.pdf

Lee, Sang Hyun, ed. *Writings on the Trinity, Grace, and Faith*. Works of Jonathan Edwards WJE Online, 21. New Haven: Yale University Press, 2003.

Legge, David. *Preach the Word*. www.preachtheword.com/sermon/evangelism02.shtml

Lesser, M. X., ed. *Sermons and Discourses from 1734–1738*. Works of Jonathan Edwards 19 New Haven: Yale University Press, 2001.
Logan, Samuel T. "Jonathan Edwards and the 1734–35 Northampton Revival." *Preaching and Revival*. London: The Westminster Conference, 1984.
Lovelace, Richard. *Dynamics of Spiritual Life: An Evangelical Theology of Renewal*. Downers Grove, IL: InterVarsity, 1979.
Lloyd-Jones, Martyn. *Preaching and Preachers*. Grand Rapids: Zondervan, 1971.
———. *The Puritans: Their Origins and Successors*. Edinburgh: Banner of Truth Trust, 1986.
———. *What is revival?* http://www.pentecostalpioneers.org/whatisrevivaljones.html
Marsden, George M. *Jonathan Edwards, a Life*. New Haven: Yale University Press, 2003.
Masters, Peter. *What the Reformers Really Said*. https://www.the-highway.com/article Nov13.html
McClymond, Michael, ed. *Encyclopedia of Religious Revivals in America*. 2 vols. Westport, CT: Greenwood, 2007.
McGraw, James. "The Preaching of Jonathan Edwards," *The Preacher's Magazine*. 32, 8, August 1957.
McMullen, Michael D., ed. *The Glory and Honor of God: 2 of Previously Unpublished Sermons of Jonathan Edwards*. Nashville, Tenn.: Broadman and Holman, 2004.
Miller, Perry. *Errand into the Wilderness*. Boston: Harvard University Press, 1956.
Minkema, Kenneth P. *Jonathan Edwards and the Great Awakening*. 1999. Unpublished paper.
Minkema, Kenneth P., ed. *Sermons and Discourses from 1723–1729*. Works of Jonathan Edwards, 14. New Haven: Yale University Press, 1970.
Minkema, Kenneth P. and Richard A. Bailey, eds. *Reason, Revelation and Preaching: An Unpublished Ordination Sermon by Jonathan Edwards*. Southern Baptist Journal of Theology, 3: 2, Summer 1995.
Merriam-Webster. *Benison*. https://www.merriam-webster.com/dictionary/benison
———. *Magnum Opus*. https://www.merriam-webster.com/dictionary/magnum%20opus
———. *Sovereignty*. http://www.merriam-webster.com/dictionary/sovereignty
Moody, *Fire*, https://www.azquotes.com/quote/867711.
Moore, Doreen. *Good Christians, Good Husbands?* Fearn (Ross-Shire): Christian Focus Publications, 2005.
Muehlenberg, Revival and Repentance, https://sbts-wordpress-uploads.s3.amazonaws.com/equip/uploads/2009/09/revival-handout.pdf
Murray, Iain. *Jonathan Edwards—A New Biography*. Carlisle: Banner of Truth Trust, 1987.
Navigators, *Moody, D.L. quote*. https://www.navigators.org/the-bible-was-not-given-to-increase-our-knowledge/.
Nelson, Allen. *Evidences of True Revival*. https://thingsabove.us/evidences-of-true-revival/
Neuman, Meredith Marie. *Jeremiah's Scribes: Literary Theories of the Sermon in Puritan New England*. University of Pennsylvania Press, 2013.
Newman, J. H., *Fifteen Sermons Preached Before the University of Oxford Between A.D.1826 and 1843 in the Definitive Third Edition of 1872*, Sermon V, uniform edition, 91–92. http://www.newmanfriendsinternational.org/newman/?p=123.
Owen, John. *Integrity*. https://www.azquotes.com/quote/1388140.

Orr, James Edwin. *The Role of Prayer in Spiritual Awakening.* (Video) San Bernardino: Campus Crusade for Christ, 1977.
Packer, J. I. *Evangelism and the Sovereignty of God.* Downers Grove, IL: InterVarsity, 1961.
———. *A Quest for Godliness—The Puritan Vision of the Christian Life.* Wheaton: Crossway, 1990.
Pang, Patrick. "*The Pastoral Preaching of Jonathan Edwards.*" Preaching 7 (January).
Parrish, Archie and R. C. Sproul. *The Spirit of Revival.* Wheaton: Crossway, 2000.
Parrish, Archie. *The Spirit of Revival Discovering the Wisdom of Jonathan Edwards.* Crossway: 2000.
Pauw, Amy Platinga. *The Miscellanies* Works of Jonathan Edwards 20: 833–1152. New Haven: Yale University Press, 2002.
Piper, John, *Desiring God,* https://www.desiringgod.org/books/the-supremacy-of-god-in-preaching
———. *The Freedom of the Will.* Indianapolis: The Bobbs-Merrill 1969. 2013 Desiring God Foundation. Website desiringGod.org
———. *God's Passion for His Glory: Living the Vision of Jonathan Edwards.* Wheaton: Crossway, 1998.
———. *Sovereignty and Responsibility.* desiringgod.org/resource-library/articles/a-response-to-ji-packer-on-the-so-called-antinomy-between-the-sovereignty-of-god-and-human-responsibility. 1976.
———. *The Supremacy of God in Preaching.* Grand Rapids: Baker, 2004.
Pratt, Glenn Ralph. *"Jonathan Edwards as a Preacher of Doctrine."* Doctorate in Sacred Theology dissertation, Temple University.
Quinlan, Chris. *Resolutions in Plain English.* http://chrisquinlan.blogspot.com/2008/10/resolutions-of-jonathan-edwards-in.html.
Ramsey, Paul. *Ethical Writings.* Works of Jonathan Edwards 8. New Haven: Yale University Press, 1989.
———. *Freedom of the Will.* Works of Jonathan Edwards 1. New Haven: Yale University Press, 2003.
Robinson, Haddon and Craig Larson. *The Art and Craft of Biblical Preaching.* Grand Rapids: Zondervan, 2005.
Robinson, Haddon. *Biblical Preaching: the development and delivery of expository messages.* Grand Rapids, Mich.: Baker, 1980.
Sanders, J. Oswald. *Spiritual Leadership.* Chicago: Moody, 1967.
Schafer, T. A. *The Miscellanies.* Works of Jonathan Edwards 13. New Haven: Yale University Press, 2003.
Simpson, A. B. "Himself" http://www.biblebelievers.com/simpson-ab_himself.html
———. "Jesus Only" https://hymnary.org/text/jesus_only_is_our_message
Skinner, Kerry. https://thinklifechange.com/revival-a-people-saturated-with-god/
Smart, Robert Davis. *Jonathan Edwards's Apologetic for the Great Awakening.* Grand Rapids: Reformation Heritage, 2011.
Smith, John E., ed. *Religious Affections.* Works of Jonathan Edwards 2. New Haven: Yale University Press, 1959.
———. *Jonathan Edwards: Puritan, Preacher, Philosopher.* Notre Dame, Ind.: University of Notre Dame, 1992.
Spurgeon, Charles. *Lectures to My Students.* Grand Rapids, Mich.: Zondervan Pub. House, 1954, 1980 printing.

Spurgeon, Power. https://www.revival-library.org/resources/revival_speakers/revival_quotes/holy_spirit_and_revival.shtml

Stamford History, *Davenport*. https://www.stamfordhistory.org/dav_james1.htm

Steele, Joseph. *A Classical Analysis of Puritan Preaching*. http://www.reformation21.org/articles/a-classical-analysis-of-puritan-preaching.php

Stein, Stephen J., ed. *The Cambridge Companion to Jonathan Edwards*. Cambridge: Cambridge University Press, 2007.

———. *Apocalyptic Writings (1723)*. Works of Jonathan Edwards, WJE Online 5, 1977.

Stetina, Karen. *Jonathan Edwards's Early Ministry and Preaching. Jonathan Edwards' Early Understanding of Religious Experience: His New York Sermons, 1720-1723*. Lewiston, N.Y., Edwin Mellen, 2011.

Stevens, Paul. *The Other Six Days: Vocation, Work and Ministry in Biblical Perspective*. Vancouver: Eerdmans, 1999.

Stitzinger, James F. *The History of Expository Preaching*. The Master's Seminary Journal TMSJ 3/1 (Spring 1992) 5-32

Stoddard, Solomon. *The Nature of Saving Conversion*, edited by Don Kistler. Morgan: Soli Deo Gloria, 1999.

Stott, John R. W. *Between Two Worlds*. Grand Rapids: Eerdmans, 1982.

Stout, Harry S. "Edwards as Revivalist"; *The Cambridge Companion to Jonathan Edwards*. Cambridge: Cambridge University Press, edited by Stein, 2007.

———. *The New England Soul: Preaching and Religious Culture in Colonial New England*. New York: Oxford University Press, 1986.

Stout, Harry S. et. al, eds. *Sermons and Discourses from 1739-1742*, Works of Jonathan Edwards 22. New Haven: Yale University Press, 2003.

Sweeney, Douglas A. *Jonathan Edwards and the Ministry of the Word*. Downers Grove, IL: IVP Academic, 2009.

Tozer, A. W. *Faith beyond Reason*. Camp Hill, Pa.: Christian Publications, 1989.

Tracy, Patricia J. *Jonathan Edwards, Pastor: Religion and Society in Eighteenth Century Northampton*. New York: Hill and Wang, 1980.

Treash, Stephen Alden. *Jonathan Edwards's principles of awakening preaching*. Unpublished dissertation; Edinburgh: University of Aberdeen, 1995.

Trumbull, Benjamin. *A Complete History of Connecticut*. 2. New Haven: 1818.

Turnbull, Ralph. *Jonathan Edwards the Preacher*. Grand Rapids: Baker, 1958.

Tuttle, Mark H. *Jonathan Edwards and the Great Awakening*. Christian History Magazine, IV. Christian History Institute, 1985.

Valeri, Mark. *Sermons and Discourses. 1730-33*. Works of Jonathan Edwards 17. New Haven: Yale University Press, 2003.

Wax, Trevin. *Tozer A. W. Prayer of a Minor Prophet*. https://www.thegospelcoalition.org/blogs/trevin-wax/prayer-of-a-minor-prophet/.

Westra, Helen. *The Minister's Task and Calling in the Sermons of Jonathan Edwards*. Studies in American Religion, 17. Lewiston, N.Y.: Edwin Mellen, 1986

Wiersbe, W. W. and Lloyd M. Perry. *The Wycliffe handbook of preaching and preachers*. Chicago: Moody, 1984.

Whitney, Don. *Jonathan Edwards's Fast Days*. https://biblicalspirituality.org/jonathan-edwardss-fast-days/

Wilson-Kastner, Patricia. *Coherence in a fragmented world: Jonathan Edwards' theology of the Holy Spirit*. University Press of America, 1978.

Winslow, Ana. *Jonathan Edwards*. New York: The Macmillan, 1941.

Wise, Taylor. *http://www.examiner.com/article/what-does-it-mean-to-be-christ-centered*
Yarbrough, Stephen R. et. al. *Delightful Conviction: Jonathan Edwards and the Rhetoric of Conversion*. Westport, Connecticut: Greenwood, 1993.

www.ingramcontent.com/pod-product-compliance
Lightning Source LLC
Chambersburg PA
CBHW070241230426
43664CB00014B/2373